NOT BY CHANCE

LEARNING TO TRUST A SOVEREIGN GOD

FOREWORD BY MARK MINNICK

LAYTON TALBERT

BJU PRESS

GREENVILLE, SOUTH CAROLINA

Library of Congress Cataloging-in-Publication Data

Talbert, Layton, 1960-
  Not by chance : learning to trust a sovereign God / Layton Talbert ; foreword by Mark
  Minnick.
    p. cm.
  Includes bibliographical references and index.
  ISBN 1-57924-639-7 (pbk.)
    1. Providence and government of God. 2. Christian life--Baptist authors. I. Title.

  BT135 .T35 2001
  231`.5--dc21

                                                    2001043680

All Scripture is quoted from the Authorized King James Version unless otherwise noted.

"Providence" from **George Herbert and Henry Vaughn** edited by Louis L. Martz (The Oxford
     Authors, 1986). Reprinted by permission of Oxford University Press.
John Flavel. *The Mystery of Providence*. Copyright 1995 Banner of Truth. Used by permission.
Robert Grant, "O Worship the King"; Robert Robinson, "Mighty God, While Angels Bless Thee"; Isaac
     Watts, "I Sing the Mighty Power of God" from *Living Hymns*, compiled and edited by Alfred B.
     Smith. Published by Encore Publications, Inc.: Montrose, Penn., 1972.
Daniel W. Whittle, "I Know Whom I Have Believed"; Daniel O. Roberts, "God of Our Fathers, Whose
     Almighty Hand"; Maltbie D. Babcock, "This Is My Father's World"; John Newton, "Amazing
     Grace" from *Favorite Hymns of Praise*. Copyright © 1967 Tabernacle Publishing Company,
     Chicago, Ill.
NASB: Scripture taken from the NEW AMERICAN STANDARD BIBLE ® Copyright © 1960, 1962,
     1963, 1968, 1971, 1972, 1973, 1975, 1977, 1995 by The Lockman Foundation. Used by per-
     mission.
NKJV: Scripture taken from the New King James Version. Copyright © 1979, 1980, 1982 by Thomas
     Nelson, Inc. Used by permission. All rights reserved.
Monopoly is a registered trademark of Parker Brothers, Inc.

Not by Chance: Learning to Trust a Sovereign God
Layton Talbert, Ph.D.

Cover and design by TJ Getz
Composition by Kelley Moore

© 2001 by Bob Jones University Press
Greenville, South Carolina 29614

Printed in the United States of America
All rights reserved

ISBN 1-57924-639-7

15   14   13   12   11   10   9   8   7   6   5   4   3   2

To Mom,

the providential firstfruits of our family's
conversion to Christ

What man intended for evil God turned to good
(Genesis 50:20)

One day you will know that this was for you

*What I do thou knowest not now; but thou shalt
know hereafter*
(John 13:7)

TABLE OF CONTENTS

FOREWORD

Recently someone handed me a tract whose fire engine red letters fairly shrieked, *Who Wants You Sick, God or the Devil?*

It's one of those questions intentionally worded to force an unthinkable conclusion—in this case, that God might ordain anyone's illnesses. But what if He does? How would you account for that?

Another tract, propped up on one of my bookshelves for many years, opens with the picture of the nine-year-old son of a missionary. He's wearing sneakers, corduroy pants, a red sweatshirt, and sports a wide, engaging grin. But disturbingly, he's sitting in a hulking electrically powered wheelchair with mammoth black controls. Josh was born three months prematurely with cerebral palsy. The tract's title asks simply, *Why?*

Most people don't know the answer to a question like that superimposed over a picture of pathos. But inevitably we all are plagued by it eventually. Life sees to that, or in those rare cases that it doesn't, impending death will.

There have been some pretty thought-provoking answers published in recent years. Several sat atop bestsellers lists for months, sold by the hundreds of thousands, and were translated into scores of foreign languages. It all generated searching office water cooler conversation, provoked debate on radio and television talk shows across the country, and served generally to keep much of the reading and listening public haunted by the fact that there have always been some mysteries to which there seem to be no certain keys. And after reading Layton's book, I've come to think that all the recent tracts, books, debate, awareness, and agonizing inscrutability can be nothing short of *providence*. It's God who provokes men to ask questions before He unveils His answers (otherwise He has no listeners).

I've known Layton Talbert for nearly twenty-five years. Since for most of these I've been privileged to be one of his pastors, I've also been keenly aware of the kinds of questions the Lord has posed him through the turns his life has been taken. From some of these he draws in these pages. Some are too personal to share. But it's apparent to me that all have been providential preparation to provoke his searching the

Scriptures, not only for his own sake but evidently for many other questioners as well, particularly among the Lord's people, whom He is intending to reassure.

It's the combination of these two qualifications—the crucible of personal experience in tandem with unshakable commitment to biblical revelation—that eminently qualifies Layton to provide sympathetic, scriptural help in these pages. He's both asked the troublesome questions personally and devoted himself to getting them answered biblically. But the biblical, not the personal, element predominates. It's this that gives *Not by Chance* its authoritative note and destines it to be a lasting contribution to answering the illusive issues of human troubles and life's mysteries. I therefore not only want to heartily recommend but to really seriously urge the Lord's people to read this outstanding work prayerfully in a sanctified spirit and with open Bibles. Search the Scriptures for yourself to see if the solutions Layton proposes are indeed God's. I'm confident that such an approach will make this book precious to many and cause them to give God praise for gloriously enlightening their darkness, for that's what providence is all about.

Mark Minnick

Pastor, Mount Calvary Baptist Church
Greenville, South Carolina

PREFACE

Only days before this book went to press, the twin towers of New York City's World Trade Center were destroyed—along with several thousand people—in an unprecedented act of terrorism. What, if anything, did God have to do with it? The Bible's answer, for any that will hear it, is not ambiguous.

The essence of biblical faith is taking God at His Word. It is incumbent upon Christians not only to say what God says about His relationship to such events but to say it the way God says it; to adjust our thinking and our expressions to God's rather than the other way around. The Bible presents an inspired paradigm of God's mind and means and actions by which we can discern His hand in the world. Apart from that revelation, we have nothing to help us understand and respond rightly to life except our own flawed, subjective notions of what seems right and makes sense to us. But God has not left Himself without witness.

The *thesis* of this book, rooted deeply in the soil of Scripture, is that even events such as these are not by chance. The *burden* of this book, particularly in the face of disturbing crises and perplexing experiences, is to "say among the heathen that the LORD reigneth" (Psalm 96:10), "the LORD reigneth" (Psalm 93:1), "the LORD reigneth" (Psalm 97:1), "the LORD reigneth" (Psalm 99:1). (The repetition of God's Word is not aimlessly redundant; we need to hear this often and to be persuaded of it.) The *subject* of this book is the providence of God over all of life.

Some of our most indispensable theological words rarely, if ever, occur in the Bible. Trinity, omniscience, incarnation, sovereignty—these important terms never appear in Scripture though they accurately reflect biblical teaching. Similarly, "providence" appears only once. But the concept of God's providence—both in doctrine and example—saturates the Scriptures.

What is providence? What factors does it involve? What events does it include? What means does it employ? What role has it played in human history? What part does it play in your life? What practical impact does it have on your relationship with God? Such questions are the focus of this book.

The Nature of the Subject

The providence of God is not an interesting theory or an abstract theological concept. It is intensely practical and radically life altering as we approach some of life's most difficult questions and disturbing experiences. It formed the bedrock belief out of which the saints of God in Scripture—from Job to Jesus, from the prophets to Paul—reacted to life's tragedies and triumphs and perplexities.

The study of providence raises hard questions. We are finite creatures struggling to comprehend the doings of an infinite God. His thoughts and ways are immeasurably beyond ours; He has already told us that (Isaiah 55:8-9). But His ways are accurately expressed—though not always fully disclosed—by Scripture. And His ways are, like Himself, *always* right and good. The earlier chapters of this book will prompt a number of theoretical questions that later chapters anticipate and address. Providence requires a patient journey of understanding. It takes time for the Word of God to work itself into our souls and to affect how we think. Our business, our need, is to adjust our minds to God's mind and to think His thoughts after Him.

The study of providence also prompts personal questions. Real-life experiences raise not merely idle curiosities but valid concerns (as the first chapter illustrates). We will find solid, certain, substantive answers to those questions only as we analyze our circumstances in the light of God's Word. And God's Word does not give an uncertain sound about these matters—if we have the courage to hear it and the humility to submit to its unambiguous assertions. The measure of a doctrine's scripturalness is never whether we can reconcile it with our limited logic or with our personal experience, but whether it is rooted in the clear, contextual statements of the Bible.

The Aim and Use of This Book

The principal aim of this book is to confront the reader with the words of God regarding the doctrine of providence. God's Word is the final authority. It is His words that produce faith (Romans 10:17) and equip our souls to resist both error and temptation (Ephesians 6:17*b*). I am not interested in propagating or defending any particular system of theology. The burden of this study is to investigate the testimony of Scripture, challenging all of us as God's people to conform our thinking and to adjust our attitudes to the plain utterances of God Himself. I invite and urge you to investigate every cited passage of Scripture in its context, to see for yourself whether these things are so.

My hope is that you will read this book with your Bible open beside you. We will survey God's providence in the pages of the Bible, tracing the doctrine through every major biblical-historical era—patriarchal, exodus, conquest, judges, monarchy, restoration, life of Christ (Gospels) and early church (Acts). We will also consider examples of God's providence in church history as well, and translate the practical reality of His providence right up into the here-and-now of our lives. At the same time, it is important to note here that this work does not pretend to be an exhaustive treatment of the subject of providence. Rather, it is a suggestive study, a primer on providence designed to heighten the reader's awareness of its ubiquity not only throughout all of Scripture but also throughout all of life, and to spark the reader's own further personal exploration in this area.

This book represents a core of material originally prepared and taught for an extended adult Sunday school series at Mount Calvary Baptist Church in Greenville, S.C. This presentation, therefore, is aimed at God's people at large and intended to be adaptable for Sunday school or Bible study use. The book attempts to be multilayered, with a lay-friendly text supplemented by endnotes often of particular interest to more advanced students of the Scriptures. An annotated bibliography also provides a sampling of additional books available on the subject of providence for the reader's extended investigation.

All truth is God's truth, and He discloses it to whom He will. Consequently, a wide variety of sources are quoted or cited in this book for the sake of crediting, corroborating, illustrating, or buttressing its arguments. Such citations and quotations focus on an author's ideas or form of expression and should in no way be construed to imply the writer's endorsement of any individual author's overall theological or ecclesiastical orientation.

An Invitation

No biblical study has ever had a more profound and personal impact on my life and faith in God, my appreciation for His ways, my confidence in His wise rule, my assurance of His constant presence, and my certainty that He really is in control of *everything*—truths of which I need constant reminding and in which I am continuing to grow. For these reasons, I eagerly invite you to take this journey through the Scriptures and trace the unmistakable outline of God's shadow on human events. May our great God magnify Himself in your eyes as you learn to trust His all-wise and always gracious providence, and to rest in His reign.

But our God is in the heavens: he hath done whatsoever he hath pleased.

The LORD hath prepared his throne in the heavens; and his kingdom ruleth over all.

Psalm 115:3; 103:19

ACKNOWLEDGMENTS

I would like to take this opportunity to express publicly my deep appreciation:

For Dr. Paul Downey, Dr. Tony Fox, and Dr. David Saxon, who labored through an early and rough stage of the manuscript and offered many kind words of encouragement.

For Dr. Robert Vincent and Tim Ashcraft, who read the manuscript specifically with a view to making detailed constructive criticisms.

For my editor, Suzette Jordan, who patiently endured the constant rewritings and additions of a slightly obsessive compulsive new author.

For Dr. Mark Minnick, my former teacher and present pastor, who graciously consented to write the Foreword, and whose careful teaching and Word-centered ministry have shaped my thinking probably far more than I am even aware. I am in significant measure a product of his tangible and intangible influence.

For my wife, Esther, and my children, Heidi, Ethan, Micah, Rebecca, and Isaac, all of whom to varying degrees had to put up with my daily descents into my study throughout the production of this book. I tried to remain accessible but was not always in the most accommodating humor. Without their tempering influence and presence in my life, this book and the writing process would be dry indeed.

PROLOGUE

The following excerpt comes from a much longer poem entitled "Providence," written by George Herbert (1593-1633), a godly minister in the Church of England, who also composed a large body of sacred poetry. The full poem can be found in Appendix A.

O sacred Providence, who from end to end
Strongly and sweetly moves, shall I write,
And not of thee, through whom my fingers bend
To hold my quill? Shall they not do thee right?

Of all the creatures both in sea and land
Only to Man thou hast made known thy ways,
And put the pen alone into his hand,
And made him Secretary of thy praise.

Beasts fain would sing; birds ditty to their notes;
Trees would be tuning on their native lute
To thy renown: but all their hands and throats
Are brought to Man, while they are lame and mute.

Man is the world's high priest: he doth present
The sacrifice for all; while they below
Unto the service mutter an assent,
Such as springs use that fall, and winds that blow.

He that to praise and laud thee doth refrain,
Doth not refrain unto himself alone,
But robs a thousand who would praise thee fain,
And doth commit a world of sin in one.

. . . .

Wherefore, most sacred Spirit, I here present
For me and all my fellows praise to thee:
And just it is that I should pay the rent,
Because the benefit accrues to me.

1

WHO IS IN CHARGE?

It were not worth while to live in a world devoid of God and Providence.

—John Flavel

Let's not start with an academic discussion of theological theories. Let's begin with true stories of real-life experiences "in the field." What do you make of these?

Sudden Death. Don and Jim had much in common. Both were young and healthy; both were married, dedicated Christians, and skilled physicians. In fact, they were partners in a medical practice. But one day in May of 1996, Jim went into full cardiac arrest in his own office. Within thirty minutes his breath had departed, his spirit was recalled by God who gave it, and Jim was standing in the presence of the Lord. Blind fate? Bad luck? A failure on God's part? Who is in control here?

Betrayal and Reversal. A young man in his teens, living in a Middle Eastern country, was kidnapped and sold to slave traders. Carried across the border into a foreign nation, he was there framed and falsely accused of a serious crime. He languished in prison for several years until, through an incredible turn of events, he was catapulted to a position of enormous power and influence within the government of that foreign country—a position he then used to rescue his own kidnappers! A series of amazing coincidences? Who is in charge here? Joseph knew (Genesis 37-50).

"Senseless" Tragedy. Charles grew up on the mission field in Africa. His grandfather had been instrumental in founding the famous Africa Inland

Mission. Charles became a dentist and was a dedicated Christian, living in the States after serving on the mission field. One day in 1995, Charles and his wife, Jean, decided to go downtown to clear up a Social Security matter. They could have done it some other day, or even planned it for some other time in the day. But they went on Wednesday morning, shortly after the Social Security office opened. The date was April 19. The place was Oklahoma City. The Social Security office was located on the first floor of the Alfred P. Murrah Federal Building. Charles's and Jean's bodies were among the last to be found in the aftermath of the infamous bombing.[1] An accident? Bad timing? A senseless and preventable tragedy?

Deliverance from Death. A young sailor was so notorious for his blasphemy and his wicked manner of life that even other sailors shunned his company, regarding him as something of a lightning rod for divine judgment. On one occasion, in a drunken stupor, he was halfway over the ship's railing about to jump in to retrieve his hat that had blown overboard when he was saved from certain drowning by one of his fellow drunken companions, who pulled him back just in time. One voyage was beset with a storm so severe that it threatened to destroy the crew at sea. The captain, convinced that they had a Jonah onboard, blamed all their calamities on this profane young seaman and felt certain that their only hope of survival lay in throwing the rascal overboard. If the captain had made trial of his plan, you would never have been blessed by the singing of "Amazing Grace." The young reprobate's name was John Newton.[2] A charmed life? A string of luck? Or is someone in control here?

Heathen Empires. The coming together of events that accumulated over a period of centuries was incredible—a common language that united the largest world empire up to that point in history; a widespread era of peace and relative tranquillity free from the chaos and confusion and distractions of war; a postal service and system of roads that equally made the rapid spread of news and information easier; the amazing "coincidence" of a heathen ruler's whim decision to order a census that would take a certain couple to a specific town prophesied centuries before to be the birthplace of Israel's Messiah. All came together in place and time for the birth of a single, special child.[3] Chance? Coincidence? Who is in charge here?

Crippling Illness. How many people do you know that are willing to leave the comforts and certainties of home and go to a mission field like Bangladesh? Tony and Faye were. Young, devoted, both trained as nurses—they were ready to leave for Bangladesh in a matter of months. Almost all their support had been raised. Suddenly they were blind-sided. Their third of four children, only three years old, was diagnosed with leukemia. That meant at least three years of excruciating chemotherapy with uncertain results. That meant no mission field—not for a long time, if ever. Three years later, six-year-old Matthew came off chemotherapy with very successful results. Now to the mission field? No. In the meantime, their newest son and fifth child, Ben, was diagnosed with a rare disease called tuberous sclerosis. The immediate effects are quite serious and the human prognosis is not good.[4] Chance misfortune? Bad karma? A perverse turn of events that someone could have averted?

Human Inventions. Though the Chinese had moveable type for centuries, it was not introduced into Europe until the 1500s—just prior to the appearance on the scene of a newly converted monk named Martin Luther. In fact, "so quickly were Luther's pamphlets set in type, printed, duplicated, and sold, that Luther said that it was as if angels were his couriers, so rapidly were his words dispersed throughout the realm."[5] Pure coincidence? Is someone in charge here?

"Avoidable" Martyrdom. On Sunday, January 8, 1956, five young, dedicated missionaries, all relatively new husbands, stepped out of their small plane onto the beach of the Curaray River to contact once again the Auca people who lived in the jungles of Ecuador. Their previous contacts had shown hopeful signs. The details of this trip had been painstakingly planned as well. But a miscalculation—one God certainly could have averted—led to a fatal misunderstanding, and they were unexpectedly attacked and murdered by the very people they had come to reach with the gospel.[6] Why? What sense did that make? What purpose did it serve? Are heathen savages in a faraway jungle beyond God's control? Is anyone in charge?

What Do We Make of This?

Most readers could, at this point, insert a similar story from their own experience or from the life of someone they know. The fact is, things happen we simply don't understand—sometimes seemingly senseless things that tax our faith and make us wonder whether anyone really is in charge after all. Or, if someone is, what He is doing. And what does what He is doing say about what He is really like?

These stories—whether from Bible history, secular history, the recent past, or personal experience—could be multiplied many times over. All of them illustrate unusual, unexpected, extraordinary events that suggest one of three explanations: (1) *pure chance*—also identified as fate, fortune, coincidence, happenstance, accident, luck, fluke; (2) *cosmic contest*—an ongoing struggle between God and Satan, which either may win on any given occasion; or (3) *divine control*—the overruling will of a single intelligent, omnipotent, omnipresent Being (God).

What Does the Bible Say?

Who *is* in charge? The doctrine of God's providence is rooted in the doctrine of God's sovereignty. Notice that in the heart of the word "sove**reign**ty" you find the word "reign." The sovereignty of God, simply stated, refers to His undisputed authority and rule over every aspect of His creation. God is the unrivaled King of all. No being, human or angelic, is capable of thwarting God or frustrating His purposes. If He does not rule supreme, if He is not sovereign, then He is not God. " 'God reigns' is a logical sequence from 'God is.' To deny God's providence is as atheistical as to deny His existence."[7]

We will take a brief survey journey through the Scriptures in search of an answer to that question. Consider carefully these stubbornly straightforward, direct statements asserting the sovereignty of God. Note the context. What do these passages teach explicitly? What events or experiences or circumstances do they include specifically? Make a list or jot some notes in the margin. And don't skip any references—all these

Spirit-inspired verses are in the Bible for a reason. Our view of God's sovereignty must be as broad and deep and comprehensive as the Bible's.

God Can Do Anything

Genesis 18:14. *"Is any thing too hard for the LORD?"* This is not a theoretical theological question posed in the sterile surroundings of an academic lecture hall. The context of this question is profoundly practical. God has just promised (for the *seventh* time)[8] that an aged and childless couple, Abraham and Sarah, will actually conceive and bear a child of their own. Think about it. If enabling the "dead womb" (as it is described in Romans 4:19) of a ninety-year-old woman to conceive and bear a child is not "too hard" for the Lord, what other kinds of equally down-to-earth applications of this truth does that invite?

The precise terminology used here is instructive. The term "any thing" translates a very common Hebrew word (*dabar*). It can mean "matter" or "thing" as it is translated here. But it is usually translated "word" and is one of the most common designations for a word or revelation from God. God had just given His word that Sarah herself—despite the "deadness" of Abraham's body and of her own womb—will bear a son. It might almost be translated, "Is any word too hard for the LORD to [fulfill]?" If it is something God has given His word on, is it possible that He will be unable to make it good? It is significant that the rhetorical question is tied directly to an explicit promise and pronouncement on God's part. He has gone on record as binding Himself to give them a son. Is it possible that what He has said will turn out to be "too hard" for Him to effect?

The phrase "is [any thing] too hard" translates a Hebrew verb (*pala'*) that means "to be wonderful, marvelous." It is used frequently in the Psalms and elsewhere to refer to God's "wonderful [wondrous or marvelous] works." The noun form of this verb serves as one of the Old Testament words for a miracle ("wonder"). Again, one could almost translate Genesis 18:14, "Is any thing [any word] too wonderful for the LORD [to perform]?" We often say that something is "just too good to be true." Is there any such category when God is under discussion? Is there anything God has given His word on—any word of assurance or promise or

5

prophecy—that is too much to expect or hope for, too good to be literally believed and actually counted on? Is there anything that is just *too* good to be true when the LORD has given His word? The question remains rhetorical for the time being, but it will resurface later in our investigation.

God Makes Everyone

Exodus 4:11. "Who hath made man's mouth? or who maketh the dumb, or deaf, or the seeing, or the blind? have not I, the LORD?" In the course of his initial call by God in Exodus, Moses respectfully offers every excuse that comes to mind in his frantic attempt to get out of an admittedly fearful task. Who am I (3:11)? What authority do I have (3:13)? What if they won't believe me (4:1)? When Moses objects that he is rhetorically ungifted and thus unqualified for so great a task, God takes the occasion to utter a sweeping claim with profound ramifications for the doctrine of providence.

We might have expected the initial question as God's way of reminding Moses that just as He had formed Moses' mouth, He would likewise give it utterance to accomplish His will. We have no difficulty accepting that God is the one who graciously gives birth to healthy people. But God goes a step further. What is striking about this claim is God's unblinking assertion that He is the Creator not only of the healthy and whole but also of the handicapped! God claims providential responsibility even for the very conditions we view as the unfortunate result of defective genetics or the tragic outcome of accidents. The language is quite direct—He "makes" them that way.[9]

Why He does so is beyond the scope of this discussion and, for the present, beside the point.[10] Remember, we are training our minds to think God's thoughts after Him, to adjust our thinking to His self-revelation. According to God, disabilities are not accidents that occur because God momentarily loses control or is suddenly taken by surprise. The mute, the deaf, the blind, the disabled are fashioned that way by the omnipotent hand of an all-wise—and always good—God for His ultimate glory (cf. John 9:1-3).

WHO IS IN CHARGE?

God Can Do Everything He Says

Numbers 11:23. "*Is the* LORD's *hand waxed short? thou shalt see now whether my word shall come to pass unto thee or not.*" Take the time to re-create this vivid historical scene in your mind's eye. The people in the wilderness whined about God's gracious (and miraculous) provision of manna. They were tired of it. They craved meat. So discontent were they that they began weeping and moaning for Moses to give them something they could sink their teeth into (Numbers 11:10, 13). God said to Moses, "The people despise Me and My provision. They covet meat? Tell the people I will give them meat. Nothing but meat for an entire month. They shall have so much meat it will make them sick. Starting tomorrow!" (Numbers 11:16-20).

"What?!" Moses was incredulous—literally (Numbers 11:21-22). He was not at all eager to make this announcement to the people. His credibility was on the line; in fact, his sanity would probably be questioned. More importantly, God's credibility was on the line. Read between the lines of Moses' reply: "Lord, are You sure about this? Remember, there are six hundred thousand of us. And that's just the men! And You are going to feed us all *meat*? From where? For a month? How? Here in the wilderness? You would have to gather together, here in the middle of this desert, all of the fish in the sea to do what You've promised!" How quickly Moses forgot—how quickly we forget—that the Lord had *opened* that sea for them and *closed* it on their enemies. Gathering from the sea a mountain of fish in the middle of a desert would not have been a big deal for God, had He chosen to do that. Had God suddenly become impotent? That is precisely God's reply to Moses' unbelief.

"Has the LORD's arm been shortened?" (NKJV). The idiom referring to the Lord's hand being "short" has reference to one's word overreaching his ability, promising more than one can deliver. "Now you shall see whether My Word will come true for you or not" (NASB). Notice how God returned again to His *word*—that is, to what He had gone on record and publicly bound Himself to do. This splendid question and challenge has timeless application to every other promise or pronouncement that God has uttered in His Word.

By the way, impossible as it appeared even to Moses, God did *exactly* what He said He would do (Numbers 11:31-34). It was a long time before any of the people could stand to *look* at a quail again without feeling sick, let alone eat one.

God Rules All Existence

Deuteronomy 32:39. "*I kill, and I make alive; I wound, and I heal: neither is there any that can deliver out of my hand.*" Over what realms or experiences does God here claim absolute authority? Eugene Merrill notes that these verses depict "the LORD as sovereign of life and death and of harm and health."[11] Peter Craigie elaborates:

> Everything that happened to the people of God happened only under his power. Life, health, and victory were a result of God's blessing. But death, disease, and defeat were equally a part of God's dealings with his people; they did not indicate any diminution of God's power. . . . An important principle emerges from this passage: when the blessing of God appears to be withdrawn, man should not question the ability of God, but should examine the state of his relationship to God.[12]

One word of caution, however. The presence of negative, adverse circumstances does *not*, in and of itself, necessarily indicate a loss of God's blessing or a rift of relationship. Joseph, Job, and Jesus suffered appallingly while in the center of God's will and in right relationship to Him. The unambiguous point of this passage is that the Lord alone rules providentially and sovereignly over all the changes of life.

God Rules All Circumstances

I Samuel 2:6-7. "*The LORD killeth, and maketh alive: he bringeth down to the grave, and bringeth up. The LORD maketh poor, and maketh rich: he bringeth low, and lifteth up.*" In case you didn't get the point in Deuteronomy, here it is again. In fact, Hannah's apparent meditation on Deuteronomy 32:39 seems to flower in a personal application of this truth to her own circumstance. Moreover, she expands God's providence to encompass the experiences of poverty and wealth, humiliation and exaltation. We too should so meditate on the specific declarations of God's Word that we, like she, come to personalize them, internalize them, glory in them, and pray and praise His own words back to Him.

Job 2:10. "What? shall we receive good at the hand of God, and shall we not receive evil?" What does Job mean by receiving both "good" and "evil" from the hand of God? Does God ever initiate sin or originate moral evil? Never (see James 1:13). As in English, the Hebrew word "evil" may denote something negative without the connotation of moral turpitude. We regularly refer to a "bad storm" (sometimes even a "wicked storm") or to something "bad" (unfortunate) happening to someone, without implying that either is morally "sinful" or "evil."

Similarly, the Hebrew word for "evil"—though it can refer to moral evil—often denotes "calamity" or "catastrophe" or "misfortune." In fact, this very word is sometimes translated "distress," "affliction," "trouble," or "adversity." It describes things that are "bad" in a nonmoral sense (such as rotten figs in Jeremiah 24:2 or contaminated water in II Kings 2:19) or "calamitous" in a nonmoral sense (such as the storm in Jonah 1:7-8; disease in Deuteronomy 7:15; or God's judgments of war, famine, beasts, and epidemic in Ezekiel 14:21). We might paraphrase Job's words this way: "Should we expect only good things from God all the time? Should we not also expect (what we consider) 'bad' things (such as hardship or adversity, loss or illness) from time to time?"[13] Who then, according to Job, is the author of the "good" we enjoy as well as the "bad" we must sometimes suffer? Whom does he say sends both? Was Job mistaken?

Job 42:2. "I know that thou canst do every thing, and that no thought can be withholden from thee." Job was not confessing God's *ability* to do anything (His omnipotence) or His *knowledge* of everything (His omniscience). God's omnipotence and omniscience were repeatedly affirmed by everyone and questioned by no one throughout the debate between Job and his friends. The issue was whether God was right, or had the right, to do what He had done to Job. Job was not here affirming God's power; he was affirming God's *freedom* to do as He pleases without any obligation to explain Himself to us (the idea is "I understand now that You can do anything You want"). Likewise, the last phrase of the verse is not referring to God's knowledge of man's thoughts, but to man's inability to restrain God's thoughts (that is, His purposes). Job does not mean that no human thought can be hidden from God, but that no thought (i.e., no intention or purpose) of God can be restrained; no one and no thing can thwart God in any thought He purposes to carry out. "I know that You can do everything, and that no purpose of Yours can be withheld from You" (NKJV).

Psalm 68:20. *"He that is our God is the God of salvation; and unto* GOD *the Lord belong the issues from death."* Though this verse is sometimes taken as a reference to resurrection, both "salvation" and "issues" are plural in Hebrew, "indicating their repeated occurrences."[14] The phrase "issues from death" literally has reference to "exits from death," or hairbreadth escapes. "God is to us a God of deliverances; and to GOD the Lord belong escapes from death" (NASB). David is not merely penning lofty poetry nor talking theoretically. He is speaking from repeated personal encounter. Think of the number of times he experienced God-given deliverances from danger and escapes from death through a variety of providential means.

God Does All He Pleases

Psalm 103:19. *"The* LORD *hath prepared* [established] *his throne in the heavens; and his kingdom ruleth over all."* Does this terminology leave any room for exceptions to God's rule or any zones outside God's dominion? Borders are nonexistent in His kingdom and nothing is beyond the reach of His scepter. What response should such a truth elicit? All His subjects—angels, hosts, ministers, creatures, and my own soul—are invited to exult in His universal sovereignty: "Bless the LORD" (Psalm 103:20-22).

Psalm 115:3. *"But our God is in the heavens: he hath done whatsoever he hath pleased."* The latter half of the verse is better translated in an ongoing sense: "He does whatever He pleases." The assertion could not be any more all-encompassing. Obstacles are nonexistent to His wishes and nothing can frustrate His purpose to do whatever pleases Him. What response should such universal sway to enact His every wish elicit? Fear of fickleness, anxiety over unpredictability, concern over potential abuse of power—these would be appropriate apprehensions were any man in such a position. But the psalmist's repeated refrain in light of this truth is "Trust in the LORD" (Psalm 115:9-18). God is praiseworthy because His rule is universal (Psalm 103) and trustworthy because His purposes are unstoppable (Psalm 115).

Psalm 135:6. "*Whatsoever the Lord pleased, that did he in heaven, and in earth, in the seas, and all deep places.*" Again, if it was true in the past, it is equally true in the present. The thought is an ongoing one—"whatever the LORD pleases he does" (NKJV) in every conceivable realm of creation. In all these various spheres the elements of earth are the tools of providence. He controls the clouds, the lightning, and the wind for His ends (Psalm 135:7)—fire and hail, snow and clouds, stormy winds all fulfill His word (Psalm 148:8) and respond to His commands (Psalm 147:15-18). Do you suppose that has any practical relevance for our attitude toward the weather?

God's Rule Is Unrivaled

Ecclesiastes 7:13-14. "*Consider the work of God: for who can make that straight which he hath made crooked?*" Who can undo what God does, or unsend what God sends? No one can alter "the shapes of things and events" that come to us from God.[15] Therefore, "*in the day of prosperity be joyful, but in the day of adversity consider.*" God appoints one as well as the other, each for His pleasure and for its own purpose. "That verse," remarks Derek Kidner, "is a little classic on the right approach to both good times and bad, which is to accept both from God for what they can give."[16] According to the verse, what two kinds of experiences does God appoint, and what should be our respective reaction to each when we experience it?

Isaiah 14:27. "*For the LORD of hosts hath purposed, and who shall disannul it? and his hand is stretched out, and who shall turn it back?*" Who is the specific object of this challenge in the context? It is Assyria—the dominant world power at the time (Isaiah 14:24-25). Who, then, is a match for God's power, or who can thwart what the "King of nations" (Jeremiah 10:7) purposes?

Isaiah 45:5-7. "I am the LORD and there is none else, there is no god beside me. . . . I am the LORD and there is none else. I form the light, and create darkness: I make peace, and create evil: I the LORD do all these things."[17] The same truth that Job confessed above (Job 2:10) now comes from the mouth of God Himself. God does not mean here that He creates or initiates moral evil; He cannot. What, then, does this passage mean by "evil"? One hint is its opposite in the context: "peace." As we have already seen in other passages, God stresses His control over the extremes of life and death, sickness and health, poverty and wealth. "Evil" here, then, refers to the opposite of "peace," namely, conflict, distress, calamity. We often assume that all good things come from God and all "bad" things come from Satan. That is a false and unbiblical assumption that gives Satan far too much credit and attributes to him far more power than he actually possesses. Contrary to popular misconception, Satan is not God's evil counterpart, but Michael's. Satan, like Michael, is "only" an angel; so he is an evil angel, not an evil god.[18] Jehovah Himself claims that He is the only God and the ultimate ruler over all our circumstances—both the "good" and the "bad." This is not the last time He will affirm this truth. Keep exploring.

Isaiah 46:9-11. "I am God, and there is none else; I am God, and there is none like me. . . . My counsel shall stand, and I will do all my pleasure [sound familiar?] *. . . yea, I have spoken it, I will also bring it to pass; I have purposed it, I will also do it."* The wedding between God's omniscience (verse 10*a*) and God's omnipotence (verse 10*b*) is His sovereignty. Yet, in one of the mysteries we will investigate later, His sovereignty employs the instrumentality of human involvement. God specifically cites the human means (Cyrus, naming this future king of Persia over a century before his birth) by which He will accomplish His purpose with Israel: *"calling . . . the man that executeth my counsel from a far country."* Elsewhere God calls Cyrus His "shepherd," adding, "I will direct all his ways: he shall build my city, and he shall let go my captives" and "shall perform all my pleasure" (Isaiah 45:13; 44:28). This passage introduces us to the intricate ramifications of such predictive statements for very specific decisions that Cyrus (and the five generations of his ancestors leading up to him) had to make in order to fulfill God's "counsel."

Jeremiah 32:17, 27. "*Ah Lord GOD! behold, thou hast made the heaven and the earth by thy great power and stretched out arm, and there is nothing too hard for thee. . . . Behold, I am the LORD, the God of all flesh: is there any thing too hard for me?*" The historical context is fascinating and instructive. The year was 587 B.C. (32:1). Judah was staring down the loaded barrel of Babylon, who would, within a year, demolish their city, take their land, and carry them into captivity (32:2-5). Under those conditions, God instructed Jeremiah to purchase a parcel of land in Judah, then publicly preserve the deed on the grounds that "houses and fields and vineyards shall be possessed again in this land" (32:6-15). Jeremiah followed God's instructions, asserting his conviction that nothing is too hard for God to accomplish (32:16-25). God affirmed Jeremiah's assertion by restating the truth in a rhetorical question (32:26-27). Why do you suppose God framed it as a question rather than as a statement? Which carries more force? Picture the maker of heaven and earth, with all His vast and varied creation stretching out all around Him, asking, "Look around Me. Look at all I have made. Look at what I can do. Do you think, then, there is *anything* that could possibly be too hard for Me?"

As in Genesis 18:14, the word "nothing" in Jeremiah 32:17 and "any thing" in Jeremiah 32:27 is literally "any word."[19] "Therefore," the passage continues, "thus saith the Lord . . ." (32:28). Both Jeremiah's assertion and God's affirmation that nothing is too hard for Him were predicated on an express word from the Lord. God proceeded to pronounce a most improbable-sounding prophecy: Nebuchadnezzar and the Babylonians would capture Jerusalem, burn it to the ground, and scatter its inhabitants in captivity throughout the world; then God Himself would regather them, restore them to their land, sanctify them internally, and make an everlasting covenant with them. Is that word too hard for God to accomplish?

Lamentations 3:37-38. "*Who is he that saith, and it cometh to pass, when the LORD commandeth it not? Out of the mouth of the most High proceedeth not evil and good?*" Human authorities are ignorant of the truth of verse

37, of course, but the fact is they are impotent to function independently or to effect their pronouncements unilaterally; they act freely, but only under divine permission. God, not the president, holds the ultimate veto pen. In verse 38, Jeremiah echoes Job's understanding that both good *and* "bad" come ultimately from God alone (Job 2:10) and introduces us again to the term "evil." The overall context and subject of Lamentations revolves around God's chastisement on His disobedient people. A good translation here might be "Is it not from the mouth of the Most High that woe and well-being proceed?" (NKJV). Jeremiah's point is to encourage God's people that both discipline *and* restoration alike come from God alone.[20] It is like the child hugging close the spanking parent. When He sends woe, He Himself is our only refuge in it and our only hope for healing and well-being. God expresses this very sentiment beautifully in Ezekiel 11:16—even when He scatters His people among the nations in disciplinary judgment, He promises, "yet I shall be a little sanctuary for them in the countries where they have gone" (NKJV).

Daniel 4:35. "And all the inhabitants of the earth are reputed as nothing: and he doeth according to his will in the army of heaven, and among the inhabitants of the earth: and none can stay his hand, or say unto him, What doest thou?" Who made this astonishing assertion? Godly Daniel? One of his Jewish companions? No, the speaker was a Gentile and the premier ruler of the dominant empire of the day—King Nebuchadnezzar of Babylon. Having delivered all the kingdoms of the known world into Nebuchadnezzar's hand, God then humbled him (Daniel 4:4-33) till he came to realize that God governs over kingdoms and kings, and that "the Most High is ruler over the realm of mankind and bestows it on whomever He wishes" (Daniel 4:25, NASB). Just as God employed the great Cyrus as His "shepherd" (Isaiah 44:28), the powerful Nebuchadnezzar was nothing more than His "servant" (Jeremiah 25:9).

If the entire population of the earth—all six billion, with all their combined technology and military might—were amassed against God, how would He regard them? Isaiah describes them as a drop in a bucket and compares them to the fine dust that has settled on a set of scales (Isaiah 40:15). Compared to God, they don't even register! Psalm 2 graphically depicts God's reaction to the pathetic "threat" of mankind marshaled in rebellion against His purposes—He laughs! Who would you say is in charge?

God's Rule Is Unquestionable

Amos 3:6. "Shall there be evil in a city, and the LORD hath not done it?" What is the understood answer to the prophet's rhetorical question? Like a master debater, Amos has been conditioning us for the correct answer to this difficult question by first stringing together a succession of easier questions to which the answer is obvious. The answer to the seventh question, as to the preceding six questions, is a clear no! And that answer should be as obvious for the seventh question as it was for the first six. We should be comfortable enough with the term "evil" by now to know that the prophet means calamity or catastrophe. This fits precisely with what God has already revealed about Himself as the sender of both "good" and "bad." Nevertheless, it is one thing to accept this truth in the abstract. It is quite another to make the application contemporary and personal. Put a name on that city and a date on that evil: "Can there be evil in Oklahoma City on April 19, 1995, and the Lord have not done [i.e., sent, permitted] it?" Can we accept that? No, that does not mean that God inspired or initiated the evil act itself. If God is all-knowing and all-powerful, could He have averted it? Certainly, yet He permitted it. Why? That answer is not within the scope of this discussion. Our first duty is to bow to the unambiguous and repeated declarations of Scripture; only then will our spirits be properly adjusted to grapple with the question of why.

New Testament Reaffirmations

Luke 1:37. "For with God nothing shall be impossible." Here is the New Testament twin to the Old Testament truth affirmed in Genesis 18:14 and Jeremiah 32:17 and 27. Embedded in this incarnation narrative is another astounding assertion. We usually celebrate this verse as an expression of God's omnipotence. Again, however, the phrase more literally reads, "For with God every saying is not impossible"—or as we would say, "with God no saying is impossible."[21] The statement is remarkable enough, but the identity of the speaker adds enormous weight to this testimony. This is no mere human opinion. This is the assurance of the angel Gabriel who, having served and dwelt in the presence of God for millennia, has had countless opportunities to witness God's words and works, confirming and reaffirming this angelic estimate of His trustworthiness.

Like the earlier passages, then, Luke 1:37 is not so much a general assertion that God is all-powerful (though He certainly is). It is an even more specific assurance that He is fully able and intent on performing every prophecy and promise He utters—every "saying." If God has said it, He can and will do it—no matter how improbable it may seem or how impossible it may sound. Remember the context here—the biological impossibility of the virgin birth! How do you suppose this angelic testimony of God applies to His "sayings" to you in the Bible?

Taken together, then, these sibling passages (Genesis 18:14; Jeremiah 32:17, 27; Luke 1:37) do convey, somewhat indirectly, an assertion of God's *ability* ("Is there anything God does not have the ability to do?"). However, given their similarity of vocabulary and context (in each case, some specific promise or pronouncement from God), the more direct intent of these passages is to make a specifically theological and intensely practical point about God's *reliability* ("If God has said it, how can He possibly fail to do it?"). The point is the absolute trustworthiness of everything God says, not only because He is powerful enough to do it, but also because His internal nature and immutable character make it unthinkable and impossible for Him *not* to do it . . . if He has said it.

Ephesians 1:11 refers to *"the purpose of him who worketh all things after the counsel of his own will."* If Luke 1:37 is the New Testament twin of the truth expressed in Genesis 18:14 and Jeremiah 32:17 and 27, then Ephesians 1:11 is the New Testament twin of the truth embedded in Psalm 103:19, 115:3, and 135:6. Paul's inspired words are as universal in scope and as focused on the ease with which God accomplishes His own pleasure as the psalmists'. "All things" doesn't leave out much, and "according to the counsel of His own will" is pretty specific.

Revelation 3:7 describes Christ as *"he that openeth, and no man shut-teth; and shutteth, and no man openeth."* What kinds of applications does this verse invite in terms of God's control?

Providence in Summary

Did you make a list of what areas of life God's providence encom-passes? According to these verses, God's sovereign rule and providence extends over everything from the miraculous to the mundane:

- humanly impossible births
- health and handicaps
- seemingly impossible provision
- life, death, and escapes from death
- wounding and healing
- poverty and wealth
- humiliation and honor
- affliction and blessing
- adversity and prosperity
- weather
- darkness and light
- calamity and peace
- woe and well-being
- closed and opened opportunities
- all the doings of collective nations as well as individual inhabitants of the earth

This is not abstract theology. These providentially governed circum-stances reflect the overwhelmingly practical experiences that affect every-one reading this book. Moreover, they are all-inclusive, encompassing virtually any kind of situation you are likely to encounter. Yet the list of

verses we surveyed is merely representative, not exhaustive. In short, Job
and John, David and Solomon, Moses and Paul, Daniel and Gabriel, Isaiah
and Jeremiah all raise their voices together in unison with the LORD Himself in affirming that He alone rules over all things and everyone. *He* is in
charge.

How seriously and literally are we willing to take our Bibles? The collective weight and force of these passages are enormous. Their meaning is
unambiguous. Their assertions are unmistakable. (See the overview
below, which topically arranges the passages we surveyed and incorporates a few others that we skipped.) God is the great King, the only Sovereign over all the earth. No scheme or sin or circumstance takes Him by
surprise. No man or demon or force of nature can thwart His power or
frustrate His purposes. He alone rules supreme. These passages should
magnify God for us, making Him BIG in our eyes. We are privileged to
know and serve the peerless Ruler of all creation. Such a realization
begets both confident exultation and sobering awe.

AN OVERVIEW OF PROVIDENCE

*A Thematically Arranged Collection of Express Verses on the
Sovereign Rule of God*

God CAN Do Anything He Says.

- Is any thing [any word] too hard for the Lord? (Gen. 18:14)
- And the LORD said unto Moses, Is the LORD's hand waxed short? thou
  shalt see now whether my word shall come to pass unto thee or not.
  (Num. 11:23)
- I know that thou canst do every thing, and that no thought can be
  withholden from thee. (Job 42:2)
- The LORD hath prepared his throne in the heavens; and his kingdom
  ruleth over all. (Ps. 103:19)

- That the living may know that the most High ruleth in the kingdom of men, and giveth it to whomsoever he will. (Dan. 4:17; cf. 4:3, 25, 32, 34; 5:21; 6:26; 7:14, 27)

- Behold, I am the LORD, the God of all flesh: Is there any thing too hard for me? (Jer. 32:27)

- Ah Lord GOD! behold, thou hast made the heaven and the earth by thy great power and stretched out arm, and there is nothing too hard for thee. (Jer. 32:17)

- For with God nothing [lit., no saying] shall be impossible. (Luke 1:37)

- In whom also we have obtained an inheritance, being predestinated according to the purpose of him who worketh all things after the counsel of his will. (Eph. 1:11)

God WILL Do Everything He Pleases.

- But our God is in the heavens: he hath done whatsoever he hath pleased. (Ps. 115:3)

- Whatsoever the LORD pleased, that did he in heaven, and in earth, in the seas, and all deep places. (Ps. 135:6)

God CANNOT Be Thwarted in What He Purposes.

- Behold, he taketh away, who can hinder him? who will say unto him, What doest thou? (Job 9:12)

- If he cut off, and shut up [in prison], or gather together [to judgment], then who can hinder him? (Job 11:10)

- Behold, he breaketh down, and it cannot be built again: he shutteth up a man, and there can be no opening. (Job 12:14)

- I know that thou canst do every thing, and that no thought can be withholden from thee. (Job 42:2)

- There is no wisdom nor understanding nor counsel against the LORD. (Prov. 21:30)

- Consider the work of God: for who can make that straight, which he hath made crooked? (Eccles. 7:13)

- For the LORD of hosts hath purposed, and who shall disannul it? and his hand is stretched out, and who shall turn it back? (Isa. 14:27)

- Yea, before the day was I am he; and there is none that can deliver out of my hand: I will work, and who shall let [hinder] it? (Isa. 43:13)

- Who is he that saith, and it cometh to pass, when the Lord commandeth it not? (Lam. 3:37)

God WILL NOT Be Thwarted in What He Pleases.

- Remember the former things of old: for I am God, and there is none else; I am God, and there is none like me, declaring the end from the beginning, and from ancient times the things that are not yet done, saying, My counsel shall stand, and I will do all my pleasure. (Isa. 46:9-10)

- And all the inhabitants of the earth are reputed as nothing: and he doeth according to his will in the army of heaven, and among the inhabitants of the earth: and none can stay his hand, or say unto him, What doest thou? (Dan. 4:35)

- And to the angel of the church in Philadelphia write; These things saith he that is holy, he that is true, he that hath the key of David, he that openeth, and no man shutteth; and shutteth, and no man openeth. (Rev. 3:7)

God Rules Providentially over "Good" AND "Bad."

- See now that I, even I, am he, and there is no god with me: I kill, and I make alive; I wound, and I heal: neither is there any that can deliver out of my hand. (Deut. 32:39)

- The LORD killeth, and maketh alive: he bringeth down to the grave, and bringeth up. (I Sam. 2:6)

- The LORD maketh poor, and maketh rich: he bringeth low, and lifteth up. (I Sam. 2:7)

- What? shall we receive good at the hand of God, and shall we not receive evil? (Job 2:10)

- In the day of prosperity be joyful, but in the day of adversity consider: God also hath set the one over against the other, to the end that man should find nothing after him. (Eccles. 7:14)

- That they may know from the rising of the sun, and from the west, that there is none beside me. I am the LORD, and there is none else. I form the light, and create darkness: I make peace, and create evil: I the LORD do all these things. (Isa. 45:6-7)

- Out of the mouth of the most High proceedeth not evil and good? (Lam. 3:38)

- Shall there be evil in a city, and the LORD hath not done it? (Amos 3:6)

A Righteous Response to the Sovereign Providence of God.

- But he said unto her, Thou speakest as one of the foolish women speaketh. What? shall we receive good at the hand of God, and shall we not receive evil? In all this did not Job sin with his lips. (Job 2:10)

- I know that thou canst do every thing, and that no thought can be withholden from thee. . . . I have heard of thee by the hearing of the ear: but now mine eye seeth thee. Wherefore I abhor myself, and repent in dust and ashes. (Job 42:2, 5-6)

- Now unto the King eternal, immortal, invisible, the only wise God, be honour and glory for ever and ever. Amen. (I Tim. 1:17)

Magnifying God

Not all magnifying devices are created equal; there are different kinds of magnification, depending on the object being magnified. We use a magnifying glass or a microscope to make something tiny look bigger to us so that we can examine it more closely. But that is not the way we magnify God. He is not tiny. He is vast beyond our comprehension. We have a different way of magnifying such things. Because of the enormous distance that separates us from them, stars and planets and galaxies appear minuscule to the naked human eye, but in reality they are colossal—in most cases, many times bigger than our own planet. Telescopes magnify those distant bodies, bringing them "closer" to the eye and helping us better appreciate their immensity. That is how God is magnified—through Scripture, through our experiences, and through our testimony to others. Not by taking something tiny and making it look big all out of proportion to reality, but by bringing up close to our senses someone who is, in a sense, "distant" but immense and magnificent beyond all comprehension.

What If It's Not God?

If God's providence does not extend over all the circumstances and changes of life—both good and bad—then what explanations does that leave to us? What are the alternatives?

1. We can conclude that we are essentially at the mercy of blind fate, capricious chance, unpredictable luck, inexplicable coincidence, or some other impersonal force. But, as the above list of passages demonstrates, that is clearly unbiblical even in some of the most seemingly minute details of life. Even a combination of divine providence over certain "significant" events, with the rest of life being ruled by chance, is not at all within the teaching and testimony of Scripture.

2. If we rule out chance and opt for God's control, but wish to deny that God exercises sovereign control over the "bad" things that happen, we must conclude either (a) that some things take even God by surprise, so that He is forced to react to certain events so as to bring some good out of them (but this denies the Bible's unambiguous and repeated assertion of God's total omniscience), or (b) that some things, even if He sees them coming, God is unable to avert (but this denies the Bible's unambiguous and repeated assertion of God's absolute omnipotence).

3. If we rule out chance *and* God's control, we are left with the disturbing option that someone *else* is actually in charge, at least much of the time—the cherished dream of the Devil and the nightmare of mankind.

In other words, we are forced to choose between an all-knowing God who is not all-powerful (a view known as finitism) or an all-powerful God who is not all-knowing (a view known as open theology).[22] The only alternatives to the Bible's assertion of God's providence over *all* things are inescapably unbiblical.

Certain writers have offered some of these alternative explanations to the biblical doctrine of God's all-inclusive providence. One of the most popular examples is Rabbi Harold Kushner's *When Bad Things Happen to*

Good People. "God wants the righteous to live peaceful, happy lives," he writes, "but sometimes even He can't bring that about. It is too difficult even for God to keep cruelty and chaos from claiming their innocent victims."[23] Can you think of a verse or two from our previous survey that directly contradicts this assertion? A Christian writer, commenting on the tragic 1982 death of seven people from cyanide-laced acetomenophin tablets, concluded that "there was no meaning in those deaths. Each was a bizarre, horrible coincidence, nothing more. Therein lies the tragedy."[24] Does this assessment square with the Bible passages above? As we will see, many more passages in the chapters to come unmask such a conclusion as inherently heathen and unbelieving.

Jerry Bridges succinctly summarizes the dilemma:

> The implicit assumption in the minds of many is: If God is both powerful and good, why is there so much suffering, so much pain, so much heartache in the world? God is either good and not all-powerful, or He is powerful and not all good. You can't have it both ways.[25]

But, Bridges concludes, "The Bible teaches us we do have it both ways." This is where we must rein in *our* logic, *our* perception, and *our* reasoning to Scripture. Faith requires that we submit our thoughts to God's, bringing our thinking into line with the unambiguous and repeated statements of God Himself in the Bible.

In short, the alternatives to the biblical view of God's all-inclusive providence are unacceptable—a God who is taken by surprise at some of our experiences (so much for omniscience), a God who is sometimes simply unable to do anything about them (so much for omnipotence), or an unrestrained Devil (so much for sovereignty).

There is, however, even more at stake here than at first appears. God's trustworthiness is rooted in His sovereignty—His absolute, all-knowing, all-powerful rule over all things. If there is *anything* He does not know, if there is *anything* He is impotent to do or to prevent, then He *cannot* be sovereign. **And if God's *sovereignty* is limited, then His *trustworthiness* is also limited.** How can we completely and implicitly trust a God in every circumstance of life—as we are repeatedly and unequivocally commanded to do throughout Scripture—if we never know for certain whether He is, in fact, in control and able to intervene. **If God is not truly sovereign, God cannot be truly trusted.** These possibilities are utterly abhorred by Scripture.[26]

If It Is God, Then . . . ?

While the passages above are unambiguous, they also raise some thorny questions. That is inevitable when finite creatures (you and I) try to comprehend the workings of our vast and infinite God. God has forewarned us of that difficulty (Isaiah 55:8-9; Romans 11:33-36). But such questions deserve to be asked and, as biblically as possible, answered.

- Why does God do or allow some of the things He does or allows?

- How or by what means does He accomplish such purposes?

- How can it be said that a good God sends calamity?

- How can it be said that a sinless God permits evil?

- If He is in control even when sinful acts are perpetrated, does that make Him somehow responsible for those acts?

- Does God's sovereign providence conflict with human freedom and responsibility?

We will explore biblical answers to these questions as we move through this study on the providence of God. Granted, accepting the fact of God's providence can be difficult at times and in certain circumstances. Like any other biblical truth, it must be accepted *by faith*. Faith is taking God at His Word, even when it seems to contradict our finite logic or limited perception or narrow experience. When we come to accept by faith the truth of God's all-encompassing providence, we may not find all the answers to our specific questions in certain circumstances; but we will find a *peace* that passes human understanding when we, by faith, submit our questions and doubts and logic to God's own revelation about Himself.

A Look in the Mirror

Who is in charge? By now we should have a handle on the resounding biblical reply to that question. God alone is sovereignly in charge and graciously in control. But why all the focus on this question in a study of providence? Because God's providence is a direct outgrowth and extension of His sovereignty. If God is not sovereign over all nations, persons, events, and circumstances, then "providence" evaporates into happenstance, coincidence, luck. It is precisely because He is sovereign that we can believe in and rely on His providence. God means for this revelation of Himself in Scripture to be carried off the page, through the mind and into your heart. Here are some questions for your own reflection, to help turn these external truths inward.

- What practical impact does God want His words regarding His providence to have on my life?

- What kinds of situations in my life does God want me to realize are under His providence?

- What circumstances am I encountering right now that I have not really thought of as being under God's control?

- What effect does God desire His providence to have on my attitude and reaction to the circumstances in my life?
  (a) Presumption? Laziness? Despair? Irresponsibility?
  (b) Submission? Faith? Encouragement? Confidence? Joy?

The passages we have surveyed (as well as the additional ones listed in the chart) are intended for our encouragement and exhortation to trust implicitly in the authority, power, and goodness of God. Each reference begs meditation, careful consideration of its context, and purposeful application to our personal circumstances and experiences. The focus of these verses is on only one side of the issue—the sovereign rule of God. But Scripture consistently counterbalances divine sovereignty with human responsibility. To ignore either emphasis for the other, however logical, is implicitly unbiblical and dangerous. The two are not mutually exclusive, but mysteriously mutually inclusive. God sovereignly controls everything according to His always gracious purpose and good pleasure. At the same time, man bears full responsibility for his actions and reactions toward God. We must be careful

> not to use God's sovereignty as an excuse to shirk the duties that He has commanded in the Scriptures. . . . Our *duty* is found in the *revealed* will of God in the Scriptures. Our *trust* must be in the *sovereign* will of God, as He works in the ordinary circumstances of our daily lives for our good and His glory.[27]

That is the right balance. It is also the scriptural balance. "The secret things belong unto the LORD our God: but those things which are revealed belong unto us and to our children for ever, that we may do all the words of this law" (Deuteronomy 29:29).

2

WHAT IS PROVIDENCE?

The doctrine of divine Providence is that all things are sustained, directed and controlled by God.

—Leonard Woods

What exactly is "providence?" You may have seen the word in older writings, used almost as a synonym or title for God Himself. However, the word "providence"

> probably has more meaning to us in this generation of "video" than it has had before. Linguistically the root of the word *providence* is two simple words: one is *before*, or *for*, or *in behalf of*; and the other is *to see*. God *pro videos*; that is, God provides because . . . He sees [before] what we need and therefore supplies.[1]

Providence, then, involves God's capacity to see (and, consequently, to act) beforehand. Obviously humans have a capacity for anticipation; indeed, "all rational beings exercise a providence proportioned to their powers."[2] We speak of "seeing it coming" or "seeing a need before it arises," and we can do these things in a very limited sense. But we are plainly not equipped to practice providence in every area even in our own lives (that would require omniscience), nor are we always able to do what may need to be done (that would require omnipotence). But providence is more than divine anticipation. Providence is not merely reactive, even to what it foresees ahead of time. It is not even merely proactive. Providence is determinative.

Providence is primarily a theological word, "the most comprehensive term in the language of theology."[3] Though the term "providence" appears only once in the Bible, our understanding of providence is drawn directly from certain Bible words. And the *concept* of providence—both in doctrine and example—saturates the Scriptures. As we discovered in the previous chapter, "Providence is presented in Scripture as a function of divine sovereignty. God is King over all, doing just what He wills. This conviction, robustly held, pervades the whole Bible."[4]

Stoking the Fire: Questions for Thought

- How can we succinctly—and biblically—define providence?
- What events does it include? Are there any events outside God's providence?
- What means does God employ in providence?
- What part has God's providence played in human history?
- What part does God's providence play in your life?
- What practical impact does/can/should it have on your relationship with God?

First, let's see how the word "providence" is used in the Bible. This will help illustrate on a very practical level what the theological concept of providence involves.

The Word "Providence" in the Bible

The only occurrence of the word "providence" in the Authorized Version of the Bible appears in Acts 24:2. The high priest, Ananias, had hired a professional orator named Tertullus to plead the Jews' case against Paul before the Roman governor Felix. Tertullus began by buttering up Felix: "Seeing that by thee we enjoy great quietness, and that very worthy deeds are done unto this nation by thy providence, we accept it always, and in all places, most noble Felix, with all thankfulness."

Ironically, "providence" refers here not to God at all, but to a man (Felix). Moreover, the historical record attests that in Felix's case it was pure flattery.[5] Still, its use in this passage gives some clues about the meaning and concept of "providence." Its use here brings certain ideas to mind: (1) foresight or forethought, (2) care, and (3) provision. This is precisely what the Greek noun (*pronoia*) means.

Though the English word "providence" occurs only once, the same Greek word is used in one other passage. Romans 13:14 reads, "Make not provision for the flesh, to fulfill the lusts thereof." What does this mean in the practical terms of that context? It denotes taking foresight or fore-thought for the flesh—planning or arranging an opportunity or manipulating circumstances so that my flesh has an opportunity to satisfy its desires.

There are many ways to "make provision" for the flesh to have opportunities to sin. You might carry the answers into an exam, or purposely stroll down the magazine aisle at the store. What are you doing when you do these things? You are exercising providence, albeit in a very negative and improper way. You are looking down the road ahead of time to arrange an opportunity to sin. Even though the image in this context is a negative one, it illustrates the dynamic of "providence."

Positive Illustrations of "Providence"

The Greek noun translated "providence" in Acts 24:2 and "provision" in Romans 13:14 appears in its verb form three times in the New Testament. In each case it is translated to "provide (for)" and has reference to taking active forethought to make certain arrangements.

Romans 12:17 ("provide things honest in the sight of all men") commands us to take every precaution to be open and aboveboard in all our dealings. Second Corinthians 8:21 ("providing for honest things, not only in the sight of the Lord, but also in the sight of men") details how Paul himself practiced what he preached in Romans 12:17 in his handling of the financial gift for the Jerusalem saints. First Timothy 5:8 ("but if any provide not for his own, and specially for those of his own house, he hath denied the faith, and is worse than an infidel") dictates the duty of caring and providing for the needs of one's family. The same idea is expressed in the Old Testament by very common Hebrew verbs such as "to see" (Genesis 22:8, 14; 41:33; I Samuel 16:1) and "to prepare" (Job 38:41; Psalm 65:9). Genesis 22 furnishes a beautifully illustrative context for our discussion of providence.

Jehovah-Jireh: Banner of Providence

Genesis 22 juts up suddenly as a pinnacle of providence early in the biblical narrative. God commanded Abraham to sacrifice his son—his only son, given by God after many long years of waiting on God to fulfill His promise. The concept of providence surfaces clearly in Genesis 22:8, when Abraham answers his son's puzzled query about what they are going to offer as a sacrifice: "My son, God will *provide* himself a lamb for a burnt offering." The word "provide" is the common Hebrew verb meaning "to see" (*ra'ah*). It could just as accurately be translated, "God himself will see to a lamb for a burnt offering." And God does just that, in a very unusual, unexpected, and "providential" way (Genesis 22:13).

God's providence on that occasion was memorialized in the name Abraham gave to the place: Jehovah-jireh. The phrase is often defined as "The LORD will provide." The word "jireh" is exactly the same Hebrew word we had back in verse 8, meaning "to see (to)." So verse 14 can be translated that Abraham named the place "The LORD will see to it" and "in the mount of the LORD it will be seen to."

It would be easy to apply this passage simply to the general notion that God always provides (that is, exercises providential oversight and provision) for His own. That is a great truth. But, as with any scriptural truth, the context itself should guide our applications—otherwise, we rob ourselves of the very specific application God intends for us to take away from that particular context.

In Genesis 22, the context portrays an obedience to the Lord that involves a willingness to sacrifice what is dearest and most cherished—and, in fact, even God-given! Here are some context-driven principles for personal application. (1) When we seek to obey God, even at enormous cost to ourselves, He "sees to it" that we are blessed (see vv. 16-18). (2) If we are on the verge of willingly sacrificing something in deference to Him, or in order to carry out His will, He will "see to" (that is, He will provide) a suitable substitute or will recompense the loss in His way and time. (3) God in His providence will provide/intervene for us when we determine to obey Him or when we willingly sacrifice for Him. "When men come to a particular test that God imposes, God helps them in His gracious providence according to their needs."[6]

What Does the Bible Say?

In the previous chapter, we surveyed some of the *propositional* statements of Scripture that *assert* God's providence. Let's look now at some *narrative* statements that *demonstrate* God's providence. Take some time to look over the passages and consider the contexts. What kinds of situations does the Bible *explicitly* attribute to God's providential intervention in these passages?

- Genesis 12:17—Preemptive disease.
- Genesis 20:6—Restraint from sinning.
- Genesis 20:17-18—Barrenness and pregnancy.
- Genesis 25:21—Conception (see also 29:31; 30:22).
- Genesis 45:4-8—Suffering as the victim of the sinful acts of others in order to be used to effect a greater good. (This introduces a difficult topic that will be discussed in detail in chapter 5.)
- I Samuel 26:12—Unusually deep sleep (to protect God's servant).
- II Kings 7:6—Auditory hallucinations and a complete misapprehension of reality.
- Daniel 2:21; 4:17, 25, 32; 5:21—Appointment of even secular governmental leaders.[7]
- Jonah 1:4, 17; 2:10; 4:6, 7, 8—Weather, animal behavior, and plant development.[8]

The variety of activities directly attributed to the providence of God is extraordinary. From issues of the largest possible scope, to the most mundane incidents, to the most personal and intimate circumstances, God exercises His providential oversight and intervention. The next step, then, is to hammer out a working definition of providence.

Defining Providence

Simply stated, providence is the word that describes the biblical doctrine of God's active involvement and intervention, directly or indirectly, in human affairs. But we want to dig a bit deeper and get more specific than that. Before formulating our own working definition of providence, however, it is worth looking at and learning from some of the definitions previously devised by others.

Nineteenth-century theologian Charles Hodge defined providence as God's

> most holy, wise and powerful preserving and governing of all His creatures and all their actions. Providence, therefore, includes preservation and government. By preservation is meant that all things external to God owe the continuance of their existence, with all their properties and powers, to the will of God. . . . The latter [government] includes the ideas of design and control. It supposes an end to be attained and the disposition and direction of means for its accomplishment.[9]

Charles Hodge's son, A. A. Hodge, put it more succinctly: "Providence includes the two great departments of the continued preservation of all things as created, and of the continued government of all things thus preserved, so that all the ends for which they were created are infallibly accomplished."[10]

The conciseness of Wilbur Tillett's definition disguises the fact that it is an extract from an eighteen-column article on the subject in *The International Standard Bible Encyclopedia*. Providence denotes the "preservation, care and government which God exercises over all things that He has created, in order that they may accomplish the ends for which they were created."[11]

WHAT IS PROVIDENCE?

Contemporary theologian Millard Erickson wins a brevity award. Providence refers to "God's care for the creation, involving his preserving it in existence and guiding it to his intended ends."[12]

Here is one of the most descriptive definitions I have come across:

> Providence is the beneficent outworking of God's sovereignty, whereby all events are directed and disposed to bring about those purposes of glory and good for which the universe was made. These events include the actions of free agents, which while remaining free, personal and responsible are also the intended actions of those agents. Providence thus encompasses both natural and personal events, setting them alike within the purposes of God.[13]

Condensing the salient features of all of the above, providence is

> the unceasing activity of the Creator whereby, in overflowing bounty and goodwill, He upholds His creatures in ordered existence, guides and governs all events, circumstances, and free acts of angels and men, and directs everything to its appointed goal, for His own glory.[14]

The Twofold Concept of Providence

Chapter 1 was dedicated to demonstrating biblically that God's providence is a logical outgrowth of His sovereignty. He can and does exercise His providence precisely because He is sovereign. Providence is, therefore, God's actual, active assertion of His sovereignty.

One point that all of the preceding definitions of providence have in common, whether explicitly stated or implicitly suggested, is the recognition that the biblical doctrine of providence is twofold. Providence is theologically defined in terms of two distinct but overlapping aspects: preservation and government.[15] These are not separate or distinct acts of providence; they merely constitute the two sides of the golden coin of divine providence. Dividing our definition, then, will facilitate our understanding of the scope and dynamics of God's providence.

Preserving Providence

God continuously preserves and maintains the existence of every part of His creation, from the smallest to the greatest, according to His sovereign pleasure.

Governing Providence

God graciously guides and governs all events, including the free acts of men and their external circumstances, and directs all things to their appointed ends for His glory.

This is, of necessity, an admittedly man-made definition. There is no single verse or passage that can be appended as biblical support for this definition. God has not given us in Scripture a "finished product" in this respect but, rather, a collection of raw materials.

Nevertheless, this definition does not represent the purely logical deduction of a theological system, nor the necessary fabrication of a rational mind seeking order and meaning in the face of otherwise inexplainable events. As we will discover repeatedly throughout this book, it represents the firm, unblinking assertion of the self-revelation of God in the Bible.

If you want "proof texts" for this definition of providence, I would submit the whole collection of passages cited in the first two chapters of this book. Such passages and a host of others like them—consisting of both propositional statements and narrative descriptions of God's providential activity—show us how providence "works." I have merely constructed from those raw materials a definition that succinctly yet accurately summarizes the scriptural doctrine.

These, then, will be our working definitions as we proceed in our exploration of God's providence. They are not entirely original. You will recognize bits and pieces of the previous definitions above. What will, I hope, be helpful is their brevity and their division of God's providence into two logically distinct but interwoven aspects of the outworking of God's activity and purpose. The remainder of this book aims to demonstrate the biblical validity and flesh out the practical applicability of this twofold definition of the providence of God.

Providence or Miracle?

The above definition of providence may raise a question. How does providence relate to miracles? Let's return for a moment to the broad description of providence as God's active involvement and intervention, directly or indirectly, in human affairs. That is a potentially very inclusive category of divine activity. In its broadest sense, providence takes many forms.

> We need to observe the different kinds of providences. There are uncommon providences, such as miracles, and there are what might be called common providences, like the refreshing rain. There are great providences, like the crossing of the Red Sea and there are what seem small providences, like a king not being able to sleep at night. There are favourable or smiling providences and there are what appear to be dark, cross or frowning providences.[16]

But this book is less about Red Seas being divided and more about insomniac monarchs. In other words, this is not a book about miracles, *per se*. Given the overlap between providence and miracle, then, how do we distinguish them? What is the difference between them?

For the sake of distinguishing providence from miracle, a definition of the latter will be helpful. *A miracle is a supernatural act in which God intervenes in the natural course of human experience, by exercising His authority over His creation, for the purpose of self-revelation.*[17] Miracles are not displays of power merely for the sake of impressing the onlookers. They are essentially *didactic* in nature and *self-revelatory* in aim. They are credentials of God's deity and reveal who He is; they not only display His power but also manifest His character (what He approves and disapproves, depending on whether the miracle is a judgment or a blessing) and reveal what He is like.[18] God's ultimate purpose for miracles is never merely to awe, nor even only to provide, but to instruct.

Providence may indeed, on occasion, employ the miraculous. Usually, however, "providence" is reserved to describe God's superintending operation in the affairs of men through the normal course of natural events and human choices. A miracle is *overt* providence. Providence might be described as God's *covert* activity in orchestrating the affairs of men and the events of history. That is the focus of this book—the more "common" and seemingly "small" providences of God, for they are the most often and easily overlooked, both in the Bible and in our own lives.

Providence or Coincidence?

Based on our working definition, then, providence obviously stands in direct contrast and opposition to luck, fate, fluke, chance, happenstance, and accident. Providence and these are mutually exclusive concepts. If there is such a thing as luck or chance, fluke or happenstance, then there is no providence in any consistent, meaningful sense of the word. If providence is real, there is no such thing as luck or chance. Sproul rightly deduces,

> The doctrine of the providence of God leaves no room for fate, blind or otherwise. God is not blind; neither is He capricious. For Him there are no accidents. . . . If chance exists, God cannot exist. If one molecule flies wild by chance, then God is not sovereign. If God is not sovereign, then God is not God. God and chance simply cannot coexist.[19]

Luck is not the only popular notion that crumbles under the weight of providence. A biblical definition of providence diametrically counters a variety of alternative philosophical notions about God's relationship to man and creation. Providence contradicts

> (a) pantheism, which absorbs the world into God; (b) deism, which cuts it off from Him; (c) dualism, which divides control of it between God and another power; (d) indeterminism, which holds that it is under no control at all; (e) determinism, which posits a control of a kind that destroys man's moral responsibility; (f) the doctrine of chance, which denies the controlling power to be rational; and (g) the doctrine of fate, which denies it to be benevolent.[20]

A Look in the Mirror

After facing little resistance from the cowering French and preparing to retire temporarily from their war in France, the English troops of Henry V are finally met by the French herald, who announces that they (and their newly hired mercenary reinforcements) are now ready to fight the English. With soldiers sick and famished and winter coming on, Henry, not wishing a battle at this time, replies, "If we may pass, we will; if we be hinder'd, we shall your tawny ground with your red blood discolour. . . .The sum of all our answer is but this: We would not seek a battle as we are; nor as we are, we say, we will not shun it." As the Frenchman departs, one of the nobles standing beside Henry confides, "I hope they will not come upon us now." To which the king replies, "We are in God's hands, brother, not theirs."[21] That's good theology.

Sound biblical theology has a way of putting our minds at ease. God intends that the Bible's teaching on His providence should have that very effect on us. You are in good hands, not with some insurance company but with your heavenly Father.

Here are some practical questions for personal reflection.

- How often do you refer to luck or chance in casual conversation?

- Are phrases like "good luck" or cynical references to Murphy's Law ("if anything can go wrong, it will")—as innocent as they may be intended—really consistent with the Bible's teaching on God's providence over all people and circumstances?

- Do you think habits of speech condition, however unintentionally, the way you or those around you view and interpret life experiences?

- If the Bible really teaches God's providence over every aspect of our lives, what effect should that have on our attitude toward *whatever* we may experience? What areas does that include?

- What assessments of and responses to past events, present circumstances, or even potential future events are biblically appropriate and consistent with the Bible's teaching on providence?

3

THE PRESERVING PROVIDENCE OF
GOD OVER MAN

There's a special providence in the fall of a sparrow. If it be now, 'tis not to come; if it be not to come, it will be now; if it be not now, yet it will come: the readiness is all.

—Hamlet, *Act V, Scene 2*

Musing on the inevitability of death, Shakespeare's Hamlet expresses a profoundly biblical truth. And he makes a superb application of that truth. We have already learned, from a wide array of Bible passages, that a gracious God rules over every aspect of our earthly experience. That is the broad picture—like looking from a distance at a massive canvas and taking in the wide sweep of a breathtakingly majestic landscape. Now we want to step closer and zoom in on one portion of the canvas of providence. Scrutinizing one segment of God's revelation in this regard will enable us to notice marvelous details painted in by the hand of the Master. Or, to return to a previous metaphor, let's extend the telescope to examine the constellation of God's providence in more breathtaking detail.

Remember our definition of the first aspect of the providence of God—His preserving providence:

God continuously preserves and maintains the existence of every part of His creation, from the smallest to the greatest, according to His sovereign pleasure.

THE PRESERVING PROVIDENCE OF GOD OVER MAN

The previous chapter pointed out that the biblical understanding of providence immediately combats certain unbiblical notions about God and His relationship to man and the world. Christians who know their Bible would unequivocally reject such antibiblical philosophies, at least in theory. Unfortunately, what we deny in theory we may, consciously or unconsciously, succumb to in practice. (Peter categorically denied, in theory, that he would ever deny the Lord.) To what extent does the biblical doctrine of God's preserving providence actually govern our thinking, affect our behavior, and inform our decisions?

Practical Deism

Deism is the belief that God created the world but that He does not involve Himself in its human affairs or earthly events. He created the world and set it in motion under certain "natural laws" but stands personally aloof from His creation. Deism is a philosophy based on human observation and reason, not revelation, and is contrary to God's revelation of Himself in the Bible.

As Christians, we reject the deistic notion that God has simply set everything in motion and stepped back to let it all run on its own with little or no intervention. But many of us fail to recognize just how intricately and actively God is involved in the maintenance and preservation of creation. Even many Christians are too ready to attribute circumstances, good or bad, to accident, chance, or even natural law. When we do so, we actually betray a kind of practical atheism.

Practical Atheism

In his superb work *The Mystery of Providence,* Puritan John Flavel spells out his purpose and target audience in these words:

> Now my business is not so much to deal with professed atheists who deny the existence of God . . . but rather to convince those that own all this [i.e., say that they believe in God], yet . . . suspect, at least, that all these things which we call special providences to the saints are but natural

events or mere contingencies. Thus, while they profess to own a God and a Providence they do in the meantime live like atheists, and both think and act as if there were no such things.[1]

That is practical atheism.

We tend to see providence only in extraordinary, unusual, surprising, coincidental, seemingly "chance" circumstances or events. We tend to think of providence as God's stepping in and changing things only when something dramatic happens—either for better (such as God's provision of a job, protection in an accident, or a successful pregnancy) or for worse (such as a job loss, an injury or illness, or a miscarriage) for His own purposes. But providence is not only God's stepping into a situation with government and guidance. Providence is, first and foremost, God's faithful maintenance and preservation of all things—or else there would be nothing to govern and guide!

How does the preserving providence of God translate into practical, everyday terms? Consider carefully the wording of Psalm 3:5—"I laid me down and slept; I awaked; for the LORD sustained me." Take a moment to note the context of Psalm 3:5, as revealed in verses 1-4 and in the subtitle to Psalm 3. David penned this poetic testimony on the run as a result of his own son Absalom's attempted coup. Clearly, his life was in danger from those sympathetic to Absalom's plot for power. Note also his sublime peace and confidence in God's providential protection expressed in verse 6. David did not consider the fact that he awoke from sleep to be an accident or a "natural law." He attributed it to God's sustaining of his life.

If we are serious about personally *applying* the truths God has chosen to include in His self-revelation to us in the Scripture, it gets just this practical. Each night you survive, each morning you awake with sound mind and healthy body (or awake at all), each day you live, each breath you draw, is the *direct* effect of the *preserving providence* of God.

Does that statement sound extreme? Do we really believe that God "micromanages" every aspect of His creation this way? Does this actually include *every* person? Does the Bible literally teach that God exercises this extent of preserving providence?

What Does the Bible Say?

Providence is not merely God's unusual, occasional intervention into an otherwise *laissez-faire* policy on His part. God does not operate on a principle of aloof noninterference, which He occasionally suspends on special occasions. Providence, as we have seen, is a two-sided coin—preserving *and* governing. The first side of the providence coin is *active, constant preservation*, day by day, hour by hour, moment by moment, and even creature by creature. But don't take my word for it.

Feel Free to Move About

"For in him we live, and move, and have our being" (Acts 17:28). What initially sounds like eloquent poetic language becomes, on closer inspection, a stunningly down-to-earth application of the doctrine of providence. Paul literally informs his audience, and us, that "in Him [God] we live, and move ourselves, and are [that is, exist]." We take life itself for granted as a "natural law." According to Paul, it is a supernatural law. Only through God and on account of His pleasure do we enjoy the ongoing privilege of life itself.[2] And that page you just turned was no accident, either. "Move" is constructed in a form that means to "possess the faculty of motion, exercise the functions of life."[3] Not everyone enjoys that privilege. When God withholds or removes our capacity for movement, for whatever reason, we have a name for it. We call it paralysis. "Have our being" is a rather elaborate translation for the simple Greek verb "to be." Without God we would never have existed; apart from His pleasure to sustain us, our earthly existence would evaporate.

Don't miss the significance of the context. Paul is preaching to heathen Greeks, in basic philosophical terms they can understand, the truth that all men (1) possess life, (2) receive their capability for bodily movement, and (3) have existence *only* "in" (that is, through and from) God. Even more significantly, he is not telling them something they have never heard. Paul is speaking (and Luke is recording) under inspiration, and the words the Holy Spirit chooses to inspire are actually a quotation from one of their own heathen Greek poets![4] Talk about providence! Paul is, under inspiration, taking a seed thought that they have been enlightened enough by God to perceive and explaining the proper context and application of that truth—not Zeus, but the true God.[5] All truth is, after all, God's truth.

The God of the Bible is the sole giver of human life and the only reason *any* of us exists in the first place. God is even the sole giver of our ability to transport our bodies and move our limbs! None of us would question that a sudden judgment of paralysis or leprosy was providential; if that is the case, then when that *doesn't* happen, according to this verse, it is *equally* due to the preserving providence of God!

Part of our problem in seeing the all-inclusiveness of God's preserving providence comes when we take for granted the normal course of our existence. We forget, or ignore, or disbelieve, that our daily good health, our wholeness of body, our soundness of mind, our bodily coordination, and the numerous essential, life-supporting bodily functions that proceed without any thought or effort or help on our part, all come from the hand of God's preserving providence. We think of God's providence only when the life or breath or health we take for granted is interrupted. The words of Scripture are neither abstract philosophy nor flowery poetry. They are truth: *"In Him we live and move and exist."*

But hasn't God kind of "wound up" everything with the power of "natural law," set everything in motion, and then taken His hands off, allowing "natural laws" to run their course, and stepping in only when it is absolutely necessary? Hasn't God created in me a sort of self-sustaining life principle so that I naturally breathe, for example? That sounds like a feasible, logical explanation. The problem is that it is not the biblical explanation.

Take a Deep Breath

Go ahead—pause in your reading for just a moment and consciously draw a breath. How long would you have survived without that breath? Did you know that Scripture has one, *and only one*, explanation for your ability to do that just now? Did you know that according to Scripture, it was the preserving providence of God that gave you that breath and sustained your life that moment? Does that sound far-fetched? Do you doubt that?

Look at these passages and—here's the challenge—adjust your thinking to bring it into line with the straightforward declarations of God's Word.

Genesis 2:7. "And the Lord God formed man of the dust of the ground, *and breathed into his nostrils the breath of life;* and man became a living soul." Man is the breath of God wrapped in clay. *But,* someone points out, *this verse is an anthropomorphism—a representation of God's creation in human terms that we can understand. That statement doesn't really count.* Well, then, what about the repeated assertions in the Book of Job?

Job 12:10. Job refers to the Lord, "in whose hand is the soul of every living thing, *and the breath of all mankind.*"

Job 27:3. Job says that God has withheld justice and vexed him, "*all the while my breath is in me, and the spirit of God is in my nostrils.*" This is classic Hebrew poetic parallelism. The second phrase is communicating precisely the same information as the first phrase, in different but synonymous terminology. In other words, "my breath is in me" equals "the spirit of God is in my nostrils." More specifically, "my breath" is parallel to "the spirit [or breath] of God." Job sees his very life breath as coming from God Himself.

Job 33:4. Elihu declares that "the Spirit of God hath made me, *and the breath of the Almighty hath given me life.*"

Job 34:14-15. Elihu again observes, "If he [God] set his heart upon man *if he gather unto himself his spirit and his breath*; all flesh shall perish together, and man shall turn again unto dust." That is, if God were to withdraw from all people the sustaining spirit and breath of life He alone supplies to them, all would die.

Yes, but that's in the Book of Job, comes the objection again, *and the Book of Job is poetry. It is the nature of poetry to express things figuratively. You can't take expressions like that literally.* Well, what about Daniel's words to Belshazzar?

Daniel 5:23. Daniel rebuked Belshazzar: "The God *in whose hand thy breath is,* and *whose are all thy ways,* hast thou not glorified."

But everyone knows that prophets often spoke in pictures, someone objects again. *Daniel's words are a kind of prophetic word picture to make a point.* What, then, about Paul's words to the Athenians?

Acts 17:24-25. "God . . . *giveth to all life, and breath, and all things." Come now,* the objector rebuts, *Paul is preaching there, and we all know how preachers are sometimes! That is just a rhetorical expression.*

The settled prejudice of unbelief can manufacture a retort for anything. We can always rationalize reasons for rejecting even the most unambiguous statements of Scripture when they seem to contradict our own good "common sense." But what *will* you do with this repeated refrain in God's Word?

To return to Paul's last statement, he makes another similar assertion in a very different context, when he charges Timothy to be faithful "in the sight of God, who quickeneth all things" (I Timothy 6:13). Contrary to our initial impression, this is not a reference to resurrection but to the fact that God is the one who continually quickens—makes alive and keeps alive—all things.[6]

All these passages are stubbornly dogmatic and unambiguously explicit in their teaching that *God alone gives every person every breath he draws.* That is not to say that God is actively, busily, continuously pumping some huge cosmic bellows somewhere to keep breath in mankind. Rather, He providentially sustains all things with the same "word of His power" by which He created all things in the first place. He is, in the intercessory words of Moses, "the God of the spirits of all flesh" (Numbers 16:22).[7]

Feel Your Head

Go ahead—nobody's looking. Better yet, take a moment to go look in the mirror. Have you ever considered counting your hairs? Probably not (even those of us who could do it much more quickly than others). But did you know that God already has? Here again, we are challenged to take an abstract theological idea and convert it—by simple, childlike faith in the very words of Jesus Christ Himself—into a very real, practical, personal truth.

THE PRESERVING PROVIDENCE OF GOD OVER MAN

Consider Matthew 10:29-31. Jesus spoke these words in Galilee when the twelve disciples were first sent out. Rejection and persecution, Jesus warned, were to be expected. In that context, Christ offered them the following assurance: "Are not two sparrows sold for a farthing? and one of them shall not fall on the ground without your Father. But the very hairs of your head are all numbered. Fear ye not therefore, ye are of more value than many sparrows."

Compare Luke 12:4-7. These words are very similar to those in Matthew 10, but actually Jesus spoke them on an entirely different occasion later in Judea. Consider the words carefully, and take them seriously:

> And I say unto you my friends, Be not afraid of them that kill the body, and after that have no more that they can do. But I will forewarn you whom ye shall fear: Fear him, which after he hath killed hath power to cast into hell; yea, I say unto you, Fear him. Are not five sparrows sold for two farthings, and not one of them is forgotten before God? But even the very hairs of your head are all numbered. Fear not therefore: ye are of more value than many sparrows.

On what does Jesus base His assurance of God's care and protection—that is, His preserving providence—over His followers? He bases it on God's preserving providence over *sparrows*, some of the smallest and most insignificant creatures in nature. And sparrows are all over the place. You could purchase them for mere pennies. Yet *not one* of *them* falls to the ground outside the providence of God, and *not one* of *them* is ever forgotten before God. Think about that the next time you find one lying on the ground in your yard or along a roadside.

Do you honestly believe that one? Does your faith stand in the wisdom and reason of men, or in the words of God? "You mean God actually cares about sparrows?" That is what Jesus said. And if it were not true, His assurance to the disciples about God's providential care over *them* would be groundless and worthless. If the illustrative assurance is false, the promised personal assurance is meaningless. So, how many sparrows are *you* worth?

Did the Son of man ever employ humor? He certainly did, on several occasions. Not knee-slapping jests or cutting gibes. It was always humor with a purpose. Simple humor can hone a truth to a keen point and make it doubly effective. There is a subtle facetiousness in Jesus' words here. If you pause to think about it, the humor makes the point even more forcefully. Picture the scenario: "I am sending you out as sheep among wolves. Some will reject your message. Some will persecute you. Some will threaten to kill you. But do not be afraid. Those sparrows you can buy in the market for a few pennies? God watches over and protects even them. He sustains their life, and not one so much as falls to the ground without Him. So be comforted. God will watch over you. After all, you are worth more than *many* sparrows."

How many is "many"? Ten? Fifty? Do you suppose you might be worth even a hundred sparrows to God? A thousand? Can you not see Jesus ending that statement with the slightest smile playing about His lips, as His words sink into the disciples? You and I alone, of all the creatures in God's creation, have been fashioned in the image and likeness of God Himself. You and I alone, of all God's creatures, were worth enough to God for Him to send His only Son as a suffering sacrifice to deliver us from death. So, let me ask you again. Just how many sparrows do you think you are worth to God?

Rain on the Unjust

The universal gift of sunshine and rain from the hand of a good God is one more manifestation of His unconditional blessing and preserving providence (Matthew 5:45). Yet His preserving providence extends beyond even those external blessings, necessary as they are, to the intimate and vital functions of the bodies of evil and good, just and unjust alike. Have you ever paused to consider the profoundest of ironies—that Christ Himself was the very one sustaining the life of His own executioners. One writer has vividly captured the pathos of the crucifixion—and simultaneously, the preserving providence of the moment:

> "On your back with you!" One raises a mallet to sink in the spike. But the soldier's heart must continue pumping as he readies the prisoner's wrist.

Someone must sustain the soldier's life minute by minute, for no man has this power on his own. Who supplies breath to his lungs? Who gives energy to his cells? Who holds his molecules together? *Only by the Son* do "all things hold together" (Col. 1:17). The victim wills that the soldier live on—he grants the warrior's continued existence. The man swings.[8]

Samuel Davies was not one to mince words. The eighteenth-century Presbyterian preacher of Virginia candidly applied the truth of providence to his hearers:

> You who can eat, and forget God; you who enjoy the blessing of the sun and rain, and the fruits of the earth, and yet go on [as] thoughtless of your Divine Benefactor as the cattle of your stall, or who look upon these as things of course or the fruits of your own industry . . . you are practical atheists. Whatever you profess in words, you do in heart and life renounce and abjure Jehovah from being the Governor of the world.[9]

"What Is God Thinking?"

A relative of mine caught me by surprise over the telephone with this outburst of incredulity. She was complaining about all the crises and tragedies and scandals that seemed at that time to be rocking the nation and world—and laying the blame for all of this at the feet of God! After all, if He is in charge, and if He is all-powerful, and if He is good, then what on earth is He doing to allow all this?[10] The obvious implication was that God was either cruel to allow it or impotent to stop it—as though the sinful choices of depraved men and women have nothing to do with it; as though their actions carry, or should carry, no consequences. When was the last time you heard someone express anger at *Satan* for his hateful part in the sin and sadness that afflicts our world? And what makes us so arrogantly assume that we *deserve* the unmixed goodness of God in the first place?

Ironically (and providentially), within two days of that comment on the telephone a massive storm system spawned a cluster of deadly tornadoes that swept right through her city, ransacking nearby areas . . . yet leaving her home unscathed. I could not help wondering if she asked herself, "What was God thinking . . . to let *me* escape those destructive storms?" Why are we so quick to blame God for all the "bad" that happens in the world, while daily we greedily and ungratefully glut ourselves on all the undeserved good we receive from God's hand without so much as a "thank you." At the root of such blindness is a mixture of ingratitude, rebellion, and unbelief in God as He has revealed Himself in Scripture.[11] As author John Blanchard observed,

> Ingratitude is a miserable trait, but a common one; Fyodor Dostoevsky went so far as to say, "I believe the best definition of man is the ungrateful biped.". . . Persistent ingratitude to such a generous Giver, who "causes his sun to rise on the evil and the good, and sends rain on the righteous and the unrighteous," is inexcusable.[12]

Quite apart from any other vice, ingratitude alone places us, at best, on the level of beasts.[13] The child of ingratitude is presumption; and lurking in the financial security we prize so highly is the subtly poisonous peril of presumption. "If everything seems to come simply by signing checks," observed C. S. Lewis, "you may forget that you are at every moment totally dependent on God."[14]

A Look in the Mirror

God is the vital life-support system of every living thing. This is as true for the arrogant atheist, the suspicious agnostic, and the selfish and ungrateful Christian as it is for the spiritually minded believer. It is as true for the young and vigorous, who suppose they have many years of life before them, as it is for the aged and frail. It is as true for you as it is for the person next to you. It is the stubborn insistence of Scripture that every breath we draw is due to the direct preserving providence of God.

- As Hamlet pointed out, we all live—and die—in the providence of God. "The readiness is all." Are you ready?

- How do you use the breath and life and body God has given to you and sustains for you each moment?

- How do we view the moment of death for ourselves, for our loved ones, or for anyone?

- Jesus taught that we manifest our relationship to the Father by being as generous with our love, blessing, good deeds, and prayers toward our *enemies* as He is (Matthew 5:43-48). How do you measure up to that standard?

4

THE PRESERVING PROVIDENCE OF GOD OVER CREATION

The providence of God is His almighty and everywhere present power, whereby as it were by hand, He upholds and governs heaven, earth and all creatures; so that herbs and grass, rain and drought, fruitful and barren years, meat and drink, health and sickness, riches and poverty, yea, and all things come, not by chance, but by His fatherly hand.

—Heidelberg Catechism

God's preserving providence over man is intimately personal, its applications intensely practical. The Scripture teaches that God—not Satan, not nature, and not us—holds our every breath in His hand. Life and health are His alone to give or withhold, to sustain or remove. Whether you are twenty-two or eighty-two, it is entirely appropriate to begin every day thanking the Lord for life and breath and health. They are from Him.

By now we should have overcome our reluctance to accept the preserving providence of God over man, right down to the breath we draw and the hairs on our head. After all, we are uniquely special—the only creature fashioned in God's image. But what about all the rest of creation? What about animals and plants? What about the weather? The solar system? Hasn't God set up the world with a kind of self-perpetuating natural law that keeps everything ticking? Just how interested and active is God in the ongoing affairs of the natural world?

What Does the Bible Say?

God's preserving providence does not extend only to humans. God's maintenance and preservation extend to every living thing, every process, every cycle, every component of His creation. The Bible speaks very plainly and directly about this.

The All-Pervasiveness of Preserving Providence over Creation

Weigh the following assertions and examine carefully the supporting passages that affirm them. The references listed are not exhaustive, but representative and suggestive. Look up the passages and you will discover that the terminology is taken directly from the passages cited.

The sustaining of every angelic being is the direct effect of the preserving providence of God (Nehemiah 9:6; Psalm 104:4; Colossians 1:16-17). The Colossians passage will be discussed later in this chapter. For now it is enough to call attention to the explicit assertion that everything, including things *in heaven* and things *invisible*—"thrones . . . dominions . . . principalities . . . powers" (biblical phrases referring to classes of angelic beings; cf. Ephesians 1:21)—were created and are granted ongoing existence by Christ in accordance with the will and pleasure of the Father. Nehemiah exclaims that God has created *heaven,* and earth and seas and all their respective living creatures, asserting that God is the one who "preserves" (maintains the life of) the inhabitants of each of those spheres.[1] Psalm 104, also discussed later in this chapter, poeticizes this truth.[2] Matthew Henry succinctly summarizes the thrust of all these passages combined when he remarks that angels "are what God made them, what he still makes them; they derive their being from him, having the being he gave them, are held in being by Him, and he makes what use he pleases of them."[3]

The continuance of the cosmos, the planets and stars in their appointed courses, is the direct effect of the preserving providence of God (Psalm 104:2;

Nehemiah 9:6;[4] Isaiah 40:22, 26; 48:13). Each night that you "lift up your eyes on high" to the heavens stretched out like a diamond-studded veil is a testimony of the Creator's ongoing preservation of what He created. He "sits on the circle of the earth"—"a figurative expression for God's providential upholding and maintaining of creation. . . . Seated as a king, He constantly upholds His creation and governs it."[5] He "leads forth" the stars in their nightly array, even calling them by names; by the greatness of His providential power, not one of them fails to appear in its appointed place (see also Job 38:31-33).

The conservation of all natural processes within the physical world is the direct effect of the preserving providence of God (Psalm 65:9-13; 104:5-13; 147:8, 15-18; Jeremiah 5:24; Matthew 5:45; Acts 14:17). The psalms in particular graphically depict God as watering and tending the earth, maintaining its fruitfulness, and ordering the weather by His word and according to His will (see also Job 38:22-29, 34-35). This is not simply poetic license or rhetorical embellishment for dramatic effect. The same truths are soberly reaffirmed by narrative statements as well.

The maintenance of all animal and plant life is the direct effect of the pre-serving providence of God (Psalm 36:6; 104:14-30; 147:9; Nehemiah 9:6; Matthew 6:26; 10:29; Luke 12:6). God preserves the life of every beast, gives food to lions and ravens, maintains the life of all living things on the land and in the seas, remembers to care for sparrows and governs over the fall of each one. Do these assertions evoke the cocked eyebrow of skepticism, or the wry half-smile of one too sophisticated to fall for such simplistic notions? Don't confuse the literal with the physical. God does not physically catch the antelope and deliver it to the lion's den, nor drop the meat into the young ravens' mouths.[6] But just as I *see to it* (do you recognize that as providential terminology?) that our bird feeders are maintained in the winter and our cupboards have what my children need so they can prepare a meal for themselves, God literally and personally maintains and provides for the life of beasts on an earthly scale.[7] More-over, He is intimately aware of their habits and their needs (Job 38:39–39:8, 26-27). Again, this is not merely the stuff of poetry. Christ

Himself, in the soberest terms of assurance, "reminds us of the providential care that God continually takes of everything that He has created."[8]

The preservation of the life and health of every person is the direct effect of the preserving providence of God (Psalm 36:6; 66:9; Matthew 10:30; Luke 12:7). This was the thesis and focus of the last chapter and needs little elaboration here. The eloquent exclamation of William Newell, however, is worth noting.

> Ghastly wonder of all the ages: man, a creature, whose very name is need, need, need; who must be "kept" from outside himself, like a newborn babe supplied with breath, with food, with air; kept in balance by a power wholly without himself; who must be warmed by a created sun; the temperature of his body kept by a marvellous adjustment; his blood kept circulating; his heart kept beating—yet the constant effort of human "science" and "philosophy" [and, indeed, of our own depraved mind and flesh] is to get as far away as possible from the consciousness of this creating, providing, maintaining Lord God![9]

In short, *all of creation* continually exists solely because of the ongoing, active, preserving providence of God. Indeed, "according to the Bible nothing in the whole universe would continue to exist for one slightest fraction of a second without God. . . . On the contrary it would cease to exist the very moment God should withdraw His preserving hand."[10]

The Scriptures leave no realm unaffected by the Lord's providential preservation. According to the Bible, the sustaining of every angel, the continuance of the entire cosmos, the conservation of all natural processes, the maintenance of all flora and fauna, the preservation of every person—created in the image of God, regenerate or unregenerate, Christian or heathen, well known or unknown—is the work of God's preserving providence.

Some of the church's great hymns (though perhaps not enough of them) celebrate the providence God exercises over every aspect of creation. Daniel O. Roberts's well-known "God of Our Fathers" opens with a reference to God's providence over the cosmos that directly reflects

Isaiah 40:26 (cited above). To get past the poetic lilt and grasp the stanza as a sentence, observe the punctuation as you read.

> *God of our fathers, whose almighty hand*
> *Leads forth in beauty all the starry band*
> *Of shining worlds in splendor thro' the skies,*
> *Our grateful songs before Thy throne arise.*

Isaac Watts's majestic "I Sing the Mighty Power of God" focuses on God's creative greatness but includes a stanza on His preservation.

> *There's not a plant or flower below*
> *But makes thy glories known,*
> *And clouds arise and tempests blow*
> *By order from thy throne;*
> *While all that borrows life from thee*
> *Is ever in Thy care,*
> *And everywhere that man can be*
> *Thou, God, art present there.*

Robert Robertson opens a hymn with the plea "Mighty God, while angels bless Thee may a mortal sing Thy praise?" For what does he wish to praise the Lord? Among His other excellencies, God's all-inclusive providence:

> *For the grandeur of Thy nature,*
> *Grand beyond a seraph's thought;*
> *For the wonders of creation,*
> *Works with skill and kindness wrought;*
> *For Thy providence that governs*
> *Through Thy empire's wide domain,*
> *Wings an angel, guides a sparrow,*
> *Blessed be Thy gentle reign.*

THE PRESERVING PROVIDENCE OF GOD OVER CREATION

And Robert Grant's "O Worship the King" expresses the fullness of soul that overwhelms anyone who finally grasps but the hem of the garment of God's providential care.

> *Thy bountiful care what tongue can recite?*
> *It breathes in the air, it shines in the night,*
> *It streams from the hills, it descends to the plain,*
> *And sweetly distills in the dew and the rain.*

It even sounds as if Grant had Psalm 104 in mind when he penned those words.

A Psalm on God's Preserving Providence over Creation

Psalm 104 is an exquisite declaration of God's preserving providence over all of His creation. Take a few moments to read reflectively through this psalm. Note the activities *explicitly* attributed to God as the cosmic Architect (vv. 1-6) of creation. Having laid solid, sturdy foundations for the earth (v. 5), God clothed it with the seas (v. 6) but set boundaries for the oceans (v. 9). The psalmist turns from these lofty contemplations to more intimate activities of God's fatherly preserving providence over creation (v. 10 ff.). The present tense throughout underscores God's ongoing, active maintenance of every aspect of His creation.

- *God* sends springs into the valleys to refresh His creatures (vv. 10-12).
- *God* waters the hills from His chambers to make the earth fruitful (v. 13).
- *God* causes grass to grow for grazing animals and vegetation for man's sustenance and pleasure (vv. 14-15).
- *God* plants trees for birds to nest in (vv. 16-17).
- *God* appointed the times and seasons of the moon and sun (v. 19).
- *God* makes the darkness (v. 20).
- *God* feeds the animals (vv. 21, 27-28).
- *God* gives and takes away the breath of all His creatures (vv. 29-30).

Twentieth-century New Testament scholar and founder of Westminster Theological Seminary, J. Gresham Machen, poses a series of searching questions on this marvelous psalm of God's providence.

> Have we outgrown that wonderful passage? Have we outgrown the conviction that God feeds the lions that roar after their prey in the night, that He provides a habitation for the birds of heaven, that all His creatures, small and great, wait upon Him that He may give them their meat in due season? Have we outgrown the words of the Lord Jesus when He said that God has so clothed the lilies of the field as that even Solomon in all his glory was not arrayed as one of these? Have we outgrown His conviction that not a sparrow falls to the ground without God, and that God feedeth them from day to day? Has scientific agriculture or the scientific study of botany or biology made these things to be out of date? Have we with our overmuch knowledge outgrown the simple conviction of Jesus and of the Psalmist that every living creature receives its meat from God. Well, my friends, if that is so, if these things have really come to be out of date, then we have lost far more than we have gained.[11]

Have we outgrown the Bible—simple faith in the unambiguous assertions of God's words? If so, where *will* you put your faith and confidence? What is left?

Key New Testament Passages on God's Preserving Providence

The New Testament contains two key, comprehensive passages relating to God's preserving providence over creation. Perhaps these passages have come to your mind sometime throughout the last three chapters. They have been purposely held in the wings. Our previous discussions have better prepared us to see them now in a new light so that their all-inclusiveness and their very specific minuteness will have a fresh impact on us.

Colossians 1:16-17. "*By Him all things consist.*" "Consist" translates a Greek word (*sunistemi*) that means "to stand together, hold together, cohere." The Greek historian Herodotus used this word to designate a "standing army"—that is, an army held together rank on rank solely by the order of the commanding officer.[12] Hold that image in your mind; we will return to it momentarily.

This verse "means nothing less than that Christ is the principle of co-hesion in the universe, making it a cosmos instead of a chaos."[13] Christ is "the unifying band which encompasses everything and holds it together. This applies not only to the largest things of the universe, but also to the smallest things of the universe."[14]

The remarks of the nineteenth-century Scottish commentator John Eadie may exercise your mind but they will feed your soul, so they are well worth the effort of reading.

> All things were brought together, and are still held together *in Him*. The energy which created is alone competent to sustain. . . . *In Him* this sustentation [sustaining] of all things reposes. *He* is the condition of their primary and prolonged being. What a vast view of Christ's dignity! *His* arm upholds the universe, and if it were withdrawn, all things would fade into their original non-existence. . . . The mighty and minute are alike to Him whose supervision embraces the extinction of a world and the fall of a sparrow. . . . Every pulsation of our heart depends on *His* sovereign beneficence who feeds us and clothes us. . . . All things which He has evoked into being have their continued subsistence *in Him*.[15]

But *how*, exactly, does Christ hold all things together? By what means does He do this?

Hebrews 1:3. "*Upholding all things by the word of His power.*" "Upholding" represents the Greek word (*phero*) commonly translated "bear" or "carry." You have probably seen images of Atlas, standing stationary with feet planted as he bears up under the great weight of the world on his back. That is *not* the image conveyed by this Greek word. The word does not refer to a static action of barely holding up or merely supporting but to a dynamic activity of movement.[16] This would be the word used if Atlas were to pick up the world and carry it along with him to a destination of his own choosing.[17]

What does Christ bear up and carry along "on their appointed course"? *All things.* Is this divine hyperbole? Inspired exaggeration? Or do we accept God at His word? But by what means does He sustain and carry along all things? *By the word of His power.* The same word by which He spoke worlds into existence (Genesis 1; II Peter 3:5; Hebrews 11:3) providentially maintains their continued existence. "The creative utterance which called the world into being requires as its complement that sustaining utterance by which it is maintained in being."[18]

Let's return for a moment to the imagery of the standing army. Have you ever seen pictures of a graduation ceremony at a military institution such as West Point or the Naval Academy? The smartly dressed graduating class maintains perfect rank and uniform order under the command of the presiding officer. But once the word of dismissal is given, chaos reigns as hats fly into the air and graduates noisily disperse in every direction. One might say the class comes "unglued." That is precisely what would happen were Christ to "dismiss" all of creation from the cohesive power of His commanding word. "He impresses upon creation that unity and solidarity which makes it a cosmos instead of a chaos."[19]

All of creation continually exists, coheres, and is carried on towards its appointed goal by the ongoing, active, preserving providence of God exercised in Christ through His omnipotent word. Do not miss the preeminence of Christ in all this. It is the unblinking declaration of the New Testament that "every living thing is sustained in being by the Lord Jesus Christ, the eternal Son."[20] The work of preserving providence over all of creation centers explicitly, in both New Testament passages, in the person and activity of the Lord Jesus Christ. An unknown poet enshrined this truth in the opening line of another of the church's best-loved hymns: "Fairest Lord Jesus, Ruler of all nature."

Christ is the center of God's self-revelation in the New Testament (Hebrews 1:1-3), the visible image of the invisible God (Colossians 1:15; Hebrews 1:3*a*), the agent and actor of creation (Colossians 1:16; Hebrews 1:2*b*), and the sole providential sustainer of all He has made (Colossians 1:17; Hebrews 1:3*b*). Consequently, He has been granted the unrivaled rank of preeminence by the Father (Colossians 1:18; Hebrews 1:4 ff.), because in Christ all the fullness of Deity dwells in bodily form (Colossians 1:19; 2:9). The final manifestation of that preeminence granted by the Father will be when every knee of every being (human or angelic) created and sustained by the Son will bow in solemn submission to His sovereignty, and every tongue in heaven and in earth will acknowledge in reverent confession His Lordship (Philippians 2:9-11; cf. Isaiah 45:23).

You may refuse Him that honor now, but you will be compelled from without and impelled from within to do so when He removes His sustaining providence and you come face to face with the terrible goodness you have spurned.

> *And then shall know both devil and man,*
> *What I was and what I am.*[21]

Or you may be persuaded to do so now and embrace His claims as the Creator of your being, the Sustainer of your life, the Savior of your needy and sinful soul, and the Lord of all. You need only respond to His call,

> *Look unto me, and be ye saved, all the ends of*
> *the earth; for I am God, and there is none*
> *else.*[22]

A Look in the Mirror

Everything and everyone owe their ongoing existence to the preserving providence of God. What practical effects should that realization have on your outlook on life and death? Your daily decisions? Your future plans? Your attitude and relationship to God? Can you think of verses that describe a biblical response to these truths? Here are a few:

- II Corinthians 6:2—"Behold, now is the accepted time; behold, now is the day of salvation."

- Proverbs 27:1—"Boast not thyself of to morrow; for thou knowest not what a day may bring forth."

- James 4:14—"For what is your life? It is even a vapour, that appeareth for a little time, and then vanisheth away."

- Ecclesiastes 9:10—"Whatsoever thy hand findeth to do, do it with thy might; for there is no work, nor device, nor knowledge, nor wisdom in the grave, whither thou goest."

- Psalm 6:5—"For in death there is no remembrance of thee. in the grave who shall give thee thanks."

- Psalm 66:8-9—"O bless our God, ye people, and make the voice of his praise to be heard: which holdeth our soul in life, and suffereth not our feet to be moved." (The middle phrase, "which holdeth our soul in life," has reference to God's preserving our life. One translation puts it more graphically: "who keeps our soul among the living.")

- Psalm 104:33—"I will sing unto the LORD as long as I live: I will sing praise to my God while I have my being."

5

GOVERNING PROVIDENCE: A CASE STUDY

No thought can enter into the mind of man better adapted to promote its piety

and peace than this—that the world is under the government of God, and all

the events of our lives under the direction of His providence.

—Orton

So far we have focused specifically on the preserving providence of God. Without that preserving providence, there would be nothing to govern and guide. But what is the point of preservation without purpose? And how is any purpose accomplished without governing and directing what is preserved? The Bible teaches that God does not preserve the life and order of His creation to no purpose. Working hand in hand with God's preserving providence is His governing providence.[1]

One of the pinnacles of the mountain range of providence in Scripture is the story of Joseph. Divine fingerprints are unmistakable throughout the narrative. Taking the time to read through the account (especially Genesis 37, 39-45, and 50) will dramatically enhance your profit from this study and your personal persuasion of the truths it uncovers. You may want to read the entire narrative through before you start this chapter or to work your way through it gradually as we go along so that the details of the text are fresh in your mind.

Before moving into the specifics of Joseph's life and looking for principles of God's governing providence, let me remind you of our definition for the governing aspect of God's providence:

> God guides and governs all events, including the free acts of men and their external circumstances, and directs all things to their appointed ends for His glory.

Notice that this definition does not say that God initiates or causes all events. If we are to maintain biblical precision in our understanding and application of scriptural truth, the terms we choose to state it are vital. We must be willing to acknowledge all that the Bible clearly affirms but at the same time insist on no more than the Bible clearly affirms.[2] Some events God certainly initiates or causes. Some events God certainly could not cause or initiate because they are inherently sinful. But Scripture is clear that God nevertheless governs over even the sinful choices and actions of people. If He didn't, that would preclude His control over a vast segment of human activity!

Can God Do Anything?

When I was in high school, a fellow student once asked me, "You believe God can do anything, right?" His confident tone made me suspicious. "It's not a trick question," he lied. Still suspicious, I cautiously answered, "Yes." "Okay," he said, "can God make a rock so big that He can't pick it up?" It was a trick question. I would like to have answered, "Of course He can . . . and then He can pick it up, too" (after all, an inane question deserves an inane answer)—but it didn't occur to me then. The absurdity of the question is even more self-evident if you ask it this way: "Is omnipotence so omnipotent that it can defeat omnipotence?" It is one of those silly pseudo-intellectual schoolboy games that atheists play to pretend that their rejection of God is logical (Romans 1:22). Here's another: Can God make 2 + 2 = 6? (Answer: No, only a product of the American public school system can.) As Charles Ryrie remarks, the question has nothing to do with power but with arithmetic. "One might as well ask if a nuclear explosion could make $2 + 2 = 6$."[3]

The point is that there are things God cannot do. Even we cannot do things that contradict our nature (such as survive indefinitely without food or water). God cannot do things that contradict His own nature any more than we can. For instance, He cannot deny Himself (II Timothy 2:13) and He cannot lie (Titus 1:2). Both of those assertions should be a great comfort to us regarding every scriptural truth we discover in the course of this book. But the Bible erects another impassable boundary more directly pertinent to our discussion of providence: God cannot be tempted to do evil, nor can He tempt any man to do evil (James 1:13). Yet the Scripture is equally clear and insistent that God rules over and uses (for His glory and our good) even those sinful actions that He neither encourages nor initiates—but that He allows.[4] Perhaps nothing illustrates this truth more clearly and explicitly than the biblical narrative of Joseph.

What Does the Bible Say?

The Bible is often misconstrued, even by Christians, as primarily a collection of sacred sayings—a series of stated truths, a textbook of systematic theology, an assortment of doctrines and proof texts. Do not misunderstand; the Bible is a book of doctrine that teaches all the truths God has chosen to reveal to man. And portions of the Bible are devoted to stating much of that doctrine in straightforward propositional form. But God has communicated His truth through an intriguing and delightful variety of literary forms. He manifested His intimate knowledge of the human heart, which He fashioned, when He did not give us merely a sterile "Book of Sayings to Live By" but a multifaceted revelation that spans virtually the whole range of human forms of communication.[5] He sovereignly and wisely chose a diversity of very human means through which to reveal Himself, and in which to couch eternal truth. In terms of its source and subject, its origin and content, therefore, the Bible is a thoroughly divine book. In terms of its varied literary forms, it is a profoundly human book.

One of the most rewarding forms of revelation to investigate is historical narrative. We call them "stories," a term that in no way undercuts their historical factuality (the word "story" itself comes from the Latin word *historia*). Knowing our nature, God gave us stories as one of the primary—and one of the most effective—means of communicating eternal truth.[6] Think about how much of your Bible, Old and New Testaments, is in the form not of doctrinal statements but of stories. Statements declare doctrinal truth; stories illustrate doctrinal truth. Doctrinal statements are like skeletons—bare bones, but absolutely essential to give form and order and interconnection to the body of revealed truth. Stories flesh out that skeleton, incarnate that truth, demonstrate how the doctrine looks and moves and acts in the real world of flesh and blood. The Joseph narrative fleshes out what God's governing providence looks like in the lives of real people in time and on earth—people like you and me—facing the same kinds of circumstances we face.

Joseph is the prince of providence. In the absence of any Bible to guide or comfort or direct or assure him, Joseph displays a remarkable knowledge of God and an implicit trust in Him that is even more noteworthy. In fact, if you will take the time to list and examine all of Joseph's references to God, you will discover an impressive theology that reveals a profound understanding of the Lord and His ways.[7] The existence and presence of God were very real to Joseph. Joseph's own words often reveal that he was profoundly conscious of God's direct involvement and activity in every aspect of daily life. In other words, Joseph had a keen sense and practical understanding of God's providence. No one's experiences more vividly reveal the providence of God at work. And no one's responses to such "dark" providences—such perplexing, disheartening and undeserved circumstances—manifest a more deep-rooted and sublime confidence in the God of providence.

GOVERNING PROVIDENCE: A CASE STUDY

Genesis 37

The story opens with an intriguing display of favoritism. Jacob is frequently castigated for his fatherly failure in showing partiality toward Joseph (as symbolized by the special robe). Granted, such preferential treatment is not a wise parental policy. What makes this passage intriguing, however, is that Jacob's favoritism has a divine parallel. Often overlooked in the narrative is the fact that Jacob's display of favoritism toward Joseph is mirrored by *God's* display of favoritism toward Joseph—manifested in the giving of two special dreams that indicated God's choice of Joseph for a unique task.

Speculation abounds regarding Joseph's handling of his obviously God-given dreams. Some suggest that Joseph brought all his trouble on himself by his lack of wisdom (at best) or his arrogance (at worst) in relating the dreams to his brethren.[8] While such inferences may be plausible, they are speculations that do not enjoy the luxury of any actual textual support. Nothing in the inspired narrative faults Joseph's behavior or attitude. The bottom line, as far as the narrative is concerned, is that they were not Joseph's dreams of self-importance; they were God-given dreams of *revelation* that simultaneously functioned as both a focal point for Joseph's faith[9] and a test of his family's submission to God's choice and purposes.

Genesis 37 fleshes out a number of principles regarding God's providence.

God, in His providence, blesses, exalts and uses whom He will

Joseph's God-given dreams initiate the topic of providence by demonstrating this biblical principle. This is not the first time God, contrary to all natural expectations, chose to exalt and use the younger in a family. Joseph's own father, the younger of twins, was chosen by God over his older brother. Nor will it be the last time God does so. (Remember, David was the youngest of eight boys.)

"That's not fair!" is a familiar complaint to the ears of any parent. A child's inherent sense of "fairness"—defined as absolute equality in all treatment, privileges, and amounts—is acute and sometimes in need of adjustment. ("Sally got six peas less than me! Why do I have to get more? That's not fair." Or, in my children's case, "Ethan got two more Brussels sprouts than me! Why does he get to have more? That's not fair." Honest.[10]) Therein lies the painful point—such a preoccupation with "fairness" is inherently "childish." It is to be expected with children; it should be otherwise with adults.

As a father, my typical reply to my children is the universal parental adage that "life isn't always fair"—and they need to learn that. My wife has sometimes remarked that such a reply might implicitly suggest to them that God is not always fair since He is in control of our life. But is God always fair? That depends on our definition of "fair." If it means—as it does to a child—that everyone always gets exactly the same things (the same quality of gifts, the same amount of dessert), then clearly no, God is not always "fair" according to our fallen perception of fairness. But God is always right and God is always good. That sometimes translates into what may appear to us to be "inequality" or "unfair" treatment. But the fact is, God also providentially superintends and often uses the unfairnesses of life to accomplish His purposes in and for us and those around us. How much of what happened to Joseph was fair? But how much of what God allowed was He right to allow?

Part of God's providential dealings in our lives is His right and freedom to bless and exalt and use whom He will—whether it happens to be you or someone else. Whether that seems "fair" to us is not the point. How we respond to God's providential choices is the point. The next principle illustrates this fact dramatically.

God, in His providence, allows and uses the anger and hatred of people to accomplish His purposes

The Bible's explicit emphasis on the brothers' demeanor toward Joseph demonstrates this principle of providence. The opening narrative highlights three facts about Joseph: his righteous character (37:2),[11] his unique relationship with his father (37:3-4), and his selection by God for an unexpected destiny (37:5-11). What was the reaction of his brothers to these facts? Note Genesis 37:4, 5, 8, 11 and mark the phrases describing the brothers' attitude toward Joseph: they *hated* him; they *could not speak peaceably* to him; they *hated him yet the more*; they *hated him even more*; they *envied* him. Do you suppose the Holy Spirit's repetition of the brothers' hatred, anger, envy, and resentment is intentional? Or do you think their reaction is perfectly understandable, legitimate, and beside the point? From both a literary and spiritual standpoint, their hostility is not beside the point. It *is* the point.

Here's an interesting observation that ties together both of these first two propositions about providence. What do these pairs have in common?

Abel and Cain	Moses and Aaron / Miriam
Jacob and Esau	David and Saul
Joseph and his brothers	Jesus and His (half) brothers

Each represents a pair or group that had every natural reason to get along. In every case but one, they are siblings. But in each case, the first was clearly chosen or favored by God in some unique way, prompting an undeserved negative, envious, sometimes even murderous reaction from the latter.

This principle is expressed most straightforwardly in Psalm 76:10: "Surely the wrath of man shall praise thee: the remainder of wrath shalt thou restrain." What a comfort to the child of God! All the heated expressions of anger and sinister strategies of hatred are under the providential governance of God. In fact, He uses those very sentiments and the actions they generate to accomplish His will. Whatever will serve His purposes and ultimately contribute to His praise is permitted and employed to His ends. Whatever will not, He restrains. God puts examples of this truth on display many times over in the Scriptures. If you think Genesis 37-50 is the record of how God managed to turn a horrible display of hostility and sibling rivalry or a series of misfortunes into something good, you have seriously misunderstood the text. Genesis 37-50 is a record of how God providentially accomplished what was His sovereign purpose all along. That will become more apparent as this chapter unfolds.

Again, many get sidetracked in this portion of the narrative by focusing on the effects of Jacob's unwise and unfair favoritism towards Joseph.

After all, if anyone should have known the folly of parental favoritism and its effects on sibling relationships, it should have been Jacob. (Remember his background growing up with Esau?) Some might even argue that none of this terrible story would have happened were it not for Jacob's foolish show of unjust favoritism toward Joseph. Is that true? Was all this, even from a human standpoint, really Jacob's fault?

Forget Jacob for a moment and suppose this scenario: What if the brothers had chosen to respond differently? You see, that is what the inspired narrative emphasizes—their attitudes toward Joseph. The focus is not on Jacob and the folly of his favoritism. (If anything, the story implies a parallel between Jacob's favor toward Joseph and God's choice of Joseph.) The thrust is this: "Here is a set of circumstances with the apparent stamp of God upon them (the dreams)—just or not, agreeable or not, comfortable or not, 'fair' or not. Now, how are you going to respond? Anger? Hatred? Envy? Resentment?"

From a human standpoint, none of Joseph's unjust sufferings would have happened if his brothers had chosen to react righteously. Nevertheless, what the larger story of Joseph illustrates is that God orchestrates all such human reactions—justified or not, sinful or not—to accomplish His larger purposes.[12] In this case, God's larger purpose was to move Joseph and, through him the entire fetal nation of Israel, into the womb of Egypt, to be nurtured and preserved from the corrupting influences of the Canaanites[13] until He determined to bring them back out by means of a spectacular deliverance that would become the touchstone event for all of God's subsequent saving activity throughout history.[14] (A "larger purpose" demands a larger sentence!) That was God's ultimate purpose for Joseph.

> It is clear, therefore, that Joseph was sent to Egypt not as an act of punishment, but as a blessing of divine providence, for Yahweh was using him to prepare the way for a period of incubation in which the nation of Israel would grow and mature in Egypt and become a suitable servant people (Genesis 50:19-21).[15]

So in this case, God's "larger purpose" had the profoundest theological implications for the rest of redemptive history. You see, though Joseph is the central figure of the narrative, something much, much bigger than Joseph is going on here.[16]

God's providence incorporates the faithfulness and obedience of His children

It would be easy to overlook this facet of the story. It is almost too obvious. But it is worth pausing to spell out. We tend to focus on the reassuring truth that God providentially rules over (and sometimes overrules) apparently coincidental or even outright negative incidents. While that is a great comfort to the child of God, it can lead to a kind of fatalism that excuses sin and disobedience. But there is another equally valid, and mysterious, side to providence.

Throughout the entire narrative, Joseph is never once cited for doing anything dishonorable or sinful. We read of the doubt and dishonesty of Abraham (the "friend of God"), the temper of Moses (the "man of God"), the adultery of David (the "sweet psalmist of Israel"). But we do not find a breath of blame uttered against Joseph for anything in the narrative (see note 8). He is consistently presented as obedient, pure, selfless, thoughtful, and genuinely God-fearing.

Obviously, I am not suggesting that Joseph was sinless. He was not. I am simply pointing out the significance of the divinely directed and selected depiction of him in the inspired narrative. There are few characters in the Bible— particularly among those who occupy as much space as Joseph does—who are presented in such consistently positive terms. Joseph faithfully served and diligently obeyed his father, fled from moral temptation, selflessly and thoughtfully ministered to others, and maintained a remarkable persevering faith in God.

At the very time Joseph was pursuing the path of duty and obedience to his father's commission, God providentially permitted this horrendous betrayal by his brothers. It was in the course of faithful service and diligent obedience that all this "bad stuff" happened. Yes, God providentially works in spite of and through all the "bad stuff." That working is God's responsibility. But God's providence also works through our obedience, our faith, and our faithfulness even in the face of all these negatives. Those responses are our responsibility.

The providence of God is never intended to lull us into a lackadaisical attitude of fatalism, as if our actions don't really matter because God rules and overrules however He wants anyway. It is revealed to maintain a glow of energizing trust that, despite all appearances to the contrary, God is governing for His glory and my good—a trust that inspires me to stay faithful, obedient, loyal and devoted to Him, and confident in Him. Spurgeon's observation on another doctrine is equally applicable to providence in general: providence "is a bed for some men's idleness; for us, it should be a couch for our refreshment."[17] God's providence, then, encompasses and incorporates the faithfulness and obedience of His children. This observation, subtly introduced in Genesis 37, will be repeatedly confirmed in Genesis 39.

God's providence often encompasses human aid

Take the time to read Genesis 37:15-17 and ponder its purpose in the overall context. It seems to be a peculiar and unnecessary addition to the narrative, does it not? Why do we need to know how Joseph found out where his brothers were? Why didn't the Holy Spirit just save some space and tell us that he finally found them in such and such a place? What purpose does this detail serve?

The Holy Spirit never wastes words. Joseph's brief encounter with this unnamed individual who just "happens" to know where his brothers have gone is anything but incidental to the story. It is pivotal. All the events that transpire afterwards hinge on Joseph's "chance" meeting with this "certain man." This is not designed to evoke panic over how many events and experiences in our lives are dependent on happenstance and come within a hair's breadth of not happening. The point is exactly the opposite! There *is* no happenstance, no chance, and no luck about it! God providentially arranged this man's access to knowledge that Joseph would need, directed Joseph to come in contact with him, then employed this anonymous individual and his knowledge to conduct Joseph to where his brothers were so that he would arrive at just the time when (1) Reuben would be there to safeguard his life, and (2) a particular caravan headed in a particular direction would happen by. That leads to the next strange twist in this tale.

God, in His providence, restrains evil plans and intentions that do not serve His purposes

Genesis 37:18-22 reveals God's providential protection and preservation of Joseph. Clearly, the immediate intention of Joseph's brothers was to murder him (Genesis 37:18-20). All the external circumstances (out in the wilderness and away from home) favored such a plot. But God, through Reuben's persuasion, prevented the deed. What was God doing? Exactly what Psalm 76:10 describes! He was restraining the deeds of human wrath that would not serve His purposes—and He was doing so, it must be noted, in incredible kindness to Joseph's brothers. Before the story ends, they will become the direct and primary beneficiaries of God's prevention of their evil intentions. Without Joseph, they would later have perished in a famine.

God, in His providence, may allow the failure of good intentions

Here is another curious bend in the road of God's providential arrangement of these events. Reuben's intention was to get Joseph safely back home to their father (Genesis 37:22). Yet we know from the story that his good intentions failed. At some point after Joseph was thrown into the pit, Reuben apparently left on some errand. We do not know precisely when he left or why, but we know that when "Reuben returned" to the pit he was dismayed to discover Joseph's disappearance. Just as God providentially used Reuben's counsel to prevent Joseph's death, God providentially employed Reuben's unexplained absence to effect Joseph's journey to Egypt. That's when Judah's counsel prevailed. And that's when the next operative principle of providence becomes apparent.

God's providence encompasses apparent coincidences

Consider the intricate orchestration of events and timing that had to take place for God to, if you will forgive the turn of phrase, "pull this off." While Joseph was looking for his brothers—who had coincidentally relocated to Dothan, which just happened to lie along a major trade route—a caravan was working its way southward down that trade route toward Egypt. When Joseph arrived, Reuben was there to persuade the brothers to spare his life; but then he inexplicably disappeared. The caravan (consisting, interestingly, of Abrahamic descendants by either Keturah or Hagar) happened to pass by Dothan not only *after* Joseph's arrival but *during* Reuben's absence. This may be coincidence, but it is providentially orchestrated coincidence.[18] And it sets the stage for the next principle of providence.

God, in His providence, may allow us to be betrayed and cruelly sinned against

This is a difficult one. Can we accept the plain affirmation of Scripture—and actually apply it to our own personal experiences and circumstances? Yet this is a conclusion to which the story inexorably drives us. I like to think of Genesis 37:25-27 as "providential relocation." Granted, it was not exactly a posh, first-class seat on a pleasure cruise. But it was God's method, employing the evil deeds of wicked men, for relocating Joseph to the place of His appointment.

Does that mean God initiated their deed? Impossible. Does that make God responsible for their sin? Unthinkable. Does that mean God temporarily lost control of the situation and will now have to take steps to try to amend the damage? Out of the question. It means that, no matter how unjustly you may be treated, there is someone in charge—setting boundaries, guiding, governing, permitting . . . and restraining, for His wise and benevolent purposes and, yes, for your good.

Before we leave Genesis 37, I wonder if you have noticed anything unusual about this chapter in your Bible. Look carefully through everything that happens. Does anything, or anyone, seem to be missing in all of these life-jarring events? Genesis 37, where the circumstances of this godly young man rapidly deteriorate from bad to worse, contains no reference to God whatsoever.

This is no narrative oversight or literary coincidence. God is directly mentioned in every chapter of Genesis up to this point (except Genesis 34 and 36, the latter of which is entirely genealogy). Is His absence from the story here an accident? No, it is reflective of our perception of reality. The nonmention of God in Genesis 37 is a purposeful literary omission that often mirrors our experience. (In chapter 8 we will focus on the extension of this omission from an entire book of the Bible.)

Often we do not sense God's presence or see His hand of intervention, especially when things seem to be going wrong. But the fact is, God is there. Like the undeniable effects of an invisible wind, you can see God's presence and activity implicitly throughout the unmistakably providential events of Genesis 37. After a brief parenthesis in the story (Genesis 38), we will be reminded explicitly in Genesis 39 (vv. 2, 3, 21, 23, et al.) that God was, in fact, present all along, just silent. And not merely present, but providentially active and intimately involved in every incident of Joseph's life. For some reader, the "silence" of and about God in Genesis 37—coupled with His "reappearance" in Genesis 39—should be a cherished token that when "bad" things come crashing down in your life, it does not mean that God has forsaken you. You are then, as much as ever, the object of God's attentive, if silent, presence.

Genesis 39

Genesis 39:2 and 3 remind us of the providential presence of God throughout the distressing developments of Genesis 37. They also communicate the blessing one experiences from God when he maintains a right attitude toward the Lord and toward his own circumstances. Joseph certainly was not perfect. Still, it is amazing that we never hear a breath of complaint leave his lips. In every new set of circumstances in which he finds himself, he gives himself to the tasks at hand with diligence and resolute cheerfulness—and all without any Bible in his hand.

Just when things seem to be going smoothly, however, Genesis 39:11 introduces us to yet another providential relocation. Like the last one, it is accomplished through the evil actions (false accusation) of a wicked person (Potiphar's wife). But it is a necessary relocation if God is to fulfill His word to Joseph (the dreams), move him into a position of blessing, and accomplish His larger purposes. Read Genesis 39:11-20. Here is another hard saying. Can you apply this principle of providence to your experience?

God, in His providence, may allow us to be falsely accused and unjustly maligned

Before you feel sorry for yourself in unjust circumstances, before you allow yourself to fume with righteous indignation over some injustice you have suffered, pause. Take time to remember and reflect, again, not only on Joseph but on Jesus—the cruelly betrayed, the unjustly accused, the falsely maligned, the undeservedly punished. Nothing you or I suffer will ever match those experiences. And their inclusion is not for our entertainment but for our instruction; God intends that we follow their example:

> For this is thankworthy, if a man for conscience toward God endure grief, suffering wrongfully. For what glory is it, if, when you be buffeted for your faults, ye shall take it patiently? but if, when ye do well and suffer for it, ye take it patiently, this is acceptable with God. For even hereunto were ye called: because Christ also suffered for us, leaving us an example, that ye should follow his steps: . . . who, when he was reviled, reviled not again; when he suffered, he threatened not; but committed himself [or, committed His suffering circumstances[19]] to him that judgeth righteously (I Peter 2:19-23).

Joseph's reaction to being wrongfully imprisoned on false charges (Genesis 39:21-23) once again awes the sensitive and sympathetic reader. No complaint or grumbling. No anger or bitter resentment to poison his spirit. Sorrow? Certainly. Confusion? Probably. But in the face of all this, an explicit trust in God (see note 7) enabled him to display an excellent and diligent spirit—and enabled God once again to bless Joseph with His presence and prosperity.[20] Joseph's attitude toward what happened to him and who was in control was central to God's ability to use and elevate him. Joseph was robbed of his reputation and position; but his character he retained and his faith he maintained. Only Joseph's location had changed; and God relocated him because He again had other ministries and greater plans for him. Genesis 39:21-23 introduces another principle, more positive in nature.

God, in His providence, gives us favor with those of His choosing

"A good man," wrote Matthew Henry in his reflections on this passage, "will do good wherever he is, and will be a blessing even in bonds and banishment; for the Spirit of the Lord is not bound nor banished."[1] The story of Joseph is repeatedly punctuated with injustice upon injustice. Try to imagine reading through this narrative for the very first time. How would you react to each twist in the story? The sympathetic reader cannot help being genuinely outraged at each successive injustice that Joseph suffers, yet amazed, humbled, and instructed when he comes to the end and discovers that it was God providentially superintending all these events and injustices and using them to accomplish gracious purposes, not only for Joseph but also for the very perpetrators of that injustice, and for their sovereignly elected descendants.

Genesis 40

Genesis 40:5-7 demonstrates that the genuineness of our faith affects our attitude toward affliction, and our attitude toward affliction affects our behavior in the face of affliction. The key to our behavior is our attitude, and the key to our attitude is our faith. Even in the midst of personal injustice, Joseph displays a self-forgetfulness that expresses itself in a genuine concern for the needs and troubles of others. In so doing, he demonstrates another principle of providence.

God, in His providence, gifts us to minister to others

Just when we think we see God's method for getting Joseph out of prison developing (Genesis 40:14-15), the story hits another unanticipated roadblock. After Joseph showed great compassion and extraordinary spiritual gifts, the butler repaid Joseph's kindness with "the unkindest cut of all." Not malice or even conscious ingratitude. Rather, he merely forgot Joseph (Genesis 40:23). In fact, we are told that the butler apparently never gave another thought to Joseph for two full years (Genesis 41:1, 9)! We do not bear ingratitude well, but forgetfulness can be even more painful to endure—the absence of any notice taken by anyone of all our labors, our sufferings, our gifts, even our help. Here again, however, God means to instruct us through the experience of Joseph.

God, in His providence, allows our suffering to be prolonged, our gifts and abilities to go unnoticed, our deeds to be forgotten, sometimes for a long time

Think about the importance of timing here, and you will see again the hand of providence at work even in the unthoughtful overlooking of Joseph. What if Joseph had been remembered immediately by the butler? Suppose the butler had spoken for him and Joseph had been promptly released. Joseph's natural inclination would certainly have been to return home if at all possible (see Genesis 40:15). But God did not want him home. He had a great and vital work to accomplish through Joseph. God was preparing and preserving all things, and especially Joseph, for a coming crisis—indeed, the crowning crisis of Joseph's life. God had other, greater, bigger, more long-term plans for him. When we feel forgotten, our sufferings unnoticed, our labors unappreciated, our gifts unused, we must remember that our experience is not unique. God's timing is perfect. Men may forget us, but God never forgets or fails to take notice. And God has a purpose.

Genesis 41

After two more undeserved years, finally Joseph's time comes—or rather, God's time for him comes—to be remembered, released, and providentially placed (Genesis 41:9, 14). This sets the stage for the next principle.

God, in His providence, causes us to be remembered and recognized in His timing, and lifts us to minister to others

Let's back up for a moment to look at Joseph's life with a wide-angle lens. When the story began, Joseph was a seventeen-year-old with a dream waiting to happen—literally. This divine dream-promise indicated that God had big plans ahead for Joseph. You might assume that such a young man would not be vaulted to such a high destiny all at once. You'd be right. You might assume instead that God's means for getting him there would involve a number of gradual steps up. You'd be wrong. It's actually a number of gradual steps *down*: (1) hated by his brothers; (2) nearly murdered but cast into a pit instead; (3) sold into slavery in a foreign land; (4) falsely accused and imprisoned; (5) forgotten two more years in prison; only then, finally, (6) vaulted to the throne of Egypt. We tend to see each downward step as a delay, a detour, a reroute. But under the providence of God, each apparent downward step, each seeming delay, is actually the most direct and necessary step toward the place of God's purpose and appointment.

Have you ever played Monopoly? I must confess an intense dislike for the game that I call "Monotony." But not long ago I pulled out the board and looked at it. When you play, you have a player's perspective—a panoramic bird's-eye view of the whole board. But imagine yourself for a moment not as a player but as the iron, the shoe, the race car, or the lead pipe (oops, wrong game! Just seeing if the editor is paying attention). In life we tend to have the perspective not of a player but of a game piece—not the panoramic bird's-eye view but a horizontal, linear, limited, board-level view—as we work our way slowly from square to square, landing on "INCOME TAX" or "LUXURY TAX" or "GO TO JAIL" (there's an appropriate one for Joseph!) or someone else's property or the uncertain "CHANCE" square. And in between, it seems we spend an interminable amount of time waiting for our turn to move again so that we can "get somewhere." But the squares on our "board" say things like "FINISH SCHOOL," "PAY OFF BILL," "WORK TWO JOBS," "LOSE JOB," "NO MARRIAGE YET," or "SERIOUS ILLNESS." There is one other significant difference: Monopoly boards have "CHANCE" squares; life's board has "PROVIDENCE" squares. God is the one moving us. He sees all our downward steps as the necessary movements of His child in exactly the right direction all the way along. And He is not rolling dice!

There was no other route that would lead Joseph from a seventeen-year-old boy in Canaan to a thirty-year-old man on the throne of Egypt in fulfillment of God's promised revelation—no other path that would adequately prepare him and place him in that position than the path down which God led him. Factor this in, too: on a human level, everything that happened to Joseph (both bad and good) happened because he consistently resisted sin and temptation.

God weaves delays into the pattern of life for my ultimate good. Think of delays from His perspective. We are so frantically time bound. God is not. You say, "But I'm twenty-five and I don't have the kind of job I thought I'd have by this time!" Joseph was thirty. You say, "But I'm thirty and I'm not married yet!" Isaac was sixty-five. You say, "But I'm thirty-five and I don't have a ministry yet." Moses was eighty. You say, "But I'm forty and I don't have children yet!" Abraham was a hundred (okay, Sarah was only ninety-five). The point is, time is a worry only to us. It never has been to God. Learn to rest in Him, walk with Him, obey Him, and cultivate contentment wherever His Hand has put you now. He has a strategy, a purpose, a method—and all the power and persuasive tools necessary to do whatever He pleases.

Our delays are God's opportunity to effect our spiritual maturity.[22] It is the very "trying of your faith" through delays that produces patience (James 1:3). "But let patience"—and by the way, this is not a "let" of suggestion or permission, but an imperative—allow patience to have its mature work. Why? Just because it "builds character"? No. "So that you may be mature and entire (literally, may have your whole allotment, every grace and skill God intends you to have for what He intends you to accomplish), lacking nothing" (James 1:4).

Our delays are God's opportunity to complete our preparation. Joseph was not ready for the throne with its enormous responsibilities and the demanding tact and insight required for governing and dealing wisely with people—not until he was done with Third Year Prison Classes.

Our delays are God's opportunity to prepare circumstances for His timing. The Lord used Joseph's "down time" to arrange an entire array of conditions that Joseph, himself now fitted for the challenges that would meet him, could step into and handle successfully. God often uses crises to create needs in people—needs that only He can then minister to and meet. So He determined not only to send famine to Egypt but also to warn Pharaoh through a dream that troubled him and that he could not figure out through his accustomed means. God then uses the failure of those traditional helps to create room for His intervention. The magicians on whom Pharaoh normally depended were specially trained in oneiro-mancy, the interpretation of dreams.[23] These advisors were the pillars on which Pharaoh was accustomed to lean in such predicaments, but here they proved useless. Indeed, it is as providential that they were unable to interpret the dream as it was that Joseph was able to. Finally God brings His servant into this vacuum. God prepares the place and the circum-stances and the crises. It is our responsibility to be sure that we have been submitting patiently to the Lord's timing and giving ourselves to what-ever preparation He subjects us so that when the time comes, we are ready to step into what God calls us to. Crises, it has been said, do not make the man (or woman); crises simply reveal what we have—or have not—been becoming in the mean time.

What, then, do we do during times of seeming delay? The biblical an-swer is "wait"—specifically, wait on the Lord. But waiting is not "doing nothing." Waiting on the Lord "is a definitive spiritual exercise" that fo-cuses your attention, submits your spirit, and teaches your soul to delight in the very presence of God Himself. "Choosing to wait on God takes you beyond the immediate problems, the painful circumstances, and gently eases you into the presence of the Lord."[24] An additional skill honed by delay is learning contentment in the midst of our present circum-stances—not seeking escape from them. Like Paul (Philippians 4:12), we learn contentment not by finally getting what we want but by adjusting our longings to match our God-ordained situation.[25] Our assignment during delays is to follow Joseph's example, to be both content and dili-gent while actively waiting on Him for His perfect purposes and His per-fect timing.

God, in His providence, employs natural phenomena to effect His purposes in people's hearts

The fruitful years came and went, allowing the silos of Egypt to be filled in anticipation of the coming famine—a famine that, from the biblical narrative's perspective, had one primary function: to move the chosen family into Egypt to become the chosen nation. Again, however, it will be helpful to step back and get a broad picture of what God had to do to accomplish this purpose.

More than four thousand miles long, the Nile is the earth's longest river. Egypt's agriculture was utterly dependent on it. The river was the lifeblood for all the cropland along the Nile flood plain and especially in the large, fertile delta region where the Nile dumped all its nutrient-rich silt. But what is the Nile's major source? Lake Victoria and the mountain rivers that flow into it. And where is Lake Victoria? In eastern central Africa between Uganda and Tanzania.

We take it for granted that God controls all the weather all the time, at least in a general way (though our frequent displeasure with the weather often belies the sincerity of our belief). But consider for a moment this one specific example of the detail involved in God's providence. In order to fulfill this specific dream-revelation to Pharaoh, God was providentially controlling the weather patterns continually for fourteen years (seven years good and seven years bad), not only over Egypt and Canaan and the surrounding nations but also over central Africa four thousand miles away.

Even more amazing is that God's providential activity in this story ranged from controlling massive weather patterns for years and years over millions of square miles to prodding the intimate inner workings of specific human hearts. Imagine in your mind's eye a satellite image of weather patterns spanning from the Mideast all the way down to central Africa. Now, from that satellite image, zoom in through the clouds onto the continent of Asia, onto the Mideast region, onto the land of Canaan, onto the village of Hebron, into the tents of Jacob, and finally into the very thoughts of Judah, Reuben, and the other brothers. As the story unfolds, God's providence is doing just that—simultaneously controlling vast weather patterns and deploying surgical strikes directly to the hearts and consciences of those men, just as Genesis 42 begins to record. And we think America has surgically precise "smart bombs"! The range of God's power and providence is a stunning thing to contemplate.

GOVERNING PROVIDENCE: A CASE STUDY

Genesis 42-44

As Genesis 42 opens (vv. 1-5), the focus of the story now turns from Joseph in Egypt to his family back in Canaan. Likewise, the lessons of providence shift from the experience of Joseph to that of his family. The notion that God unfailingly blesses His children with material abundance has always had its advocates. Biblical examples to the contrary abound, however. It is corrupt-minded and truth-deprived men who preach the health-and-wealth gospel that godliness and gain go hand in hand (I Timothy 6:5). The truth is found in the next principle of providence.

God, in His providence, may allow His own people to suffer need

We don't like this one. Famine and starvation are serious threats. But there are even more important issues. God must often use a material crisis to get our attention so that He can then redirect that attention to our deeper spiritual needs. This is precisely what He does with Joseph's brothers, who for years had sought to squelch their unquieted memories. Read Genesis 42-44 attentively and you will witness a remarkable phenomenon: the awakening of conscience. Every time some distressing turn of events arises, the brothers instantly attribute it to God's judgment for their unresolved sin committed against Joseph over twenty years earlier (see Genesis 42:21, 28 and 44:11-16).

God, in His providence, causes us to face the consequences of our sins and actions

God leads the brothers, through distress, to (1) identify the deed that has triggered their predicament (42:21), (2) acknowledge that God is dealing with them (42:28), and (3) confess the iniquity of their deed (44:16). As Judah pours out the story to this "Egyptian" (unaware, of course, that he is simultaneously confessing to the very one he so wickedly wronged), he reveals the specific conviction he and his brothers keenly sense years later, his genuine concern for Jacob's feelings, and a striking change of character.

God, in His providence, can effect a total transformation of character, though it be years later

The mark of genuine and humble repentance is not merely an admission of guilt but a willingness as well to submit to whatever consequences God (through your circumstances) deems appropriate. Joseph's brothers showed this willingness to accept what they understood to be the consequences for their sin against Joseph—and against their father, Jacob. Perhaps most amazing is, of all people, Judah's willingness to take Benjamin's place as a slave (see 44:18 and compare to the "old" Judah in 37:26). What a supernatural transformation has taken place in these brothers!

Genesis 45, 50

Read 45:4-8 and you cannot fail to hear the reassuring repetition falling earnestly from the lips of Joseph: "God did send me," "God sent me," "it was not you that sent me but God." Joseph had a penetrating grasp of the providence of God. Finally the resolution comes. Reconciliation is made. Equilibrium is restored. And the whole "mystery" of providence is spelled out by Joseph in plain language, with no Scripture to teach him such truths. Yet he displays a profound understanding of God and His ways that, quite frankly, shames us by its implicit and unflinching childlike faith.

Genesis 50:15-21 beautifully underscores the truth that what man means for evil, God intends for good. Even wicked acts committed against us with evil intent are turned, by God's providence, to God's purposes—which are always good. Nevertheless, despite all Joseph's assurances and kindnesses to them, the brothers still could not bring themselves to believe that Joseph bore no lingering ill will against them. Little did they understand how deeply Joseph—through all his trials—had come to believe and rest in God's providence. They could not help wondering if perhaps Joseph was not saving his revenge until after their father died. So they fabricated a "dying request" from Jacob to Joseph that he should forgive them and not avenge the evil they had done to him. No doubt grieved that the brothers still suspected the sincerity of his forgiveness and wondered what revenge he might secretly be plotting against them, Joseph once more showed his quality and his faith.

In case you haven't noticed throughout the story, this last episode makes one final allusion to the providential fulfillment of the dreams that started this whole story in the first place! Joseph's brothers "fell down before his face" (50:18). The dream-prediction that his brothers despised and derided initially (37:5-11) they repeatedly fulfilled unwittingly (42:6; 43:26, 28; 44:14) and, in the end, finally obeyed consciously and submissively. God always has a way of providentially impelling men to bow in submission to His purposes.

The psalmist catches this truth of God's providence in this story when he attributes the experiences of Joseph directly to the doing of God. Psalm 105 opens with a call for praise: "O give thanks unto the LORD; call upon his name: make known his deeds among the people." Notice what were some of those deeds of the Lord, and who was responsible for these events (vv. 16-19):

> *He* called for a famine upon the land; *He* broke the whole staff of bread.
> *He* sent a man before them, even Joseph, who was sold for a servant,
> whose feet they hurt with fetters; he was laid in iron, until the time that
> His word came; the word of the LORD [tested] him.

A Look in the Mirror

Was Joseph's treatment right? Was it fair to Joseph? What would be your natural reaction to such hatred and betrayal and neglect? How would you feel about your brothers? More importantly, how would you feel about God? Have you ever experienced betrayal, false accusation, being forgotten or unnoticed? How much revelation did Joseph have on which to base his understanding and interpretation of his circumstances? Yet how did Joseph respond? Now think about how much revelation about God you have, and your responses to similar kinds of injustices.

If you ever feel unfairly treated, unjustly maligned, wrongly accused, ungratefully forgotten—compare your experience to Joseph's. Measure your response to his. And if that doesn't work, compare yourself to the ultimate example of unparalleled, undeserved, unjust suffering—Jesus Christ. C. S. Lewis once candidly observed, "We are not necessarily doubting that God will do the best for us; we are wondering how painful the best will turn out to be."[26]

God's best may sometimes be painful. But by eternal standards our affliction is light and momentary, producing a far greater weight of glory (II Corinthians 4:17). How do we measure our present affliction by those eternal standards? By looking not at the things that can be seen but at the things that cannot be seen; for visible things are only temporary, but the things that are invisible are eternal (II Corinthians 4:18). Look at Paul. Look at the martyrs. Indeed, look "unto Jesus" (Hebrews 12:1-3). All our pain in the providence of God must ultimately be measured by the providentially governed suffering of Jesus Christ. And even if you, like the sparrow, "fall" in the midst of His will, it will not be "without your Father" (Matthew 10:29-31). Nor, if you know Him, will it be the end.

6

THE MYSTERY OF PROVIDENCE

God's providence is powerful. . . . It is so powerful that it even brings good out of evil; making bad men and fallen angels to serve God's designs, while they intend no such thing: giving the greatest efficiency to causes apparently the most contemptible; and infallibly securing the very best ends. . . . All conspiracies and combinations against providence are vain. . . . He who rejects the mystery of providence must ever be in perplexity.

—William S. Plumer

I hope you have been taking the time to read and ponder the quotations at the head of each chapter. They have not been included as an afterthought or inserted for decorative purposes. They have been selected as concise and classic expressions of the various aspects of providence that each chapter addresses. They are some of the "pearls of providence" (see Appendix B). We now return to a question raised earlier in our definition of God's governing providence. How does God providentially govern human deeds and decisions without violating human will?

God's providential control over our external circumstances is often difficult enough for us to accept. Nevertheless, we have seen many explicit examples of this truth in Scripture. Once again, our job is to bring our thinking into line with the clear affirmations of God, not to adjust the Bible's assertions to fit our preconceived perceptions. But how is it that God "guides and governs all events, *including the free acts of men*"? This chapter explores that facet of God's providence in more detail. It will not provide a detailed explanation of the dynamics and mechanics of that divine operation; that remains largely shrouded in silence, which is the reason this chapter is titled the "mystery of providence." Nevertheless, numerous biblical examples unmistakably buttress the truth that God's providence encompasses, but does not violate, "the free acts of men."

Part of the mystery of providence resides in the fact that God rules and reigns over all things according to His will and pleasure (Ephesians 1:11), yet man is still fully responsible and accountable for his choices and actions. In other words, God exercises His providence and accomplishes His will *through* the free and voluntary choices and attitudes of men and women. Were this fact limited to God's persuasive working in *believers*, that would be amazing enough. But it is equally true of the wicked. God never prompts evil men to sin, yet even their rebellion against Him and their hostility against His people is providentially governed and employed by God. (The clearest example of this, found in the events surrounding the Crucifixion, will be the specific focus of chapter 11.)

What Does the Bible Say?

The working of providence pervades the entire Exodus account—from the hiding, finding, and nursing arrangements of the infant Moses (Exodus 2) to the plagues that directly assaulted the supposed domain of Egypt's gods (see Exodus 18:11).[1] There is, for instance, the strikingly direct statement of divine involvement in Israel's escape. The LORD, the text says unblinkingly, "took off their chariot wheels" so that it was obvious to the Egyptians that the LORD Himself was fighting against them (Exodus 14:24-25). But the greater mystery of God's providence—His operation through human choices and attitudes without violating human will and responsibility—is underscored in the encounters with Pharaoh.

THE MYSTERY OF PROVIDENCE

The Holy Spirit is not capricious or careless in His use of words. It is incumbent upon us, therefore, to handle the text of Scripture attentively and accurately. If we are to form a correct understanding of the facts of the story (and, consequently, to arrive at sound theological conclusions), it is vital that we carefully observe the details—and confine our conclusions to the information explicitly communicated by those details. We must joyfully be slaves to the text.

Who Hardened Pharaoh's Heart?

The hardening of Pharaoh's heart is a recurring and, indeed, dominating, theme in the narrative of Exodus. The *idea* is first hinted at when God commissioned Moses at the burning bush. After explaining Moses' task and message, God assures him, "And I am sure that the king of Egypt will not let you go. . . . And I will stretch out my hand, and smite Egypt with all my wonders . . . and after that he will let you go" (Exodus 3:19-20). How did God know this? Obviously, because He is omniscient. He knows all things. But how will He *accomplish* this? He reveals that bit by bit as the story unfolds.

The next eleven chapters of Exodus (4-14) contain *eighteen* explicit references to the hardening of Pharaoh's heart (and one reference to the hardening of the hearts of Pharaoh's soldiers). It would be helpful to underline or highlight them in your Bible; that way you can locate them easily and the force of this Spirit-inspired emphasis will arrest your attention whenever you read the account. Repetition in God's Word is purposeful, not accidental or insignificant. The Holy Spirit uses repetition to rivet our attention to an important point.

It is not enough, however, merely to notice the emphasis on the hardening of Pharaoh's heart. Because the Holy Spirit's repetition is purposeful and His wording is deliberate, it is essential to notice in each reference specifically *who* is hardening Pharaoh's heart. A definite progression of development is evident in each of the references. Close attention to the text is imperative. I hope you will read through this section with your Bible open beside you.

The following references are listed chronologically and include a literal translation of the key phrase in each verse. In most cases, the rendering will merely reinforce and emphasize what you can see for yourself in your own Bible. In a few cases, however, the literal rendering may differ slightly from what you see in your text. In addition, the subject of the verb is indicated in all capital letters, since it is particularly important to notice in each case who is the one actually doing the hardening.

God warns that He will harden Pharaoh's heart (Exodus 4:21; 7:3)

The first reference comes in the form of God's prior announcement to Moses (before Moses ever confronted Pharaoh) that, when the time came, He would harden Pharaoh's heart: "I [GOD] *will* harden his [Pharaoh's] heart" (4:21).

On the way to the next reference, however, notice that Pharaoh's *own voluntary initial response* to God's demand through Moses was a negative one: "Who is the LORD, that I should obey his voice to let Israel go? I know not the LORD, neither will I let Israel go" (Exodus 5:2). In other words, even before God commences His providential hardening of Pharaoh's heart, Pharaoh's free and independent inclination was to rebuff Israel's God and reject Moses' request.

The next reference to the hardening of Pharaoh's heart is another reassurance from God to Moses that He was *going* to do this. The wording of the text indicates that God Himself had not yet begun to harden Pharaoh's heart: "I [GOD] *will* harden Pharaoh's heart" (7:3). God's providential hardening was yet to come. First, however, Pharaoh repeatedly reconfirmed his own innate inclination and hardness of heart.

Pharaoh hardens his own heart (Exodus 7:13, 14, 22; 8:15, 19, 32; 9:7)

The next reference is both crucial and problematic. It is crucial in what it communicates, but potentially problematic because of its traditional translation. The text literally reads that "the HEART of Pharaoh hardened" (7:13).

First, there is no "he" (either expressed or implied) in the Hebrew text of this verse. The very same Hebrew construction also appears in

7:22, 8:19 (8:15 in the Hebrew text), and 9:35. In every one of these cases, the Authorized Version translates this Hebrew phrase, "Pharaoh's heart was hardened." The indefiniteness of this translation in these three passages is much closer to the Hebrew than the translation of the identical Hebrew construction in 7:13.

In addition, the Hebrew verb form here is not an active voice, but neither is it passive or reflexive. In other words, grammatically speaking, the Hebrew does not say that "he [God] hardened" Pharaoh's heart (active voice); nor does it say that Pharaoh's heart "was hardened" by some outside force or influence (passive voice); nor does it say that Pharaoh's heart "hardened itself" (reflexive voice). Rather, the Hebrew text is *describing the condition* of Pharaoh's heart and its *reaction* to God's demand. We would say that Pharaoh's heart "hardened" or "stiffened." Or it could be translated that Pharaoh's heart "was hard" or "was stubborn." That is, his heart was unmoved by the miraculous display and unyielding to the accompanying demand. Textual commentaries reveal a consistent consensus that the proper translation of 7:13 is something akin to "Pharaoh's heart hardened" or "Pharaoh's heart was hard."[2]

The theological ramifications of the wording of this text are significant. After all, this is the first reference to the *actual* hardening of Pharaoh's heart. If God's twofold prediction that He would harden Pharaoh's heart were immediately followed by the assertion that "he [God] hardened Pharaoh's heart," that would raise a question. Was that "fair" to Pharaoh? Was God forcing him to do something he would not otherwise have chosen to do, "programming" him to respond in a way that, if left to himself, he might have avoided? And this is not just about Pharaoh. Remember, an entire nation also was severely judged for his steadfast refusal. If God "made" him respond contrary to what he otherwise would have chosen and then judged him for that artificially imposed choice, wouldn't that impugn God's justice?

This is not an attempt to tinker with the text in order to make it fit more comfortably with a preconceived theology. It is exactly the opposite. This is a conscious effort to be as accurate as possible with the text and allow its wording to dictate our theology. And according to the text, the *first* one to harden Pharaoh's heart was not God but Pharaoh.[3] In fact, as we will see, the first *seven* consecutive references recounting the actual hardening of Pharaoh's heart reveal that *Pharaoh first hardened his own heart* or that *his heart hardened*. This does not change the fact that God did, in time, add His judicial hardening to the process. But in doing so, He was not forcing Pharaoh to choose contrary to his own desire or inclination. He was merely confirming Pharaoh in his hardness, in keeping with the choices and inclinations Pharaoh had himself already expressed—the "free acts" he himself initiated.

We have seen, then, the first reference to the actual hardening (7:13). The next six consistently maintain the same emphasis—Pharaoh hardened his own heart:

- "the HEART of Pharaoh (is) hard" (7:14)
- "the HEART of Pharaoh hardened" (7:22)
- "PHARAOH hardened his heart" (8:15; 8:11 in Hebrew)
- "the HEART of Pharaoh hardened" (8:19; 8:15 in Hebrew)
- "PHARAOH hardened his heart" (8:32)
- "the HEART of Pharaoh hardened" (9:7)

God finally hardens Pharaoh's heart (Exodus 9:12)

Only after these seven references to Pharaoh's own hardness of heart do we find God actively intervening for the first time: "the LORD hardened the heart of Pharaoh" (9:12). Matthew Henry issues a fearful and solemn warning about the hardening of Pharaoh's heart: "Willful hardness is commonly punished with judicial hardness. If men shut their eyes against the light, it is just with God to close their eyes. Let us dread this as the sorest judgment a man can be under on this side of hell."[4] Have you shut your eyes against any light from God's Word?

Pharaoh further hardens his heart (Exodus 9:34, 35)

After a single reference to God's hardening of Pharaoh's heart, the text returns to describe how Pharaoh personally perpetuated the hardening process:

- "PHARAOH hardened his heart" (9:34)

- "the HEART of Pharaoh hardened" (9:35)

God further hardens Pharaoh's heart (Exodus 10:1, 20, 27; 11:10; 14:4, 8)

The heart-hardening that Pharaoh himself initiated, God then judicially extended not only on Pharaoh himself but also, in the end, on his armies (see 14:17 below), in order to accomplish all His purposes. God's hardening was nevertheless in keeping with Pharaoh's own previously expressed wishes and inclinations.

- "I [the LORD] have hardened his [Pharaoh's] heart" (10:1)

- "the LORD hardened Pharaoh's heart" (10:20)

- "the LORD hardened Pharaoh's heart" (10:27)

- "the LORD hardened Pharaoh's heart" (11:10)

- "I will harden Pharaoh's heart [to pursue]" (14:4)

- "the LORD hardened the heart of Pharaoh" (14:8)

- "I will harden the hearts of the Egyptians [to pursue]" (14:17)

Since all men are "made for the honor of the Maker," notes Matthew Henry, reflecting on the Egyptians' self-destructive pursuit of the Israelites against their better judgment, "those whom He is not honored *by* He will be honored *upon*." Then he adds for our application and encouragement, "what seems to tend to the Church's ruin is often overruled to the ruin of the Church's enemies, whose pride and malice are fed by Providence, that they may be ripened for destruction."[5]

GRAMMATICAL SYNOPSIS OF
THE HARDENING OF PHARAOH'S HEART

Here is a summary of all the passages describing the hardening of Pharaoh's heart. Verses in parentheses denote the reference in the Hebrew Bible.

Reference	Subject	Verb	Object
4:21	Yahweh	(will) harden	(Pharaoh's) heart
7:3	Yahweh	(will) harden	(Pharaoh's) heart
7:13	(Pharaoh's) heart	hardened	[none]
7:14	(Pharaoh's) heart	(is)	hard [predicate adjective]
7:22	(Pharaoh's) heart	hardened	[none]
8:15 (8:11)	Pharaoh	hardened	(his) heart
8:19 (8:15)	(Pharaoh's) heart	hardened	[none]
8:32 (8:28)	Pharaoh	hardened	(his) heart
9:7	(Pharaoh's) heart	hardened	[none]
9:12	Yahweh	hardened	(Pharaoh's) heart
9:34	Pharaoh	hardened	(his) heart
9:35	(Pharaoh's) heart	hardened	[none]
10:1	Yahweh	hardened	(Pharaoh's) heart
10:20	Yahweh	hardened	(Pharaoh's) heart
10:27	Yahweh	hardened	(Pharaoh's) heart
11:10	Yahweh	hardened	(Pharaoh's) heart
14:4	Yahweh	(will) harden	(Pharaoh's) heart
14:8	Yahweh	hardened	(Pharaoh's) heart
14:17	Yahweh	(will) harden	(Egyptians') hearts

But how?

How did God harden Pharaoh's heart? Through what mechanism? At least part of the answer involves the extension of opportunity. God gave Pharaoh opportunity, from the first request in chapter 5 all the way through the sixth plague, to reveal his own inward obstinacy and pride. Once Pharaoh had displayed his will repeatedly, God continued His demands and miraculous works, confirming an irreparable hardness and rebellion in Pharaoh's willful heart. The world will witness such hardness on a much wider scale in response to the coming tribulation plagues.

Revelation 16:9, 11, and 21 describe a similar stubbornness reflected in man's progressively vehement and blasphemous revolt against the divine sender of those plagues and the only one who can deliver them through their repentance of the very deeds that have brought His judgment in the first place.

Is It Fair?

The apostle Paul anticipates this very question in Romans 9. After citing God's words to Moses in Exodus 33:19 ("I will have mercy on whom I will have mercy," Romans 9:15) and God's words *through* Moses *to* Pharaoh in Exodus 9:16 ("I have raised thee up, that I might show my power in thee," Romans 9:17), Paul concludes that God has mercy on whom He chooses and hardens whom He chooses (Romans 9:18). Now comes the anticipated objection in the next verse: *You will say to me, then, "If that is the case, why does God still fault those whom He hardens? For who has ever resisted His will?"* Paul's answer in verse 20 bluntly brooks no argument: *On the contrary, O [mere] man, who are you to talk back to God?*[6]

That may not seem to be a satisfying answer, but it is an appropriate and sufficient—and inspired—answer. By it, Paul underscores his point that God is not only unanswerably sovereign and free but also that He is unquestionably righteous and good. The oft-missed concluding emphasis of the passage is not on His hardening, but on His mercy and compassion shown out of free grace to the undeserving. Note the positive direction the argument takes in Romans 9:23-30.

Incidentally, Scripture nowhere teaches that God actively hardens everyone to whom He does not show mercy. Pharaoh is presented as an individual example not a universal pattern, an exception not the rule. God does not show mercy on some and then harden everyone else; He does not need to. Apart from His gracious drawing and intervention, the rest will naturally follow their own fallen inclinations.[7] That is precisely the point the Exodus narrative makes about Pharaoh's own free and independent initial responses to God. And it is precisely the same point that the Genesis narrative makes about Esau's attitude toward the birthright. Paul alludes to this example as well to illustrate his point.

God Himself reveals that He loved (chose) Jacob and hated (rejected) Esau (Romans 9:13; cf. Malachi 1:2-3). Yet, read the Genesis narrative and you will discover that God's selectivity was not arbitrary or capricious or unfair, but perfectly in keeping with Jacob's and Esau's own values and desires. Jacob had an eye and aspiration for the future benefits of the birthright; Esau so disdained and lightly esteemed his privilege that he was willing to exchange it in desperation for immediate physical gratification (Genesis 25:29-34; cf. Hebrews 12:16-17). Repeatedly, their own choices and actions revealed their inner values and validated that God's "election" was perfectly in keeping with their own private wishes.[8] So it is with Pharaoh.

As we have seen from the details of the narrative in Exodus, God's hardening of Pharaoh was not unfair but in keeping with what Pharaoh first manifested regarding his own will and inward disposition. In his poem titled "Providence," George Herbert expresses this truth with profound simplicity: "All things have their will, yet none but thine."

Charles Haddon Spurgeon, universally hailed as the "Prince of Preachers" and a staunch Baptist Calvinist in nineteenth-century London, once asserted that "the divine will is accomplished, yet men are perfectly free agents." How can we reconcile these twin theological truths? The bottom line, if we have the honesty and courage to accept it, is that we cannot. Spurgeon elaborates:

> "I cannot understand it," says one. My dear friend, I am compelled to say the same—I do not understand it either. . . . Certain of my brethren deny free agency, and so get out of the difficulty; others assert that there is no predestination, and so cut the knot. As I do not wish to get out of the difficulty, and have no wish to shut my eyes to any part of the truth, I believe both predestination and free agency to be facts. How they can be made to agree I do not know, or care to know; I am satisfied to know anything which God chooses to reveal to me, and equally content not to know what he does not reveal. . . . Believe these two truths and you will see them in practical agreement in daily life, though you will not be able to devise a theory for harmonizing them on paper.[9]

Other Examples of God's Providential Hardening

Pharaoh does not stand as the lone example of God's providential working in and through free human will. The Holy Spirit records an amazing array of remarkable occasions on which human deeds or decisions are "from the Lord." Again, you will multiply your benefit from the following section if you will turn to each passage in your Bible and read it in conjunction with the brief discussions below.

Sihon, king of Heshbon (Deuteronomy 2:30)

In reply to Moses' peaceful and reasonable request (Deuteronomy 2:26-29), Sihon refused to allow the passage of God's people through his land and instead came out to fight against them. The preceding study of God's dealing with Pharaoh provides a paradigm by which we can rightly understand what happens in similar subsequent cases. Having made up his own mind to oppose Israel, Sihon's obstinacy was confirmed by God who "hardened his spirit and made his heart obstinate"—because God purposed to judge him via Israel's conquest. "God sometimes ruins His enemies by their own resolves."[10] The next passage corroborates and expands on this aspect of God's providential working in the nations whom Israel was commanded to dispossess.

The Canaanites (Joshua 11:19-20)

With the exception of the Gibeonites, no other city sought to make peace with the newly arrived, conquering nation of Israel. Clearly, there were understandable human explanations for this. The inhabitants of the land were fighting for their homelands and their independence from the domination of these apparent newcomers. The bottom line, however, is that God confirmed their own willful resistance because "it was of the LORD to harden their hearts, that they should come against Israel in battle, that he might destroy them utterly, and that they might have no favour." God was working providentially not only to execute His pronounced judgment on the wickedness of pagan, truth-rejecting nations. By hardening them in their own purposes to war rather than to parley with Israel, God was also protecting His own people from the temptation to disobey God, to accommodate His (and their) enemies, and to expose themselves to the evil influence of those nations.

Samson (Judges 14:1-4)

Samson illustrates the fact that even men mightily used by God may be deeply flawed by arrogance and selfishness. That is intended not as an encouragement but as a sober warning. The biblical portrait of Samson repeatedly highlights his selfishness. When God decided that it was time to deliver His repentant people from their subservience to Philistia, He began "seeking an occasion" against the Philistines—an opportunity to set that deliverance in motion. What device did God use to accomplish this purpose? The answer astonishes us, even troubles us. But the text says that the Lord used Samson's inappropriate, unlawful, and unwise determination to take a Philistine wife—even over the rightful objections of his parents.

Did God incite that desire in Samson, or fan the flames of his illicit and unlawful craving? Impossible! The clarion canon of James 1:13-16 once again forbids such a conclusion. That it was "of the Lord" does not mean that God was "leading" Samson to do this but that this development, this turn of events, this success of Samson's selfish and foolish designs was allowed and providentially used by God. God permitted Samson's own selfish purposes to prevail and employed even Samson's sin as the catalyst by which he would initiate Israel's deliverance from under the heel of Philistia. You know the rest of the story of Samson. He paid a terrible price both in life and in death. His "domestic" life was restless, unfulfilling, and in constant turmoil; and his career ended in miserable and humiliating enslavement. Samson is a reminder that God *can* use *anyone*—but to the degree that we "force" God to use us in *spite* of ourselves and our sin and our disobedience, we are the losers. Like Samson, "you and I have enough evil residing in us that if God were to let us have our own way, we would destroy ourselves."[11]

Eli's wicked sons (I Samuel 2:22-25)

The behavior of the sons of Eli the priest was scandalous, but his feeble rebuke was too little too late. These boys appear to have been raised with minimal discipline, little respect for authority, and light regard for things holy. So it was no surprise that they ignored their father's warning of God's judgment. The surprise comes in the Holy Spirit's insertion that their hardhearted disregard of Eli's admonitions was cemented by God's determination to slay them: "they would not listen to the voice of their father, for the LORD desired to put them to death" (NASB).

Did God prompt or initiate or approve of the sins of Eli's sons? Clearly not. They were like the obstinate, idolatrous, rebellious Israelites centuries later who prompted God to utter the frightful verdict "Ephraim is joined to idols: let him alone" (Hosea 4:17). When God leaves you alone in your sin, beware; judgment is crouching at the door. God often ultimately gives people what they want, and sometimes God's greatest judgment is to give people what they insist on.

Ahithophel's good counsel (II Samuel 17:14)

Did you know that God sometimes works to *defeat* sound, sensible counsel? When men pursue a course of rebellion, God may close their ears to good advice because He intends to bring disaster on them. The wider context of this verse pulls back the curtain to reveal part of the machinery of God's working. God was simultaneously answering David's prayer (II Samuel 15:31) and even utilizing David's own strategy (II Samuel 15:34) to accomplish His providential purpose—to defeat Ahithophel's counsel in order to undermine Absalom's coup in order to punish Absalom and reinstate David. Sometimes God's providence works solo, sometimes hand in hand with man. Providence never negates the importance of prayer and prudence on our part. They, too, are tools of providence (as we will see in chapter 13).

Solomon's adversaries (I Kings 11:14-25)

God employed the long-nursed bitterness of two of David's former enemies in order to chasten Solomon by "stirring up an adversary" against him (vv. 14, 23). Note the Spirit-inspired explanation of the human circumstances that led to the actions of these two enemies of Solomon. God is not the author of bitterness but, like human wrath (Psalm 76:10), He can give it enough leash to make use of it for His own purposes.

Rehoboam's impudence (I Kings 12:15, 24; II Chronicles 10:15; 11:4)

      Rehoboam refused to listen to the people's sensible request, "for the cause was from the LORD" to divide the kingdom. The Hebrew word translated "cause" contains a picturesque idiom. The word means "turn." There are, of course, different ways of "turning" (and different Hebrew words to describe them). For example, "turn" may mean to flip over (turn a pancake), to veer in a particular direction (turn the car), or to rotate (turn around). This particular Hebrew word specifically carries the idea of rotating. We would refer to this as a "turn of events" or a "turning the tables." And this development, this "turn" of events, was "from the LORD." God determined to use Rehoboam's arrogant impudence as the hinge on which the door of opportunity would swing for Jeroboam to come to power in fulfillment of His word (I Kings 11).

Ahaziah's visit to Joram (II Chronicles 22:7)

      Ahaziah (wicked king of Judah) allied himself with Joram (evil king of Israel) against Syria. God had determined to judge both through Jehu, anointed to become the next king of Israel. When Joram was wounded in battle, he was taken to Jezreel to recover. Ahaziah decided to visit him there; but God was at work in that free decision on Ahaziah's part. Verse 7 is a little difficult to decipher: "And the destruction of Ahaziah was of God by coming to Joram."[12] In other words, Ahaziah's own decision to visit Joram was providentially orchestrated by God so that He could slay Ahaziah and Joram at the same time through Jehu, "whom the LORD had anointed to cut off the house of Ahab."[13]

Amaziah's stubbornness (II Chronicles 25:20)

      Emboldened by a victory over the Edomites, Amaziah (king of Judah) challenged Joash (king of Israel) to battle. Despite Joash's warning (vv. 18-19)—a parabolic version of "Don't mess with me; you don't know who you're fooling with!"—Amaziah persisted in his arrogant stubbornness. Why did Amaziah foolishly refuse to heed Joash's warning?

Because "it came from God, that he might deliver [Judah] into the hand of their enemies." God did not "goad" Amaziah into ignoring Joash against his better judgment; He did not have to. He simply let Amaziah follow his own way. "The toxicity of [the human] heart is so potent that when God wants to judge a man, all He has to do is turn that man over to his own heart."[14]

But why would God want to deliver Judah into the hand of idolatrous Israel? Poetic justice. Because of *Amaziah's* idolatry. Amazingly, after the Lord gave Amaziah victory over Edom, Judah began worshiping Edom's defeated gods (vv. 14-16). How ludicrous! How absurd! But how sadly and typically human. When men resolve in sinful stubbornness to turn from the Lord, the fountain of life and truth, the only alternatives are self-made, humanly hewn broken cisterns (Jeremiah 2:11-13).

Marauding bands against Judah (II Kings 24:2-3)

When Jehoiakim rebelled against Nebuchadnezzar, "the Lord sent against him bands" of Chaldeans, of Syrians, of Moabites, and of Ammonites. In fact, He "sent them against Judah to destroy it" according to His prophetic promise of judgment. Do you think that these heathen troops had any inkling that their purposes were being directed and prospered by the Lord? Nevertheless, the inspired insistence on the hand of providence behind all this is reiterated: "Surely at the commandment of the Lord came this upon Judah."

Darius and Artaxerxes (Ezra 6:22; 7:27)

Finally, a positive example! The Jews who returned to the land after the seventy-year exile began to rebuild the temple at Jerusalem. Due to local harassment and a change in governmental leaders and policy, however, the work ceased. But God raised up Darius and "turned the heart of the king" toward them; he "strengthened their hands" and charged them to finish the temple construction (6:22). Under the reign of Artaxerxes (some sixty years later), the Jews blessed God for putting it into "the king's heart to beautify the house of the Lord" in Jerusalem (7:27). Both of these monarchs were, as far as we know, heathen men upon whose hearts God moved to accomplish His purposes on behalf of His people.

A Look in the Mirror

Did you notice what all the examples above have in common? It is striking. And, quite honestly, I did not plan or arrange it this way. In every case of God's mysterious providential working in and through the free choices of men, the central figures are all leaders—judges, priests and, most of them, kings. This observation—and the obvious divine arrangement of these examples in Scripture—illustrates a truth about God's providence that is capsulized in Proverbs 21:1: "The king's heart is in the hand of the LORD; like the rivers of water; He turns it wherever He wishes" (NKJV).

The imagery of this proverb is striking. Remember the verses back in chapter 3 that taught us how God holds man's breath in His hand (e.g., Job 12:10; Daniel 5:23)? Here God holds the king's heart—any and every king's heart—in His hand. When we read here about "rivers of water," we probably tend to think of the course of a river, which is fairly established and unchangeable, randomly created by natural forces. But "rivers of water" refer here to man-made canals or irrigation ditches. Just as a farmer digs his irrigation ditches and can redirect the flow of water wherever he wants it to go, God bends, extends, and stretches out the heart of earthly rulers, either to accomplish His pleasure or to restrain His displeasure. Has God ceased this providential working in the hearts of human power brokers in our day?[15]

I have reminded God of this reassuring principle on many prayerful occasions when I faced a decision from some authority figure. The first time I can remember was when I was a high school student working a part-time job and trying to save up money for college. My employer informed me that he could not afford to give me a raise he had previously promised. I left his office, walked out on the loading dock, and prayed Proverbs 21:1 back to the Lord. He knew my need, and I believed the heart of my unsaved employer was in His hand to move it wherever He chose. Later that day he called me back into his office and gave me the raise.

The point of this illustration is not that God will always do what we want Him to do if we pray on the basis of Proverbs 21:1. The point is to remind and reassure us that God will always accomplish what *He* pleases through the choices and decisions of even the most godless and powerful authority. (For another example, see Nehemiah 1:11–2:6.) It is our duty both to draw comfort from that assurance and to submit ourselves to whatever He chooses to do through the "king's" heart as from His hand—whether it is what we want or not.

What personal applications can you draw to your own life or present circumstances from the examples of people like Pharaoh, Sihon, Samson, Eli's sons, Absalom, or Rehoboam? How does the truth of Proverbs 21:1 extend to your situation, and how does it affect your prayers regarding the various relationships in your life? Does God's providence rule over the decisions and actions of your government (Romans 13:1-7)? Your employer (Colossians 3:22-24)? Your parents or your children (Ephesians 6:1-4)? Your brother or sister in Christ?

A POETIC INTERLUDE ON PROVIDENCE

The juxtaposition of chapters 6 and 7, on the mystery and means of providence, provides an appropriate juncture to interject a few more stanzas from George Herbert's poem, "Providence."

In these stanzas, Herbert expounds on God's ability, through His providence, to employ many means (including, as we will see in chapter 7, people and beasts). All such men and means have and exercise their own will, yet in so doing they all perform God's will. God's providence rules over all, whether by command or permission. If only we had spiritual eyes to see and spiritual ears to hear God's "skill and art" as displayed in the amazing works of providence around us, "what music it would be!"

> We all acknowledge both thy power and love
> To be exact, transcendent, and divine;
> Who dost so strongly and so sweetly move,
> While all things have their will, yet none but thine.
>
> For either thy command or thy permission
> Lay hands on all: they are thy right and left.
> The first puts on with speed and expedition;
> The other curbs sin's stealing pace and theft.
>
> Nothing escapes them both; all must appear,
> And be disposed, and dressed, and tuned by thee,
> Who sweetly temper'st all. If we could hear
> Thy skill and art, what music would it be!

7

THE MEANS OF PROVIDENCE

As there are tools of all sorts and sizes in the shop of Providence, so there is a most skilful hand that uses them, and . . . they could no more produce such effects of themselves than the axe, saw, or chisel can carve a rough log into a beautiful figure without the hand of a skilful artificer.

—John Flavel

The workshop of a skilled master craftsman is a treasure-trove of tools. Arranged on his walls is an endless array of implements, each designed and manufactured to perform a particular function. Toolboxes reveal yet more contraptions, gadgets, and devices—some differing only slightly from others in size or design. His "furniture" of saws, drills, lathes, and planes stands ready to perform the specialized tasks for which each was fashioned. The tools themselves are powerless to produce anything of value, use, or beauty. Those same tools in the hands of the clumsy or untrained or inexperienced are ineffective at best and, at worst, potentially dangerous. It takes the hands of what John Flavel called "a skilful artificer" to manipulate these tools to accomplish what he envisions and purposes in his mind.

The means at God's disposal for the providential working out of His purposes are as limitless as His own imagination. In fact, one element that we tend to use to distinguish between "providence" and "miracle" is the spectacular nature of the event or the means employed. Sometimes, however, this distinction can be artificial.

Picture a discouraged prophet who, after a miraculous manifestation of God's power, flees for his life when threatened by a powerful woman. He is accustomed to personal danger. But he never dreamed that after such an incontestable spiritual victory he would still face persecution and rejection. He seems suddenly doubtful or forgetful that the same God who worked such miracles for and through him could continue to protect him from personal threats. God imparts a vital lesson to Elijah (and to us) about the means He uses.

Alone in a wilderness mountain, Elijah is treated to a succession of sensational phenomena in I Kings 19:11-12—a rock-rending wind, a convulsive earthquake, and a blazing fire (like the one God had sent only weeks earlier in answer to Elijah's prayer on Mount Carmel). But the Lord was not in any of those momentous displays of power. Instead, He manifested His power and presence in a "still small voice," a "gentle whisper."

Providence is the whisper of omnipotence, the small voice of a great and active God. He quietly employs the ordinary, foolish, weak, base, and despised things of this world to confound His enemies and to accomplish His purposes. Take a moment to ponder I Corinthians 1:27-29.

> But God hath chosen the foolish things of the world to confound the wise; and God hath chosen the weak things of the world to confound the things which are mighty; and base things of the world, and things which are despised, hath God chosen, yea, and things which are not, to bring to nought [nullify, put out of action, render ineffective] things that are: that no flesh should glory in his presence.

We will return to this passage more than once as the chapter progresses.

What Does the Bible Say?

Many events in the Bible *imply* God's providential involvement. But let's confine ourselves to incidents that the Scripture *explicitly* attributes to God's providence. In hopes of whetting your curiosity to scour other portions of Scripture for similar examples, I want to direct your attention to just one section of God's Word—the historical record in the Books of Kings.

Again, I do not want you to take my word for it. Look up the cited passages and note carefully the wording of the text. I am eager for you to discover for yourself what I have found in the Scriptures. These examples will persuade and minister to you to the extent that you are willing to take the time to be confronted with God's words, not just mine.

God Providentially Uses People

People are one of the means of God for providentially effecting His purposes. That He accomplishes this without coercing their own will, infringing on their voluntary choices, or prompting them to sin is one of the mysteries of providence that we investigated in the previous chapter. There we saw several examples of the fact that God frequently uses men and women to bring about His designs. Here we discover that, often, the people God uses are the ones we might least expect—the weak and the insignificant, as well as the powerful and the corrupt.

A wicked king (I Kings 16:11-13)

God pronounced a prophetic judgment against the wicked Israelite king Baasha (see 16:1-4). Whom did He use to fulfill that prophecy? A godly prophet or righteous ruler? God used another wicked king, Zimri, to execute His judgment against the house of Baasha. Does that mean God led or prompted Zimri to go on his bloody rampage? Certainly not. The barrier of James 1:13-16 blocks that reasoning and prevents us from arriving at that erroneous deduction. God simply permitted Zimri's voluntary choices to effect His will. For another explicit example of God's employment of a man who turned out to be wicked, see God's use of Jehu to execute judgment on Joram (king of Israel) and Ahaziah (king of Judah) with the house of Ahab (II Kings 9). For the clear assertion of providence, see the account in II Chronicles 22 (addressed in chapter 6).

A poor and starving widow (I Kings 17:9-16)

Through whom did God supply Elijah's need of food and drink during a severe famine (of His sovereign sending)? A wealthy friend? A neighboring king? No, God supplied His prophet's needs through a poverty-stricken widow who was herself on the verge of starvation. What could be more unlikely? Yet God instructed Elijah to leave the dry brook bed of the Cherith and go to Zarephath, where *He* had "commanded a widow woman there to sustain" him. An unknown starving widow sustained God's prophet while Ahab's forces searched the land for him. God uses the weak to confound the mighty. Ironically, God's providential provision for *her* need (vv. 15b-16) came *through* her provision for Elijah's need. Her self-sacrificing obedience to "the word of the Lord" (v. 15) was the human key that unlocked the door of God's providential provision not only for Elijah but also for her. This passage, by the way, beautifully and accurately illustrates the New Testament assurance expressed in Philippians 4:19 ("But my God shall supply all your need according to his riches in glory by Christ Jesus").[1]

God Providentially Uses Animals

God also makes use of dumb beasts in His providence. He used Balaam's ass (Numbers 22) and apparently employed hornets to drive some of Israel's enemies out of the land (Joshua 24:12). Here are some other examples from the Books of Kings.

Ravens (I Kings 17:4-6)

Reflecting on this passage of the ravens feeding Elijah, Matthew Henry shares his confidence in a truth he learned deeply from personal experience: "Let those who have but from hand to mouth learn to live upon Providence. . . . He that could furnish a table in the wilderness, and make ravens [the] purveyors, cooks and [servers] to His prophet, is able to supply all our need according to His riches in glory."[2] This is not a theoretical thought from an armchair theologian. Matthew Henry knew firsthand what it was to experience "hand to mouth" circumstances. In 1662 his father, Philip Henry, a Nonconformist pastor, was turned out of his pulpit when the Act of Uniformity was passed in England (requiring all ministers to conform to all the forms of worship practiced by the Church of England or face fines, jail, and even banishment). His livelihood deprived and his furnishings confiscated, Philip Henry and his family joined the ranks of some two thousand other suddenly unemployed Nonconformist ministers (including John Bunyan) who suffered persecution and deprivation for their faithfulness to the cause of Christ.

A lion and a donkey (I Kings 13:1-32)

The Word of God sometimes paints some startling images. Picture the strange setting described in I Kings 13:24-25. An eerie silence surrounds a lion and an ass, standing together beside the crumpled form of a human body on the edge of a dusty road. The lion has just attacked the man, pouncing upon him as he was riding along on the donkey, mauling and killing him. But he is not eating the carcass. Stranger still, the ass did not bolt when the lion attacked; in fact, it doesn't even seem to be afraid of the lion at all!

Both animals stand together beside the road, motionless except for an occasional swishing of the tail or turning of the head, as if obeying some silent command. And for how long? This uncanny scene lasted for some time. Several people "passed by and saw" it, then reported it to others in the city before the old prophet (to whose lie the slain man of God had fatally listened, 13:11-19) came upon the same sight. This is no natural phenomenon or accidental coincidence. Everyone knew what had happened and understood why (13:26). What a sovereignly preserved portrait of a providentially arranged event! God's providential tools? A lion and a donkey—both of which seem to have resisted their natural instincts at the inaudible command of their Creator.

Dogs (I Kings 22:38; II Kings 9:30-37)

Part of God's pronounced judgment against both wicked Ahab and bloody Jezebel was that dogs would play a role in their final disgrace. Dogs were to lick up Ahab's blood in the same place that they had lapped up the blood of Naboth, the innocent man cruelly murdered by Jezebel's henchman so that the pouting Ahab could acquire Naboth's prime real estate (I Kings 21:19). Likewise, God said, dogs would eat the cursed corpse of cruel Jezebel (I Kings 21:23). This is not at all what you would expect at the death of wealthy, powerful, royal personages. It was utterly unlikely, contrary to all expectation. But the mouth of the Lord had spo ken it, and in each case it came to pass exactly "according" to His word. Such incidents also illustrate a principle we will see in more stunning de tail in the next chapter—God's minute attention to and inclusion of often unnecessary details, as a further evidence that these events are not accidental but providential.

God Providentially Uses Inanimate Objects

Let's return to I Corinthians 1:27 for a moment: "But God hath cho sen the foolish things of the world to confound the wise." Do you notice anything unusual? God chooses foolish *things*? The Greek word for "fool ish" is neuter here and is rightly translated "the foolish things."[3] In con trast, "the wise" is masculine in form and refers to wise people. In other words, God sometimes uses foolish *things* in this world to confound wise *people*![4]

God once rained hailstones from heaven to defend Gibeon (Joshua 10). On another occasion, Gideon's son Abimelech was slain with a prov idential piece of millstone thrown by a woman over the wall of her be sieged city (Judges 9). Here are some other "foolish things" that served as tools in the hand of God's providence.

A wall (I Kings 20:28-30)

God had decided to deliver the Syrian forces of Ben-hadad into the hands of Israel and promised through a prophet to do so. Why? To bless Israel because they were good? Hardly. Notice who is the king of Israel (20:2). Ahab! No, God would do it to magnify Himself in the eyes of the Syrians and to teach them something about Himself (see v. 28). He in formed Ahab, therefore, that He would deliver Syria into his hands, even though Ahab's forces were like two little flocks of goats compared to the Syrians, who "filled the countryside."

How did God accomplish this? Initially, by enabling the Israelites to destroy a hundred thousand Syrians in battle. Then God added a final touch when He caused a *wall* in Aphek to fall on twenty-seven thousand "of the men who were left." Accident or providence? Perhaps God employed some human error in construction or some force of nature or some miscalculation of judgment. However it happened, God was superintending the situation in verse 30 to accomplish the purpose He had already pronounced in verse 28.

Dry ditches (II Kings 3:9-20)

The kings of Israel, Judah, and Edom faced a severe situation. Having joined together to put down the rebellion of Moab, their forces faced an impending battle in the midst of a drought that threatened man and beast. Elisha was called on to inquire of the Lord for them. Through him, God directed them to dig ditches throughout the valley—a seemingly pointless task in the dry dirt. What a foolish thing to do, wasting their precious energies and resources on such an absurd exercise . . . of faith. But the next day "there came water by the way of Edom," apparently from the nearby mountains. Drought problem solved!

But God often "outdoes our hopes" (as Matthew Henry puts it). God always has a way of doing "exceeding abundantly" above our expectation (Ephesians 3:20). He used those same ditches to solve their battle problem as well. But since that involved yet another category of providential means, we will reserve the rest of this story for later.

God Providentially Uses Coincidence

By definition, "coincidence" means simply "to fall together"—two (or more) incidents converging on the same point in place and time. It is a mistake to attribute providential "co-incidence" to happenstance or luck. God is the Master of coincidence, purposefully and providentially arranging events so that they do coincide.

This truth is unmistakably implied in the events of Esther 6—the king's insomnia, the selection and reading of a particular volume of the governmental chronicles, the previous oversight of Mordecai's reward, the arrival of Haman at just the right moment, and even Haman's own arrogant misconstruing of the king's question—all of which we will examine in detail in the next chapter. The same truth is quietly reaffirmed in the story of Ruth, whose "hap was to light on a part of the field belonging unto Boaz" (Ruth 2:3)—an exquisitely subtle way of saying that Ruth "just happened" to glean in the part of a field that belonged to the only man who could and would meet the desperate needs of both Ruth and Naomi.

The principle is illustrated again in the story of Gideon (Judges 7:10-15). God encouraged the anxious Gideon—whose forces were already frightfully reduced to a paltry three hundred men—to sneak over to the Midianite camp, where He would arrange an incident that would reassure Gideon and his men. Sure enough, they *just happened* to approach a section of the camp where they *just happened* to be able to overhear a particular soldier who *just happened* to be recounting a peculiar dream he *just happened* to have had the previous night that *just happened* to pertain to the upcoming battle and that his fellow soldier *just happened* to interpret as symbolic of their imminent overthrow by Gideon's forces. Such serial "coincidences" *just happen* to be the hand of Providence.

The Books of Kings likewise contain similar examples of God's flawless timing, illustrating His providence over "co-incidents."

A random bow shot (I Kings 22:34)

This passage embodies one of the simplest and most sublime expressions of providence to be found in the pages of Scripture. As we saw earlier, Elijah prophesied God's judgment on wicked Ahab, a pronouncement accompanied by a very specific prophetic detail—in the same place that dogs had licked up the blood of the murdered Naboth, the dogs would lick up Ahab's blood (I Kings 21:19). Not a very respectable death for a king. Kings have great state funerals. How could this grisly prediction possibly be arranged?

Ahab and Jehoshaphat later joined forces to fight against Syria in battle. After hearing Micaiah's prophetic warning that God intended through this battle to take Ahab's life (I Kings 22:13-28), Ahab took what he thought was a precaution for his protection. It was a freely chosen strategy that actually secured his downfall. Rather than remaining in his royal apparel (thus attracting the attention of the enemy), he dressed in the armor of a common soldier and entered the fray. At least now he would not be the object of a direct and planned assault against him personally as the commander.

A shrewd plan. Now he's safe, right? The anonymity and simplicity of the narrative statement is exquisite: "*a* man drew *a* bow at *a* venture." Just a common, unnamed soldier taking a random shot into the fray. All unknown to him, God providentially superintended his aim, the exact angle of his bow, the precise tension on the string—and, simultaneously, Ahab's own free movements across the field of battle. For that arrow had Ahab's name and address on it, and God delivered it with flawless and fatal precision. It smote the king of Israel *between* the joints of his armor. There is no hiding from God, no evading the word of the Lord, no out-maneuvering of providence.

Despite all of his careful precautionary measures, Ahab could not elude God's intent. God Himself persuaded Ahab to go to battle in the first place because He had determined to judge him there (22:19-22). What about the prophecy that dogs would lick up his blood? Details don't escape God. The blood from Ahab's mortal wound pooled in the bottom of his chariot (22:35). When they washed it out in Samaria, "the dogs licked up his blood . . . according unto the word of the LORD which he spoke" (22:38).

A well-timed tale (II Kings 8:1-6)

To honor her conscientious care for His prophet Elisha, God blessed a barren Shunammite woman with a son. Later, when God revealed to Elisha an approaching famine, the prophet in turn warned the woman to sojourn elsewhere for the duration of the drought. After the famine, she returned to discover that her house and land had been confiscated in her absence. She purposed to implore the king of Israel for the return of her property.

It just so happened that, at that very time, the king had asked Elisha's former servant Gehazi to tell him about "all the great things" Elisha had done (v. 4). When the woman appeared to appeal to the king, Gehazi was describing how his master had once restored to life the son of a Shunammite woman. Suddenly, right in the middle of Gehazi's tale, there she was—the very woman whose story Gehazi happened to be telling the king. A stroke of luck? Or God's providential synchronization of circumstances to secure a blessing for this woman? "Providence is to be acknowledged in ordering the circumstances of events, for sometimes those that are minute in themselves prove of great consequence."[5]

God Providentially Uses Human Imagination

Have you ever wondered what Paul meant in I Corinthians 1:28, when he said that God can use even "things which are not"—things that do not exist—in order to nullify the effects of things that do exist? How does that work? This is my favorite category of providential means because it most magnifies God's infinite imagination and unlimited resources. Ours is a God, Paul says, who (literally) "calls the things that do not exist as existing" (Romans 4:17). How does He do that?

A visual illusion (II Kings 3:21-25)

Remember the dry ditches discussed above? Now it is time for the rest of the story. When the Moabites rose up early in the morning, "the sun shone upon the water" in the ditches, "and the Moabites saw the water on the other side as red as blood." This was not a miracle; it was a providential mirage. The rays of the early morning sun reflecting on the groundwater in the ditches looked to the Moabites like blood. Thinking that the armies of the three kings had fallen to fighting among themselves, Moab flew heedlessly upon the spoil—so they thought. They didn't realize their error until it was too late, and their disarray was their downfall. God's providential tool in this case was an optical illusion.

An auditory hallucination (II Kings 7:6-7)

The city of Samaria was under siege, surrounded by a massive enemy army (6:24). Famine conditions were critical; some had even been reduced to cannibalism in their desperation (6:25-30). The king, at his wits' end, threatened the prophet Elisha (6:31-33), as though he were responsible for their predicament. What possible prospect could there be for escape? On top of all this, Elisha had the audacity to utter a prophecy of deliverance and provision so unbelievable that one of the king's servants flatly proclaimed its fulfillment to be an utter impossibility—even for God (7:1-2).

But God is never at a loss for tools. If no other means are at hand, He simply *creates* a means. God intervened in a humanly hopeless situation through an incredible method—*an auditory hallucination.* That very evening He caused the Syrians to *imagine* that they heard the noise of a vast military host.[6] Mistakenly concluding that the Israelites had hired the Hittite and Egyptian armies against them, the Syrians deserted everything and ran for their very lives . . . from no one!

So convinced were they of the imminent arrival of this imaginary host that they left behind their entire camp—tents and food, weapons and spoil. Then God used, of all people, four starving lepers, outcasts from their own community, to make the fabulous discovery; they in turn reported it to those in the city. The king sent out a cautious search party to see if it was a trap. It wasn't, and pandemonium ensued. What about the king's aide who disbelieved Elisha's prophecy of God's provision? He saw its fulfillment but did not partake of it. Paying the pronounced price for his unbelief, he was literally trampled at the city gate by the people stampeding out to the spoil (cf. 7:1-2 and 7:17-20).

A Final Sketch

This chapter has not been about artificially inserting God into strange events in an attempt to explain those unusual occurrences. In every case the Scripture underlines God's direct involvement in these episodes. As John Flavel observed in the opening quotation of this chapter, there is no shortage of tools in the workshop of God's providence. The unlikeliest of people, animals, objects, and even imaginary phenomena all serve God's purposes. The Book of Jonah provides an amazingly condensed compilation of such means that God providentially employs to perform His bidding and accomplish His designs.

Jonah: Five-Minute Portrait of God's Providential Means

Have you ever had your portrait done at a fair or festival by a speed artist? I haven't, but I have watched one at work. The result may not be something you'd frame and hang in your living room or pass down to future generations as a treasured family heirloom. Nevertheless, a skilled artist has the knack of capturing your most prominent features so that, in about five minutes, you have a remarkably recognizable representation of yourself.

Jonah presents a five-minute portrait of providence. Have you ever noticed the tools of providence employed in the story of Jonah, and how explicitly each incident is connected to the direct intervention and activity of God?

After Jonah's initial disobedience to the Lord's call (when he took a ship sailing in the opposite direction God wanted him to go), "the LORD *sent out* a great wind into the sea," a "mighty tempest" that threatened the ship itself and the lives of all those on it (1:4). Once Jonah was cast overboard ("and the sea ceased from her raging"), "the LORD *had prepared* a great fish to swallow up Jonah" (1:17). When that encounter had accomplished its designed effect, "the LORD *spake* unto the fish" and it unceremoniously deposited Jonah onto a nearby beach.

Jonah finally made it to Nineveh. But he still balked at what God wanted to do through him, so God wanted to make a point. Consequently, "the LORD God *prepared* a gourd" (4:6), a plant to shade Jonah from the heat. But the very next day "*God prepared* a worm" (4:7) to eat the plant and destroy the very gift He had just given to Jonah. To make matters worse (and to make His point more keenly), "*God prepared* a vehement east wind" to chase away the clouds so that the hot sun "beat upon the head of Jonah." There are a number of implications and applications of what God was doing in Jonah's life. But our primary interest here is in God's providential use of means to accomplish His will.

The Holy Spirit's inspiration of the wording of this story is not accidental or insignificant. God directly, personally, and providentially employs such common, "natural" means as **weather** (1:4), **whales** (1:17, 2:10), **weeds** (4:6), **worms** (4:7), and **winds** (4:8). (I know Jonah 1:17 says "great fish" and not "whale," but I needed a "w." Besides, if God providentially controls "great fish," He certainly providentially controls whales, too.)

A Look in the Mirror

Hard times hit everyone. God's children are not immune. If the times are hard enough, our initial response may not be discernibly different from others'. When we lose our scriptural perspective on the character of God and the reality of His providence, we sometimes misread the meaning of our circumstances.

I have read of a dear wife and mother whose family was forced by financial hardship to move from their home in search of livable conditions elsewhere. Not long after they had relocated, her husband died suddenly and inexplicably, leaving her a widow. She still had two healthy young sons, each married to a lovely daughter-in-law who also cared for her. But within just a few years, both of her sons died as suddenly as her husband had. This began to look like more than coincidence; this began to look like judgment—bitter providences from a God she had somehow greatly displeased. That is what she thought, and that is what she told everyone. Read it for yourself in the first chapter of the Book of Ruth.

"It grieves me deeply for your sakes," Naomi apologized to her widowed daughters-in-law, "that *the hand of the LORD has gone out against me*" (Ruth 1:13, paraphrase). When she returned to her homeland and her old acquaintances barely recognized her, she replied, "Do not call me Naomi ["pleasant"]; call me Mara ["bitter"].[7] *For the Almighty has dealt very bitterly with me*. I went out full,"[8] she explained, "but *the LORD has brought me home again empty*. Why call me Naomi anymore, since *the LORD has testified against me* and *the Almighty has afflicted me?*" (Ruth 1:20-21, paraphrase).

The repetition is unmistakable. Naomi makes *five* distinct statements reflecting her perception of God's dealings with her:

- *the hand of the LORD has gone out against me*
- *the Almighty has dealt very bitterly with me*
- *the LORD has brought me home again empty*
- *the LORD has testified against me*
- *the Almighty has afflicted me*

What is Naomi's problem? She does not appear resentful or angry with God. She seems rather to have sunk into a kind of shoulder-shrugging despair. She doesn't know why God has done all this to her but she knows it has been God doing it, and she assumes it is all her fault. She feels like a walking lightning rod, endangering those around her (1:13).

Naomi has forgotten the gracious character of God. He is neither cruel nor capricious, chastening without explaining. *She has misread God's posture towards her.* Consequently, *she has misinterpreted the meaning and intent of her circumstances.* Through every painful turn of events, God was moving her back into a place where He would provide amply for her very real material needs through Boaz (Ruth 2-3). More than that, He was strategically moving her into a position that would attach her indirectly to the privileged lineage of the Messiah (Ruth 4)!

The gloomy clouds of threatening circumstances hide what the child of God can see only by faith in the repeated assurances of God's Word— the smiling grace and kind purpose of God. William Cowper[9] captured this common experience in the following lines:

> *Judge not the Lord by feeble sense,*
> *But trust him for his grace:*
> *Behind a frowning providence*
> *He hides a smiling face.*
>
> *His purposes will ripen fast,*
> *Unfolding every hour;*

THE MEANS OF PROVIDENCE

The bud may have a bitter taste,
But sweet will be the flower.

This is not to say that God does not often chasten through difficult circumstances. He certainly does. But remember, if you are a believer, you are *in Christ*. That means God's posture toward you is as unchangingly loving and gracious as His posture toward Christ. God's love for believers is neither rooted in nor dependent on how faithful or obedient we are. When we are tempted to lament that God would be more inclined to hear and answer our prayer if only we walked more faithfully each day as we should, we are succumbing to an insidious misconception—that our faithfulness somehow *merits* God's love and attention.

God's love for us is immovably grounded in promises He has made to us *through Christ*. All God's promises to us are centered in Christ, so all those promises are firm, constant, and reliable only if, and only *because*, we are "in Christ" (II Corinthians 1:20). God does not love us because of any merit that we possess or any faithfulness that we maintain, but precisely and purely because we are "in Christ." [10] We are "accepted in the Beloved" (Ephesians 1:6). To doubt God's love toward us, then, is to doubt God's love for His own beloved Son. When this thought thoroughly captures God's people, it engenders neither arrogance nor presumption, but profound love and loyalty in return. [11] And it enables you to discern, beyond the frowning providences of present circumstances, God's smiling face.

Consider briefly one more example of a believer who despairingly misread the divine intent of the circumstances that surrounded him like gathering storm clouds. Here is Jacob's perception: his most beloved son is dead; another son is being held hostage in Egypt; their own land is still held in the dusty grip of drought and famine; the supply of food recently imported from Egypt has run out; and the only way they can get more from Egypt is for him to release his youngest boy to go with the others to Egypt and risk losing him too. Jacob sees himself hopelessly hemmed in, stuck in the middle of a rock, a hard place, an anvil, and a hammer. That perception naturally evokes from Jacob a cry of anguish and frustration: "All these things are against me" (Genesis 42:36).

That was Jacob's perception, but here is the reality: his beloved son is *not* dead; his other son is *not* being cruelly treated in Egypt but better cared for than his family (*by* his son who was not dead); the drought and famine they are experiencing in their own land is graciously designed by God to drive them down to Egypt, where He intends to provide for and protect them; and his youngest boy—without being lost or sacrificed—is the ticket to get them down there. In other words, everything that Jacob saw as *against* him, God was actually doing *for* him. Jacob did not yet recognize it, but what appeared to him as the blackest clouds looming on the horizon actually signaled God's approaching showers of mercy and blessing. To the stanzas already cited above, Cowper pens,

> *Ye fearful saints, fresh courage take,*
> *The clouds ye so much dread*
> *Are big with mercy, and shall break*
> *In blessings on your head!*

God loves impossible situations! God thrives on humanly hopeless circumstances. He delights to shock us with "impossible" pronouncements and prophecies. How do we respond to statements and promises of Scripture that seem equally impossible to apply to our own situations? After reading the kinds of accounts we have traced throughout this chapter, how can we ever doubt God's ability to intervene in our circumstances? Even if *we* cannot imagine any possible way for God to alter our situation, *He* can. There is no limit to His imagination or to the means and tools at His disposal. And if no means of intervention or provision exist, He can create one! Cowper's hymn reflects this facet of the truth as well:

> *Deep in unfathomable mines*
> *Of never-failing skill,*
> *He treasures up his bright designs,*
> *And works his sovereign will.*

Whatever difficulty or uncertainty you may find yourself facing right now, God means for you to reflect on these testimonies of His providence and ask, "Is *anything* too hard for the Lord?" Cowper confidently concludes,

> Blind unbelief is sure to err,
>   And scan his work in vain:
> God is his own interpreter,
>   And He will make it plain!

8

SILENT PROVIDENCE

This mysterious reality which we call providence, this sovereign manipulation of all the ordinary, non-miraculous doings which make up the ordinary ongoing of human affairs, so as to bring about, by natural processes, those results which are divinely predetermined, is the mightiest of all miracles.

—J. Sidlow Baxter

The story of Joseph is a full-screen, feature-length film on providence, with surround sound and as technicolor as his coat. God's providence is expressly displayed and His presence and control over circumstances loudly asserted. The story of Esther is more like a silent movie with captions; the picture is just as vivid but the sound is turned down. To see God's sovereign involvement when He appears to be hidden, you have to read between the lines. The Book of Esther holds special interest for us because it is so much like our own experience of God's providence.

The events of our lives are not narrated for us, confirming the presence of God and clarifying exactly what He is doing. In the story of Esther, you see amazing things happening, yet you never hear God's name mentioned. "The absence of pomp and parade in God's providence has struck many. How noiseless are most of his doings."[1]

As in Genesis 37, it is no accident that a distinguishing feature of the entire Book of Esther is the absence of any explicit reference to God. Yet, to the attentive reader, God is unquestionably present and active. The believing eye can with little difficulty trace the unmistakable outline of the silent Sovereign's shadow over this scene and see the movements of His invisible hand in seemingly insignificant and incidental details.

Introduction to the Book of Esther

Before we dive into what the Book of Esther has to say about God's governing providence, it will be helpful to lay some groundwork for understanding the book's historical context and literary construction.

Unusual Characteristics of the Book of Esther

Several exceptional features mark this portion of God's Word. It is one of only two Bible books named for the woman heroine in the story. It is never quoted in the New Testament. And there is no clear indication of exactly who penned the book.

Some have suggested that Mordecai was the author. Even though Esther 10:2-3 indicates that Mordecai's career is over at the time of writing, God could have used him to pen most of the account. Others think perhaps Ezra or Nehemiah may have written it. It is not entirely unlikely that it could have been recorded by a Gentile since the writer appears to have had intimate, first-hand acquaintance with a number of historical features. Consider the intricate detail of the court scenery described in chapter 1: the beautiful tapestries (including details of how they were hung and fastened), the couches, the types of stone that comprised the mosaic floor tiles, even the tableware. The author also had explicit knowledge of the Persian names of the king's chamberlains and wise men. These factors, along with the absence of any direct reference to God, may suggest someone (possibly a Persian) who was closely associated and intimately familiar with the king's court from the beginning of the story—perhaps even one of those mentioned later (Esther 8:17) who converted to the true God as a result of witnessing these extraordinary events.

By all accounts, however, the most unusual feature of this narrative is the absence of any direct reference to God. He is never once mentioned by name or by pronoun. Why?

Some have attempted to explain this curious characteristic by insisting that Esther, Mordecai, and the other Jews in Persia were living in disobedience to God.[2] The story of Esther opens in the year 482 B.C. (Esther 1:3). The Jews had been permitted to return to Judah about fifty years earlier (538 B.C.). Many thousands had returned; the temple had long since been rebuilt in Jerusalem (completed in 516 B.C.), though the city walls were not yet finished and the city languished in disrepair until the time of Nehemiah (444 B.C.). Rather than remaining in Shushan, some argue, these Jews should also have returned to Jerusalem, "where they belonged." While God did graciously work in their behalf, He did not wish to countenance their sin of remaining in Persia by giving any explicit indication of His approval or presence among them. So He withheld His name from the narrative.

This assumption, though rational, is speculative. The book itself contains no hint of such disobedience, which would have been a very simple detail for God to insert in the narrative. We do not know Mordecai's age, but certainly Esther was in Persia because she was born there long after the original return. It is not as if the Jews whose parents had, for whatever reason, remained behind could pick up and make the arduous and dangerous four- to six-month trek whenever they pleased. One *might* be able to blame their parents, but not them.

Moreover, the inspired description of Esther and Mordecai is a positive one. They are clearly the human heroes of the story. The Lord later made similar use of two other Jews living in Persia, Ezra and Nehemiah. Ezra did not return to Judah until he was old enough to have acquired a reputation as an expert scribe of the law and to be officially commissioned by the Persian king Artaxerxes (458 B.C.). Nehemiah was also officially commissioned by Artaxerxes as governor of Judah (444 B.C.), but not before he had spent a considerable portion of his life in Persia—long enough for him to rise to the highly trusted position of personal butler to the Persian king.

Finally, far from reflecting on their alleged disobedience for staying in Persia, the events of the book actually demonstrate how God preserved the lives of those who *had* returned to Jerusalem *through* the presence and providential placement of principled people who had remained behind. It is important to remember that the decree of destruction arranged by Haman threatened *all* the Jews who lived throughout *all* the king's provinces (3:13; 8:5). That included Judah. Had it not been for Esther on the throne back in Susa, the Jews in Jerusalem would have been destroyed by their enemies in the neighboring communities.[3] And, according to the accounts of Ezra and Nehemiah, they had plenty of enemies who would have been all too eager to eradicate those troublesome Jews who had invaded "their" territory by moving back into Judah.

I have deliberately chosen to describe the absence of God's name in the Book of Esther as the "nonmention" of God. What, then, is the point of this nonmention of God? What could be the purpose of a book in the Bible that records the deliverance of God's people from destruction through a series of seemingly "chance" events without ever mentioning God? What effect does this apparent absence of God have on the story and its impact on the reader?

In the course of storytelling, it is one thing to say, "God did this," or, "Then God caused such and such to happen." That is what characterized the story of Joseph—constant, explicit reference to God's activity behind all the circumstances Joseph experienced. But it heightens the dramatic effect and underscores the undeniable reality of God's presence and activity when such unpredictable events in such an unlikely story are related with *no direct reference to God at all*. In the former, the narrator tells the reader what God did. In the latter, the reader is compelled to conclude on his own, "That *had* to be God. Only God could have done *that*." *That's* the point! That is why I refer to the "nonmention" of God in Esther, not the "absence" of God. God was *not* absent—it just looked that way sometimes.

Likewise, God is not absent today—it just looks that way sometimes. In that important respect our experience parallels the days of Esther. The Book of Esther records events that transpired only fifty years before the end of the Old Testament era. Through the record of Esther, God vouchsafed to His people in the twilight hour of Old Testament revelation the assurance that "in post-Biblical times . . . where the presence of God was not overt, His word not direct, and His face not revealed, still, behind the veil of purim,[4] God's providence toward His people would uphold them."[5]

Don't we find ourselves in a strikingly parallel, "post-biblical" situation today? God's presence is not overt; He no longer communicates His Word directly to men; and His primary *modus operandi* is now, as it was in the time of Esther, silent providence. "Heaven has now been dumb for eighteen [now nineteen] long centuries," observed Sir Robert Anderson, in which time "the world has never witnessed a public manifestation of His presence or His power."[6] The Book of Esther, therefore, becomes a valuable paradigm for understanding God's invisible presence and silent activity in our own day.

Function of the Book of Esther

The literary character of the Book of Esther is divine drama, a suspenseful demonstration of providence. The plot revolves around the deliverance of the Jews from genocide. The overarching theme of Esther is the governing providence of God—*God governs all events, including the free acts of men and their external circumstances, and directs everything to their appointed ends for His glory.*

The purpose of Esther is threefold.

- Historical—to recount the events that led to the Feast of Purim (see 9:20-22, 27-28).

- Theological—to highlight God's providence in ruling and overruling in the affairs of men and to demonstrate His protective care for His people.[7] This is where the nonmention of God becomes a crucial part of underscoring that purpose. There are two paradoxical but complementary implications of the nonmention of God:
  1. It underscores *God's* activity in the seemingly chance circumstances of everyday life.
  2. It emphasizes *man's* role and responsibility in the course of human history.[8]

- Practical—to illustrate a variety of truths related to God's providence as it affects our lives and circumstances.

Synopsis of the Book of Esther

Esther, a Jewess, becomes queen of the Persian empire (478 B.C.). Haman, an upstart prince, plots the genocide of all Jews throughout the empire because of a personal affront by Mordecai, who is (unknown to Haman) Queen Esther's elder cousin. Mordecai learns of the plot and persuades Esther that she must risk her life to intercede with the king to save her people. Esther reveals to the king both the plot and the villain. Haman is hanged on a gallows he had built for Mordecai. Esther and Mordecai take measures authorized by the king to reverse the plot and establish a feast to commemorate their deliverance from destruction (a feast still observed by Jews today).

Chronology of the Book of Esther

Because it is such a readably short story, we tend to think of the events in Esther as occurring over a relatively brief period of time. That is not the case. The whole story covers a period of about ten years. We know that Ahasuerus (his Aramaic name; he is better known by his Greek name, Xerxes I) began his reign in 485 B.C. Here are some dates you can plug into the text to help you keep track of the chronology of the story:

- 482 B.C.—Opening feast and deposing of Vashti (Esther 1:3)
- 478 B.C.—Accession of Esther to throne[9] (Esther 2:16)
- 473 B.C.—Haman's genocidal plot (Esther 3:7)

Key Events in the Book of Esther

Have you ever paused to enumerate all the vital hinge events on which this story of suspense and intrigue turns? Again, imagine reading this narrative with fresh eyes and let it surprise you. A series of crucial defining moments drives the overall plot, steering the course of the story and affecting its outcome:

- The *unexpected* deposing of Vashti and consequent accession of Esther to the throne of Persia (Esther 1-2).

- The *fortuitous* discovery by Mordecai of an assassination plot against the king (2:21-23).

- The *unfair* lack of recognition for Mordecai's loyalty in informing the king, as his deed is *recorded* but *not immediately rewarded* (2:23b).

- The *unexplained* promotion of an arrogant prince named Haman (3:1).

- The *unanticipated* decision of Mordecai to risk all for principle (3:2-5).

- The *staggering* malice of Haman in plotting genocide (3:6-15).

- The *crucial* confrontation between Mordecai and Esther (chapter 4).

- The *unusual* time-delay "strategy" of Esther in approaching the king (5:1-8).

- The *unwitting* digging by Haman of his own "grave" (5:9-14).

- The *unpredictable* insomnia of the king (6:1).

- The *random* selection of the record of Mordecai's deed to read to the king (6:2).

- The *well-timed* determination to reward Mordecai (6:3).

- The *coincidental* appearance of Haman at the king's court at that precise moment (6:4).

- The *ironic* role reversal between Mordecai and Haman, unwittingly attributable to Haman's own egotism (6:4-14).

- The *surprising* payday banquet for Haman (chapter 7).

- The *timely* reversal of Haman's plot (chapter 8).

- The *curious* naming of a memorial holiday (chapter 9)

- The *gratifying* exaltation of Mordecai (chapter 10).

All of this introduction fills out the context and sets the stage for a closer and more profitable look at what the Book of Esther contributes concretely to the doctrine of providence.

What Does the Bible Say?

The overarching theme of the governing providence of God in Esther is buttressed by several supporting emphases that highlight the ordinary means through which God providentially accomplishes extraordinary things.

The Nonmention of God

Jacob, the patriarchal ancestor of Esther and Mordecai, once awoke from a revelatory dream and exclaimed, "Surely the Lord is in this place, and I knew it not!" (Genesis 28:16). That is the effect the nonmention of God is intended to have on those who read this marvelous account. We have already discussed how the nonmention of God underscores both divine activity and, simultaneously, human responsibility. The narrator does, however, include at least three *implicit*, "veiled" references to God's presence and activity.[10]

Esther 4:13-16. Mordecai presents three consequences for Esther if she refuses to intervene on behalf of her people: (1) deliverance would come "from another place" (implying someone else was at work); (2) retribution would be certain—"thou and thy father's house will be destroyed" (implying certain and inescapable judgment); and, (3) Esther would be missing the opportunity and duty, indeed the very purpose, of her position—"thou art come to the kingdom for such a time as this" (implying a larger purpose at work; who placed her there?). Though God is never directly mentioned, His active presence is unmistakably insinuated "between the lines" of Mordecai's arguments. Many also see Esther's reference to fasting, which is almost invariably connected with prayer elsewhere in the Old Testament, as the most obvious veiled hint of their appeal to God and their consciousness of His presence.[11]

Esther 6:13. When Haman reports the embarrassing experience of having to honor Mordecai publicly, Haman's wife and friends see this as an ominous sign. They warn him that since Mordecai "is of the seed of the Jews," Haman's unexpected humiliation can only portend his own ultimate overthrow. Why is this connection drawn between Mordecai's lineage (which was obviously already known) and this inauspicious turn of events? The record that these Gentiles interpret this event as an omen marking the turning of the tide of "fate" against them signals a *tacit* recognition of the reality of the God of the Jews and of His evident activity on behalf of His people.

Esther 8:17; 9:2-3. Some have suggested a "hidden theology" in the phrases "the fear of the Jews" and "the fear of Mordecai" (cf. Genesis 31:42).[12] What is inherently "fearful" about the Jews or Mordecai, unless they represent something (or someone) bigger? These statements, too, constitute veiled references to God Himself and His intimate connection with His people. This "fear" on the part of the heathen who witnessed this plot reversal made them unable to withstand the Jews, led the Gentile authorities to help the Jews, and resulted in many of the heathen converting to Judaism.

What's the point? Scrutinize the details of the story and you cannot miss the unmistakable footprints of the presence of a silent but active God. Whenever God seems absent or silent in your life, look closely and carefully enough at the daily details of your circumstances; you will see the same footprints of God's gracious presence and providence.

Wrath

This may sound like a strange subtheme, but its presence makes a vital contribution to the development of the story. Remember Psalm 76:10—"Surely the wrath of man shall praise thee: the remainder of wrath shalt thou restrain." Nothing demonstrates this truth more vividly than the story of Esther. The narrative recounts four expressions of wrath. Each one is a vital hinge on which the story turns, redirecting the events that are crucial to the outcome.

The wrath of the king against Vashti (1:12; 2:1)
A variety of explanations have been offered as to the reason for Vashti's refusal to obey the king. In the end, all of them are speculations, and to focus on that part of the story is to miss the larger point. Regardless of the king's request (appropriate or not) and regardless of the

queen's reason (justified or not), her refusal and the king's displeasure, resulting in his decision to dethrone and replace her, was the human means God employed to vault Esther to a position of influence in anticipation of the coming danger.

The wrath of Bigthan and Teresh against the king (2:21)

The beauty of this detail lies in the fact that it is utterly peripheral to the plot of the story and is connected to the outcome by the slenderest of threads. We know nothing of these men or the nature of their grievance against the king, yet God used their wrathful plot (and Mordecai's incidental discovery of it) to weave into history an exquisitely "unnecessary" part of the story. If you think about it, the ironic reversal in chapter 6 (where Haman must honor Mordecai) is as nonessential to the outcome of the story as it is delightful to read. It is icing on the cake. The heart of an artist delights in creating things not merely for function or necessity but for their own sake and beauty. Providence, the crafter of history, sometimes fashions events purely for the delight of His people and for the reflection of His own glory.

The wrath of Haman against Mordecai (3:5; 5:9)

This particular manifestation of wrath is, of course, the fulcrum of the entire story.

The wrath of the king against Haman (7:7, 10)

The final display of wrath was God's human tool for bringing His judgment upon Haman, drawing this scene of history to a gratifying and appropriate conclusion.

The story of Esther presents one of the most striking illustrations of God's providential *use* of the hatred and hostility of man, and His *restraint* of any such expressions that will not ultimately serve His glory. Indeed, "even the most disreputable characters and the most flagrant violators of His will are bent into the service of His ultimate purpose."[13] God does not, however, prompt evil human wrath. He does not need to. But He can turn the anger instigated even by the Devil himself to His own purposes. These four references to wrath are not accidental. In every case, the wrath is manifested at a key juncture in the story. And in every case God demonstrates His providential governance over such human emotions, threats, and plots.

> The same fury and rage whereby men think to dishonor God and overwhelm His Church, He turneth to the contrary, and maketh out of that same fury His own glory and the deliverance of His Church to shine. The Lord is a wonderful workman. He bringeth about His purpose in such sort that He can draw light out of darkness, and bring forth His own praise out of their greatest rage.[14]

This is not merely ancient biblical history. God's use of man's wrath for His glory is regularly demonstrated throughout church history. One famous and delightfully vivid example is the case of Voltaire, the renowned eighteenth-century French infidel, who "predicted that within a hundred years Christianity would be swept off the face of the earth and the Bible would be found only in museums. The British and Foreign Bible Society later bought his Paris house as a depot for the distribution of Bibles."[15]

Adjust your view of reality to the Bible's explanation of what is really going on, and you will see examples of this principle played out in your own experience.

Destruction

In Zechariah 2:8 God warns that whoever touches His people touches the apple of His eye—a curious phrase. We use that cliché to denote something particularly precious in our sight. Literally, it refers to "the little man of the eye," that is, the pupil (which reflects the image of whomever we are looking upon). Any movement towards our eye—any action that threatens this most delicate and sensitive organ—elicits an instinctive and immediate protective reaction on our part. Likewise, any action that threatens God's people elicits from Him the same kind of immediate protective reaction. The New Testament parallel to that truth is hinted at in the story of Paul's conversion (Acts 9:1-5), in which Christ identifies Himself inseparably with His people ("I am Jesus, whom thou persecutest"). Whatever affects them affects Him.

As we have already discovered, the basic plot of the story revolves around Haman's genocidal scheme to destroy the Jews. That Haman's intent was nothing short of holocaust is evident from the frequent piling up of three unambiguous words to describe his intention "to kill, to destroy, and to annihilate" all the Jews. In Esther 3-8 you find *eight* references to Haman's plot to "destroy" the Jews (3:6, 9, 13; 4:7, 8; 7:4; 8:5, 6). This threat dominates the narrative into chapter 8 because, even after Haman's death, the decree was still in effect and had to be countered.

Through the providence of God, however, Haman's cabal is not merely halted but reversed. The tables are turned in Esther 8 as you read *eight* references to the Jews' "destruction" of their enemies (8:11; 9:5, 6, 10, 11, 12, 15, 16). Though some have entertained the misconception that the Jews' vengeance amounted to a cruel and heartless retaliation, there are actually several evidences to the contrary. The original decree could not, by law, be reversed; so the Jews' response was strictly one of attacking in self-defense those who actively sought their destruction.[16]

"Chance"

This motif of apparent "chance" (the quotation marks around that word are crucial, for one man's chance is another man's providence) is one of the most obvious but overlooked thematic elements in the entire narrative. Proverbs 16:9 observes that "a man's heart deviseth his way: but the Lord directeth his steps." Verse 33 adds that "the lot is cast into the lap; but the whole disposing thereof is of the Lord." This principle plays out in one of the historical purposes of the book discussed above. From a strictly historical standpoint, the function of the Book of Esther is to explain the background behind this curiously named Jewish feast. (Purim is mentioned five times in the last seven verses of Esther 9.) But first let's look again at the pervasiveness of this "chance" motif throughout the development of the story.

Esther is filled with events that, on the literary surface (helped by the nonmention of God), appear to be pure coincidence. Who could have predicted or expected these remarkable "chance" events as the story unfolds?

- The king's call for Vashti and her refusal (1)
- Vashti's dethronement and the accession of a young Jewess, Esther, to the throne of Persia (1-2)
- Mordecai's discovery and reporting of an assassination plot against the king, and its entry into the king's chronicles without immediate reward (2)
- The lot ("Pur") cast by Haman to determine the most auspicious timing for his genocidal scheme (3)
- Esther's hesitation at the first banquet, substituting for her request an invitation to a second banquet, and the resulting events in the meantime preceding the second banquet (5-6), most notably
- The king's insomnia, the reading of the account of Mordecai's unrewarded deed, and Haman's ironically timely arrival (6)
- The falling out of the king and his most favored prince (7)
- The reversal of what seemed to be certain destruction for the Jews (8)
- The naming of the Feast of Purim (9:23-32)

The Feast of Purim takes its name from the *pur*, or lot, that Haman cast to determine the best time for his satanic strategy. The Feast of Lots. Have you ever wondered why *that* name was chosen to denote a feast celebrating the Jews' deliverance from destruction? Why not the Feast of Deliverance? Or the Feast of Esther? Or the Feast of Protection? Any number of options would appear to be more obvious candidates than the obscure reference to a Persian word that essentially refers to dice! After all, the *pur* appears only once in the course of the entire story (3:7). Yet when the time came to name this new feast, attention fastened on this peculiar, minor detail (9:24, 26).

But God's providence smiles even in the very naming of the feast. "Purim"—the very symbol of chance, luck, fate, randomness—became eternally memorialized as the ultimate "anti-chance symbol, the symbol of that which God so readily controls to *His* ends."[17] The Feast of Purim, still universally celebrated by Jews, embodies an ironic reminder of the fact that *God*—not chance or luck or fate or dice—is in charge, controlling even the most seemingly insignificant details, objects, and incidents. The naming of the Feast of Purim commemorates the truth that the unbeliever's chance is the believer's providence. *Nothing*, however large and threatening or seemingly random or capricious, is outside God's calm and constant control.

Reversal

Uncanny reversals are the stuff of the story of Esther. Such reversals in human fortunes are the domain of God, not chance, luck, or fate. It is God who changes the times and the seasons, and enthrones and dethrones kings (Daniel 2:21) . . . and *queens*. It is God who declares "the end from the beginning," determining "from ancient times things that are not yet done," with the confident assertion of sovereignty, "My counsel shall stand, and I will do all my pleasure" (Isaiah 46:10).

Esther contains several fascinating examples of literary reversal.[18]

- Haman hates Mordecai (3)—Haman honors Mordecai (6)

- Decree against the Jews (3)—Decree against the Jews' enemies (8)

- Shushan is perplexed (3:15)—Shushan rejoices (8:15)

- Jews mourn (4:3)—Jews rejoice (8:17)

- Haman rejoices and boasts (5:9-12)—Haman mourns and fears (6:12; 7:6)

- Haman makes Mordecai's gallows (5)—Haman is hanged on those gallows (7, 9)

Perhaps even more intriguing is the overall chiastic structure of the major movements of the story. "Chiasm," a literary device often employed in the Bible, is a kind of inverted parallelism. Suppose you have four lines of poetry. In normal parallelism, the first and second would be parallel to one another; likewise the third and fourth. But in chiastic parallelism, the first and fourth are parallel; likewise the second and third. It is not successive parallelism, but parallelism from the outside in, so to speak.

Chiasmus can also be employed as the framework for constructing an entire work of prose. It is like laying out two slices of bread for a sandwich (mayonnaise and mustard optional)—on each slice you lay a piece of roast beef, then on each of those you lay a slice of tomato, on each tomato you lay a leaf of lettuce, then on each leaf of lettuce you lay a slice of cheese. Now close the sandwich together and you have a culinary chiasmus. Each layer corresponds to the layer in the same place on the opposite side of the sandwich.

The Holy Spirit is an omnisciently imaginative inspirer of Scripture. A study of the literary forms of the Bible unveils a God who was concerned to communicate truth and to communicate it beautifully. The way the story of Esther as a whole is chiastically structured and put together reveals an ingenious and intentional emphasis on reversal:[19]

Opening & Background (1)
King's First Decree (2-3)   danger
Clash Between Haman & Mordecai (4-5)   rising tide
"On that night could not the king sleep" (6:1)   crisis moment
Mordecai Triumphs over Haman (6-7)   turning tide
King's Second Decree (8-9)   deliverance
Epilogue (10)

Is all this "technical" analysis a waste of time? Absolutely not. The literary structure itself, the brilliant style and form simultaneously penned by man and inspired by God, reinforces the message. As such, the more we discover and notice about the content as well as the form in which God crafted His revelation to us, the more it reflects back on His glory and skill. Recognizing such structures helps the reader understand what it is that gives many passages their appeal and impact, and often aids in rightly assessing the emphasis and interpreting the point of such passages. God often reinforces the message of His words through the form or style or structure in which He has communicated it.

A Look in the Mirror

Take some time to think through and apply some of the lessons we can draw from the story of providence that unfolds through the Book of Esther.

Remember that God controls and directs the free acts of evil men— including the wrath of His enemies and the enemies of His people—for His own praise and purposes (Psalm 76:10).

The story of Esther unveils different "kinds" of wrath with different causes. God governs all of them:

Embarrassed pride. The wrath of the king against Vashti (1:12; 2:1) that was used by God to effect Esther's accession to the throne.

Political malice. The wrath of Bigthan and Teresh against the king that led them to plot his assassination (2:21) was used by God to provide the occasion for Mordecai's life-saving service to the king, ultimately resulting in the reward of chapter 6.

Offended arrogance, personal animosity, and racial hostility. The wrath of Haman against Mordecai (3:5; 5:9), which plotted the destruction of all Jews, proved to be Haman's own undoing, for God ultimately turned it against him and all those like him to their own destruction.

Mistaken indignation. The wrath of the king against Haman, whose behavior towards the queen was misconstrued as an improper advance toward her (7:7, 10), was the tool God used to seal the doom of Haman. The almost humorous scene illustrates that God not only uses impressions but sometimes even *mistaken* impressions to accomplish His purpose.

Recognize that God is in control when you do not get what you think you deserve, or even what you may rightly deserve (Esther 2:23).

God is the recorder and rewarder of all your works. Therefore, "whatever you do, do it heartily, as to the Lord and not to men, knowing that from the Lord you will receive the reward of the inheritance; for you serve the Lord Christ" (Colossians 3:23-24, NKJV). Men may forget or fail to notice, but "God is not unrighteous to forget your work and labour of love" (Hebrews 6:10). These are not merely convenient proof texts. The Lord intends them for serious meditation and personal application.

Resting in the providence of God, determine to do right because it is right, regardless of the consequences (Esther 3:2 ff).

"Those that walk in holy sincerity," remarked Matthew Henry, "may walk in holy security, and go on in their work, not fearing what man can do unto them."[20]

Realize that God is in control of who and where you are (Esther 4:13-14).

You do not have opportunities for influence by accident. God-given opportunities bring God-intended responsibilities. Do all the good you can wherever God puts you. Apply this to your situation among family members, your neighbors, and your coworkers.

> We should every one of us consider for what end God has put us in the place where we are, and study to answer that end; and, when any particular opportunity of serving God and our generation offers itself, we must take care that we do not let it slip; for we were entrusted with it that we might improve it [i.e., put it to good use, use it to good purpose].[21]

Be sensitive to God's leading, and give God time to work providentially (Esther 5:1-8).

Don't rob yourself or others of the opportunity to see all that God can do. Allow Him to accomplish all He wants in His time. Whether Esther's initial hesitation was the result of feminine intuition, fearful apprehension, a calculated strategy to butter up the king, a ploy to pique his curiosity, or her response to an inexplicable divine impression simply to wait, we are not told. But Esther's delay through the employment of two banquets set the stage for the events of chapter 6—the literary and dramatic climax of the entire story—which never would have happened had she immediately presented her request.

Several years ago my wife and I were looking to buy a house that could accommodate not only our children but also my mother (then in the early stages of Alzheimer's disease). Homes with mother-in-law suites were not easy to find. After several months of searching, our agent found one that was just about to come on the market. It was a lovely home right in our price range—and with a perfect mother-in-law addition newly built on! Surely, we thought, this was the answer to our prayers. We stood in the carport with our agent, who was leaving on a business trip the next day, debating what to do with this house that was bound to sell quickly once it hit the market. Shouldn't we go ahead and make an offer? Our agent clearly thought so. But the rush of it troubled me.

Suddenly, involuntarily, the story of Esther's banquets leapt into my mind! Our anxiety over the apparent necessity of this hasty decision took on a new light. "Wait a minute," I thought. "If this is the house the Lord wants us to buy—if this is really where God *intends* for us to live—then this house will be available tomorrow. Can't God hold a house for us for a few days, while we have time to make a responsible and fully informed decision? Is that too hard for Him? Let's wait, and pray, and investigate more closely, and if God truly intends for us to live there, He will have no trouble keeping it open for us. Let's give God time to work." As it turned out, the house did not sell for some time; and when it did, we weren't the ones buying it. The neighborhood, we subsequently discovered, was less than ideal for bringing up young children. It was far from church. And not long after, God opened up *another* house with a mother-in-law suite that really *was* perfect—including a large basement for my study and for home schooling our children. I never drive past that other house without thanking God for prompting us to wait and to give Him time to do His "perfect work" in our behalf.

Be assured, despite all apparent odds and even apart from all human intervention, that the king's heart is like a channel of water in the hand of the Lord; He turns it wherever He wishes (Esther 6-8; cf. Proverbs 21:1).

"God can turn the hearts of men, of great men, of those that act most arbitrarily, which way he pleases towards us."[22] If this is true of kings, it is certainly just as true of presidents, governors, judges, legislators, managers, employers, parents, or anyone else.

Be patient; payday always comes eventually and providentially (Esther 6-7; cf. Galatians 6:7).

Good will be rewarded and evil will be punished (Ecclesiastes 8:12-13; Psalm 62:12)—often when we least expect it and in ways we would never dream. We may not see it personally but God's providential timing is flawless; and this life is not all there is.

Be content; vengeance belongs to God and His providence, not to us (Esther 8:10-12; 9:10, 15, 16; cf. Romans 12:18-21; Deuteronomy 32:35).
Some people act as though they have extracted their "life verse" right out of the middle of Romans 12:19—"Vengeance is *mine*; *I* will repay!" (There's a good lesson on the importance of context.) David is often criticized for his "imprecatory" psalms in which he prays, often quite specifically and graphically, for God's judgment on his enemies (e.g., Psalm 59, 69, 109). Such expressions, however, actually reflect David's remarkable humility, patience, and trust in the Lord. After all, he was a king with undisputed royal authority. He could have taken immediate vengeance for any personal affront whenever he wished, but he regularly refrained. Lesser men in that position frequently stooped to abusing their power, turning their throne into a whipping post. Instead, David committed the judgment of his enemies to God.[23] So must we. That takes grace. The point is not so much that we learn to pray biblical imprecatory prayers, but that we adopt a Christlike humility that commits our souls, our cause, and our enemies to one who judges righteously (I Peter 2:19-23)—because we ourselves were once enemies of God, brought back to Him only at enormous cost to Himself (I Peter 2:24-25).

Be trusting; God's providential protective care for His people runs deep (cf. Zechariah 2:8).
This is no less true for His people today (Acts 9:1-5a). The Bible often describes God as being "jealous"—beginning in the Ten Commandments (Exodus 20:5). Is God really *jealous?* The question is not whether God is jealous (the Bible says flatly that He is), but what does "jealous" mean? Our problem in understanding this divine attribute is the negative, even sinful, connotation of the English word "jealous." Yet jealousy is entirely appropriate in certain contexts. Thus, the Hebrew word can be defined as (1) a negative, improper envy (never used of God), or (2) a positive, legitimate zeal, which generally has as its object either (a) the protection or defense of another, or (b) the affection or devotion of another.

The objects of God's "jealousy" are (1) His name, that is, His character and reputation (Ezekiel 39:25; 20:9, 14, 22, 29; 36:20-23; 39:7; 43:7), and (2) His people and the land He promised them (Joel 2:18; Zechariah 1:14; 8:2). God is jealous for His people's welfare and for their singular loyalty and devotion to Him. God's jealousy (Exodus 34:14; Deuteronomy 4:24; 5:9; 6:15) is not a suspicious, fretful passion; rather, it emphasizes the depth of His commitment and the seriousness of His relationship to His people in every age.

Be persuaded that, with God, there is no such thing as chance (Esther 3:7; 9:23-28).

The lot may be cast, but every result is from the Lord (Proverbs 16:33; cf. Proverbs 16:9). There is no wisdom or skill, understanding or intelligence, advice or scheme that can succeed against the Lord (Proverbs 21:30). Our duty is to make responsible plans and preparations, but safety and success come from the Lord (Proverbs 21:31). God is in control—not luck or fate, dice or demons, force or fortune.

Elizabeth Barrett Browning penned a thought that I have come to love. Picturesquely and succinctly, it sums up the essence of providence. Even when God appears absent and silent, He is most assuredly very present and active. If we look attentively and thoughtfully, we will see His shadow in the most mundane experiences of life. Only those who have eyes of faith can see the invisible hand of God's providence; and only those who see will respond rightly.

> *Earth's crammed with heaven,*
> *And every common bush afire with God;*
> *And only he who sees, takes off his shoes—*
> *The rest sit round it and pluck blackberries.*[24]

Do you notice the burning bushes around you? Do you have eyes to see God's presence and activity in the common, everyday experiences of your life? Do you, like Moses, worshipfully remove the shoes of your heart at the evidences of God's daily providences? Or are you blind and deaf to the Lord's fresh mercies to you each day, presumptuously plucking the berries of God's providential care and protection, oblivious of the miracles of life and breath, health and provision of which you are a daily partaker? Let us pray for ourselves the prayer that Elisha offered for his servant when they were hopelessly surrounded by their enemies (II Kings 6): "Lord, open our eyes that we may see." Look intently and you can make out the hoof prints of God's horses and chariots in the hills surrounding you. Look closer still and you will see traces of flames in the blackberry bush of God's providence right in front of you.

9

PROBLEMS OF PROVIDENCE

God's providence is supreme, and therefore sovereign. . . . He is the sole arbiter of events and destinies. . . . So that it is as clear that God rules alone as that he rules at all, that he rules everywhere as that he rules anywhere; that he governs all agents, all causes, all events, as that he governs any of them. To surrender in whole or in part his control of the universe would be to admit that he was not God.

—William S. Plumer

We have explored several examples of God's providence—His secret working in and through the free acts of men, directing all events in order to accomplish His will. That raises another important question: where does sin fit in?

Where, exactly, *does* sin fit into the equation of providence? Does it fit in *anywhere*, or is sin outside the realm of God's providential control? What part does Satan play on the stage of providence? How does God providentially maneuver through all this murky terrain of free will, sinful impulse, human wickedness, and Satan's prompting without becoming sullied Himself?

The problem can be illustrated, for example, in the Lord's use of "evil spirits" in the lives of Abimelech (Judges 9:23) and Saul (I Samuel 16:14), and a "lying spirit" in the life of Ahab (I Kings 22). David's numbering of the people presents a similar problem that raises a slightly different but related question. Carefully compare the wording of II Samuel 24:1 and I Chronicles 21:1. Who "moved" David to number the people? God or Satan? The answer is "yes." That answer may not satisfy all our curiosities, but it is the only thoroughly biblical answer.

What Does the Bible Say?

One of the best contexts from which to address the problems of providence is the Book of Job. The explicit juxtaposition of God and Satan shoves this aspect of providence to the forefront and carries us to the very threshold of a crisis question. By now we should be persuaded of God's governing providence over all things. But let's return to a question raised earlier and seek to dissect a biblical answer: when "bad" things happen, is it God or man or Satan?

No matter how familiar you may be with the story, please take a few moments to acquaint yourself once again with God's own words. For the purpose of this discussion, read at least Job 1-2 and 42.

Who's Responsible for This?

Who is responsible for what happened to Job? God or Satan? Note carefully the contrast between God's "hand" (Job 1:11) and Satan's "hand" (Job 1:12). Satan challenged God, "Put forth *thine* hand now, and touch all that he hath." God replied, "Behold, all that he hath is in *thy* power," literally, "*thy* hand" (exactly the same word as in 1:11). Notice again the same contrast in Job 2:5 and 6. Satan: "Put forth *thine* hand now." God: "Behold, he is in *thine* hand." Which is it? Is Job in God's hand or Satan's hand?

As we already discovered through the study of Joseph, God is ultimately responsible for *everything* that happens to us. And not just "ultimately" responsible in a broad, theoretical, aloof way, but genuinely, ultimately responsible. He *must* be if He is both just *and* omnipotent. If something "bad" happens that we do not understand, we are immediately tempted to question either God's omnipotence for not preventing it or (more commonly) His justice for permitting something we see as undeserved or even unfair. (Incidentally, it is the latter that Job eventually came to question.)

But was the "bad" that Job suffered merely nonmoral, "natural" catastrophe? Fire from heaven, a great storm of wind, physical disease—are these to be attributed to natural causes, Satan, or God? Moreover, was Job the victim of morally neutral calamities only? Or was Job also the victim of sin?

In addition to suffering the effects of "natural" calamities (Job 1:18-19; 2:7-8), Job (like Joseph) was also the victim of violent sins committed against him, against his servants, and against his property. Marauding bands of Sabeans and Chaldeans *murdered* Job's servants and *stole* all his livestock (Job 1:14-17). Later, he was even subject to an explicit solicitation to sin by his own wife (Job 2:9). So now who is in charge, God or Satan?

At this point we may be tempted to conclude that God may have been in control of the natural calamities, but all the suffering as a result of the sins of others against him had to be inspired and controlled by Satan. God cannot be the originator of any sin or temptation to sin. But we return to the original question: who, if anyone, was *ultimately responsible* for what happened to Job? Were God *and* Satan jointly in control? Do they share the responsibility/blame? Who is ultimately in charge?

Again, there is only one biblical answer. God is in charge. God is ultimately responsible. This is not simply an abstract theological deduction for the sake of preserving a tidy systematic theology. It is the explicit assertion of the text itself. After Job's sufferings were over and God's blessings returned, Job's friends and relatives "bemoaned him, and comforted him over all the *evil* that the LORD had brought upon him" (Job 42:11). Perhaps, someone might object, that was just a human misconception on the part of his family and friends. Maybe they were mistaken. But those are not the words of Job's family or friends. Those words reflect the perspective and statement of the Spirit-directed narrator.

Nevertheless, if you want even more explicit, inspired, textual proof from the mouth of God Himself, look at the Lord's own answer in Job 2:3. The words of God to Satan here are stunning. He points out to Satan that, despite the tempter's worst efforts, Job had maintained the integrity of his faith *"although thou [Satan] movedst me [God] against him [Job], to destroy him without cause." Satan* moved *God?* Satan moved God *against Job?* Satan moved God against Job *to destroy him without cause?* How can that be? Yet that is what *God* says. Let's look at this crucial passage more closely.

A Closer Look at a Key Verse

Job 2:3 is a crucial theological key to the whole book of Job and, in a broad sense, to our understanding of the problem of providence throughout the Bible. Its remarkable admission is elevated by the fact that God Himself is the one speaking. Job maintained his integrity, God told Satan, "even though you moved Me against him to destroy him undeservedly." Let's dissect the terms of the text that are central to this problem of providence.

"Movedst" (סות) means "to allure, entice, incite, provoke." The word is used eighteen times in the Old Testament in different senses.

Sometimes people do this to other people in an evil sense of seducing or enticing them to do something wrong.

- Jezebel *stirred up* Ahab to do evil (I Kings 21:25).
- Ahab *persuaded* Jehoshaphat to join him in battle (II Chronicles 18:2).
- A friend or relative might *entice* someone else to serve idols (Deuteronomy 13:6).

Sometimes people do this to other people in an innocent sense of motivation.

- Achsah *persuaded* her husband to ask Caleb for an inheritance (Joshua 15:18).

Sometimes God does this to people in the sense of prompting or directing, either directly or through secondary means.

- He *moved* Israel's enemies to leave Jehoshaphat alone in battle (II Chronicles 18:31).

- He *moved* David against Israel to number them (II Samuel 24:1; cf. I Chronicles 21:1).[1]

Only once does anyone ever do this to God. Only in Job 2:3 is **God** the **object** of this verb. By God's own admission, Satan *incited/provoked/motivated/persuaded* Him against Job to swallow him up undeservedly. Whichever particular translation you want to choose, the meaning of the word is as clear as it is startling. God Himself admits in this verse that He has been "moved" by Satan to do this to Job. To do what?

"Destroy" (בָּלַע) is a graphic word that literally means "to swallow up" or "to gulp down." The imagery is quite vivid. In Numbers 16:32, the earth "opened her mouth and *swallowed up*" those who rebelled against God's leadership through Moses. Jonah 1:17 records that God prepared a great fish to "*swallow up*" Jonah. God admits that what He did to Job, at Satan's incitement, was not unlike these kinds of utterly overwhelming experiences. Why did God say He was moved to do this? To what end, or for what cause?

"Without cause" (הַנָּם) can mean either "without compensation" or "without cause, undeservedly."[2] Saul sought to destroy David *without cause or provocation* (I Samuel 19:5). David refused to offer a sacrifice from that which was *without cost* (II Samuel 24:24). Perhaps the most instructive use of this phrase here is the messianic reference in Psalm 69:4, "They hated me without a cause." This prophetic reference to Messiah's suffering focuses on the single event of history that puts all our suffering, even Job's, into proper perspective. Who could ever suffer more cruelly and undeservedly than the spotless, holy, harmless Lamb of God? Henceforth, we must gauge our attitude toward our own suffering not by the experiences of others but by the experiences of Christ.[3]

Back to the Question
So, who "did" all this to Job, God or Satan? The answer is yes. Whether we are comfortable with it or not, the mystery of Job 1:11-12

and 2:5-6 stares us unflinchingly in the face. God placed Job in Satan's "hand" and "power."[4]

Then who is responsible for all this? The answer of the Scripture is God. Whether we are comfortable with it or not, the divine declaration of Job 2:3 and 42:11 is unambiguous. Significantly, throughout the book neither Job nor his companions ever doubted that God was behind what was happening to Job. They all understood implicitly, and even expressed explicitly, their settled certainty that "the hand of the LORD hath wrought this" (Job 12:9). Neither Job nor Joseph ever questioned that God was in control of *all* his circumstances and experiences. Why should we?

You may divide this up into God's "perfect" will versus God's "permissive" will if it helps you understand it better. There is both scriptural and moral ground to do so. But when we talk about what God only "permitted" to happen to Job, we must remember to factor in one more vital piece of information: who *started* it all? We typically tend to think that all Job's problems were brought upon him by the Devil. But from the standpoint of what the narrative reveals, *none* of this would have happened if *God* had not initiated it. God spoke first, not Satan (1:7). God first brought up Job's name and character, not Satan (Job 1:8). Knowing all that it would entail and how it would end, God not only permitted Job's circumstances but also initiated the whole process of Job's suffering.

Principles of Providence

Combining what we have learned so far, let's draw some guidelines to govern our thinking about the operation of God's providence.

God is *not* responsible for my (or anyone else's) wrong actions or choices. That is free will (which, apart from God's intervening grace, habitually chooses in accordance with its fallen nature) and human responsibility.

God *is*, by His own admission, responsible for what happens to me, even when it involves the sinful actions and choices of others (the "free acts of men" in our definition of providence). That is providence. Remember Joseph. Remember Job. Remember Jesus.

God is the ultimate cause of every moral right (for no moral right can originate from fallen man) but the cause of no moral wrong (for no moral wrong can originate from an unchangeably holy God). Yet He sovereignly controls and orchestrates both to accomplish His purposes. How does He do this?

How exactly does God providentially manipulate both righteous and evil acts and inclinations? Man possesses a vast, nearly unlimited capacity for evil that is part of human depravity resulting from the Fall. In fact, God's assessment of humans both before and after the Flood was that the imagination of the thoughts of their hearts was only evil continually (Genesis 6:5; 8:21). It is as if God opens the lid on this bottomless pit of potential depravity just so far, filtering what escapes, so that only what will further our ultimate good and serve His purposes is providentially allowed to come out. The rest is just as providentially restrained.

"No wild beasts rend and devour their prey more greedily than wicked men would destroy the people of God that dwell among them, were it not for this providential restraint upon them."[5] Theologian Millard Erickson helpfully outlines and illustrates four ways in which God, in His providence, "can and does relate to sin: he can (1) prevent it [Genesis 20:6]; (2) permit it [Psalm 81:12-13]; (3) direct it[6] [Genesis 50:20]; or (4) limit it [Psalm 124:1-3]."[7] God knows the nature and proclivities of man, permits only certain expressions of his native depravity, restrains the rest, clothes all His purposes with what He permits, and turns it all ultimately to His praise (Psalm 76:10). Given the depth of man's depravity, the wonder is not that God permits harm and difficulty and even devastation to befall us; the wonder is that He *prevents* and *restrains* so much.

But Why?

No one who reads the Book of Job can avoid this question. Job himself raises it some twenty times throughout his speeches. It is his central question. And it is usually our central question.

A thorough answer to this question would require a thorough study of the theme and message of Job—and that would take another entire book. It may be worthwhile in this context, however, to catch a glimpse of the larger providential picture that provides at least a partial answer to the question of why. To do that, it will be most helpful to go first to the New Testament. There we discover that at the root of much of what God does is His desire to display aspects of His character to an entire spiritual world that we never see and rarely consider.

Throughout the magnificent theological tapestry of Ephesians runs like an azure thread a subtheme that is designed to alter our perspective on all of life. It is contained in the phrase "in the heavenlies" (Ephesians 1:3, 20; 2:6; 3:10). Notice, in addition, the repeated references to "the praise of his [God's] glory" (Ephesians 1:6, 12, 14). Who does all this praising? Just believers? Ephesians 2:7 goes on to declare that in the ages to come God will "show"[8] the exceeding riches of His grace through His kindness to us in Christ. Show to whom? Just to us?

Then Ephesians 3:8-11 throws opens a "wardrobe door"[9] to a whole new world and begins to answer these questions. Verse 10 literally reads, "In order that now may be made known to the principalities and to the powers in the heavenlies, through the church, the manifold wisdom of God." God displays His wisdom not *to* the church but *through* the church. To whom? To *principalities and powers* (cf. Ephesians 1:21), to spiritual rulers and authorities in heavenly places. In other words, *God is doing things to and for and in and through us in order to manifest to all other created spiritual intelligences (angels) His perfections, for their benefit and for His glory.* This is part of His eternal purpose—or, as Ephesians 3:11 puts it literally, the divine "purpose of the ages."

Making explicit reference to Ephesians 3:10, Charles Bridges begins his classic work on *The Christian Ministry* with these opening words:

> The Church is the mirror that reflects the whole effulgence of the Divine character. It is the grand scene in which the perfections of Jehovah are displayed to the universe. The revelations made to the Church—the successive grand events in her history—and, above all—the manifestations of "the glory of God in the Person of Jesus Christ"—furnish *even to the heavenly intelligences* fresh subjects of adoring contemplation.[10]

Why does God need to "show" these kinds of things to angels? We tend to assume that because angels dwell in God's presence, they must be privy to all His counsels and understand everything God is doing and why He is doing it. But this is clearly not the case. We are told that angels look with eager and quizzical interest into some of God's works and dealings with men (I Peter 1:12). They are His servants, just as we are. There are things God does that they do not understand, just like us. And there are things God does to reveal Himself to them, just as He does to reveal Himself to us.

First Corinthians 4:9 paints an even more vivid picture of this reality. The apostle affirms that God had "set forth" the apostles. This colorful technical term refers to bringing a person into an arena for a public exhibition.[11] There, Paul says, they are made a "spectacle." This Greek word is *theatron*—from which we get "theater." A theater for whom? For the world, for men, *and for angels*! Shakespeare was right—all the world *is* a stage! Men are the actors and angels are in the audience. But this is no ordinary play. The intention is not to entertain the audience with a story, but to instruct the audience—not merely about the players but primarily about the Director; and not merely through the action of the play itself, but through the interaction between the players and the Director.

Now all this may be very intriguing but what does it have to do with Job? Is there any suggestion of this celestial audience in the Book of Job? Reread Job 1:6 and 2:1. The words between God and Satan (Job 1:7-12; 2:2-6) were spoken in the presence of all the "sons of God" as they appeared before the Lord. The "test case" of Job, therefore, must take place in as wide an audience as the challenges were issued.[12]

I pointed out earlier that, in the face of such troubling experiences, man's instinctive, natural, central question is usually "Why?" It is rarely central to God's answer, however. When, after thirty-seven chapters, God finally broke His silence and "answered Job out of the whirlwind" (Job 38:1), the *one* question He did *not* answer was "Why?" From our perspective, finding out why is the whole point. From God's perspective, explaining why—for the time being—is beside the point (cf. John 13:6-7).

The whole point, for now, is genuinely understanding who is in charge and bowing in submissive trust to the scepter of His providence.

Practical Ramifications

We can easily become small-minded and man-centered in our theology when we think of God as acting almost solely for our benefit. But that leaves much of life utterly baffling and inexplicable. The fact is, we are not the center of the universe—God is. We are not even the center of God's redemptive activity—*God* is. This is not to minimize our genuine value and importance to God; but it is to maximize the all-importance of God Himself and the ultimate aim of all creation—His glory and preeminence (Colossians 1:16-18). Further, it is to maximize our perspective on the real spiritual world around us, the presence of a multitude of beings other than us for whose benefit God does certain things. They, too, will share in glorifying God for what they learn about Him through His dealings with men (see Hebrews 1:6; Revelation 5:8-14).

This is what is going on in Job—the celestial audience at the original live "production" of the drama of Job, consisting of all the spiritual intelligences in the heavenlies. And according to Ephesians 3:10 and I Corinthians 4:9, this is what is still going on today in the midst of circumstances that we often find perplexing. God is concerned to display to *all* His created beings, human and angelic, the flashing facets of His matchless character.

Job suffered to prove, among other things, that there *are* people who genuinely worship and serve God "for nothing" other than for who and what He is. What do we prove when we, like Job, suffer perplexing difficulties? *We are proving that we are some of those people!* We are demonstrating before an onlooking earthly and celestial audience a great deal about ourselves, about the integrity and sincerity of *our* faith in and relationship to God, and about the (trust)worthiness and desirability of God.

Every difficulty we or someone we love faces, every trial we endure, every loss we bear, every experience of the severest pain and suffering—and even the misunderstanding and rejection it may bring from friends or relatives or even Christian brethren who may, like Job's friends, assume we are being chastened for some serious sin—every such experience is a fresh opportunity to stand in the company of Job and to affirm that our faith in and our worship of and our devotion to God is rooted in soil far deeper than personal advantage or material blessing or physical well-being. The legacy of Job is uniquely the inheritance of those who suffer like Job, not in degree but in kind.

A Look in the Mirror

First, is it correct to view God as doing "bad" things (i.e., not moral evil but undesirable experiences) to us? And do such experiences indicate a lapse in God's love or favor?

As finite, earth-focused mortals, we often need to adjust our thinking. We need to adopt God's perspective as it is reflected in His Word. We must think God's thoughts after Him. It is not that God "did" this to Job. Rather, He *entrusted* this experience to Job, just as God entrusted to Joseph the terribly trying circumstances that he experienced.

God does not entrust severe trials to just anyone. That sounds strange to our ears, but it is so. In the cases of both Joseph and Job, we know something of the outcome and God's reasons for doing what He did. When we are the ones in the vise of hardship, calamity, or heartbreak, we cannot see the outcome, and rarely do we have any real idea of the reasons. *But that's why God has given to us the stories of Joseph and Job and others.* The outcomes and purposes may vary from one person and one circumstance to the next. But the Josephs and Jobs of the Bible enable us, in the midst of our own circumstances, to see "the outcome of the Lord's dealings, that the Lord is full of compassion and is merciful" (James 5:11, NASB).

Nowhere is this truth more tenderly illustrated than in the illness of Lazarus. Read John 11:1-6 and notice carefully the wording of the text. The sisters' message to Jesus in verse 3 was, "He whom thou *lovest* is sick." The Greek word translated "lovest" here is *phileo* and refers to an emotional attachment of fondness and affection.[13] The sisters appealed for Jesus' intervention on the basis of His emotional affinity with the family.

In John 11:5, however, the Holy Spirit emphasizes the true nature and depth of Jesus' love for them: "Now Jesus *loved* Martha, and her sister, and Lazarus." Here the word is not *phileo* but *agapao*—the Scripture's word for the fullest, most selfless and giving kind of love. *Agape* is not the emotional attachment of affection but the volitional attachment of commitment.

Jesus did not merely harbor an emotional fondness for that family. His love surpassed affection, meaningful and tender as that is; it expressed itself in a settled, self-giving commitment to them and to their best interests. That fact gives the point of the passage even more weight and poignancy: "But Jesus *loved* Martha, and her sister, and Lazarus. **Therefore**, when he heard that he was sick, *he remained* at that time *two days* in the place where he was" (John 11:5-6, independent translation). The Holy Spirit did not phrase it this way capriciously.

The account admits Jesus' affection for this family but further asserts a love on His part that strengthened the cords of emotion with the chains of commitment. It was *on account of this love* that Jesus *purposely delayed* His response to their deep and urgent need. Jesus did not delay *despite* His love for them. Neither was His delay a contradiction to His love. Still less was His delay a sign of His impotence to meet their need. The trial and delay, leading from Lazarus's illness to his death, was *because* of His love for them. "Now Jesus *loved* [them] . . . *therefore* . . . *he abode two days still*."

Jesus' delay was, in fact, a *manifestation* of His love for them, for their ultimate greater good and His glory. We rarely perceive this divine motive at the time of suffering. Mary and Martha could not at first fathom that truth in the hour of their grief. They must have felt the keen knife-edge of confused disappointment in Jesus' delay. When they knew, *they knew*, that He *could* have done something about Lazarus, but He didn't (John 11:21, 32). But God is never, *never* late, my friend. And John 11 is in your Bible to assure you that if and when He seems to delay deliverance or relief, it is *because* He loves you and wants to work your greatest good and His greatest glory. Submit in grateful humility to His love and in quiet, confident patience to the perfect timing of His providence.

"I adore and kiss the providence of my Lord," wrote Samuel Rutherford in words of profound worship and mature faith, "who knoweth well what is most expedient for me, and for you, and your children."[14] The well-known English hymn writer William Cowper (1731-1800) was periodically plagued with deep bouts of depression. Out of his experience emerged ringing words of triumphant conviction that we still sing:

> *Judge not the Lord by feeble sense,*
> *But trust Him for His grace:*
> *Behind a frowning providence*
> *He hides a smiling face.*[15]

Second, was it "bad" for God to take away everything Job had "without cause"? Was it right?

Again, the foundational Bible principle that God is incapable of sin or injustice applies here. But beyond this, Satan could not "move" God to do anything that was evil in itself. Even though Satan's purposes in seeking Job's destruction were evil, God's purposes in permitting it were positive and good.[16] More importantly, it is neither "bad" nor unfair for God to remove any or all of the blessings He has freely and undeservedly bestowed on us in the first place.

To what do we attribute Job's loss and suffering? To providence. But to what do we attribute Job's *initial* health and prosperity? To inheritance? To chance? To hard work? Granted, Job had done nothing to deserve the removal of all God's blessings. God Himself acknowledged that Job's suffering was in that sense undeserved and "without cause." *But neither had Job done anything to deserve the giving of those blessings in the first place. Nor have we.* All God's gifts and blessings are out of His sovereign pleasure and gracious goodness. Job's responses indicate that he himself clearly understood both of these truths (Job 1:21; 2:10). Do we?

The key to reacting with a right spirit when things seem to go "wrong" is to cultivate a right sense of humility for all of God's continuous, undeserved goodness while things are going well. Simply put, nothing good we have is deserved in the first place, and anything God does with it is always right.

Each new day brings us face to face with God's goodness, though many of us forget it, ignore it, or are brutishly unaware of it. God manifests that goodness in many ways: through acts of benevolence toward us, through the withholding of deserved judgment, through His willingness to forgive repeated offenses. The goodness of God is designed to have a certain impact on our spirit and behavior.

God's goodness does not necessarily indicate His blessing on one's life or His approval of one's actions. That Pharisee-like assumption infected the mindset of many of Jesus' religious enemies. It infects many today, pagan and believer alike. Some assume that their wealth or success is an evidence of God's approval of their ministry or manner of life. Paul describes such people as "supposing that gain is godliness" and warns us to keep our distance from them (I Timothy 6:5). God's goodness is not a validation of our lifestyle nor a commendation of our merit (cf. Psalm 50:21); it is a commentary on His nature. The Bible asserts that the righteous and the ungodly alike benefit from the goodness of God.

"The Lord is good to all" (Psalm 145:9). He gives sunlight to the evil and to the good; He sends rain on the just and on the unjust (Matthew 5:45). He gives breath to the blasphemer, wealth to the wicked, bread to the pagan, and rain on the crops of the ungodly. Why? We might reason that a strategy of fire and brimstone and misery and affliction would be a more appropriate and effective means of getting the attention of evil men. Wrath and judgment are, after all, necessary and ultimate expressions of the holy character of God. But Paul explains God's rationale in Romans 2:4-6. Men and women who continually abuse God's goodness to them are putting God's retribution on layaway (vv. 5-6). But that is not God's wish or intent. Do you lightly disregard the riches of His goodness and patience? Don't you realize that the goodness of God is intended to lead you to repentance (v. 4)?

Hardening oneself against a mean, cruel, spiteful God would be understandable. But how can anyone resist the wooing of God's goodness that is daily poured out upon all of us in life and breath, sun and rain, food and shelter (Acts 17:25-28)? How does one reject the overtures of God who holds our life breath and all our ways in His hand (Daniel 5:23)? God's kindnesses to all do not display divine sentimental weakness. They are weapons in the arsenal of the Almighty that are graciously intended to lead us to the surrender of repentance—a change of mind about our ways.

Presumption eats daily from the very hand of God and then, when it is extended in a call to surrender and repent and return to Him, bites that hand. Guard your heart against presumption and ingratitude. Bless the Lord "and forget not all His benefits" (Psalm 103:2). Your daily blessings come directly from the hand of God's gracious providence. Presumption against man—whether expressed as rude arrogance or insolent ingratitude or brazen audacity—is universally offensive to anyone with any degree of manners and breeding. But presumption against the benevolence, forbearance, and forgiveness of God is not only the height of folly; it is the deepest affront any creature can offer. And it is ultimately self-destructive.

Third, what is the biblical measure of suffering that helps us put all our difficulties, no matter how severe, into proper perspective?

Christ suffered under the providential hand of God infinitely more than we could ever endure. If you want to put your suffering into perspective, go to the cross. Measure your suffering not by others' circumstances but by Christ's. And as we will discover in chapter 11, the crucifixion of Christ was—in astoundingly minute detail—a manifestation of the providential supervision of God.

10

PROVIDENCE IN THE INCARNATION OF CHRIST

History, when rightly written, is but a record of providence; and he who would read history rightly must read it with his eye constantly fixed on the hand of God.

—Hollis Read

When the fulness of the time was come, God sent forth his Son.

—Paul the Apostle (Galatians 4:4)

Pieces of a jigsaw puzzle make little sense by themselves. Any piece in isolation is unfinished, incomplete. Each piece raises questions that can be answered only as it is fitted into its proper connection to the other pieces. As you begin interlocking individual pieces, the picture gradually becomes clearer. Some pieces God has purposely withheld, retaining their secrets in His hand. But He has granted enough of the puzzle for us to form very definite and clear ideas about the nature and working of His providence.

We have seen various segments of this puzzle pieced together in the events and lives recorded in the Bible. But God saved the crowning works of His providence for the incarnation and ministry of His beloved Son.

The next two chapters will highlight God's activities in relation to the coming and mission of Jesus Christ.

God providentially "set the stage" for the entrance of His Son into the world. Nothing was overlooked; no expense was spared. The preparation for this grand drama was not the work of a few weeks or months or years. God's preparation for the "fullness of time" was literally centuries—indeed, millennia—in the making. This divine casting and staging encompassed social, political, religious, and even philosophical elements; it ranged from individual to international preparations; and it included both broadly circumstantial and intimately personal issues. Some of these details are explicitly outlined in Scripture. Others are discovered only as we look at the textbook of history.

What Does History Reveal?

History is the illustrated encyclopedia of God's providence. Upon its pages the observant eye can trace the outline of the invisible hand of God. "To the believer the 'amazing coincidences' of history are but manifestations of God's intervention for His omniscient, benevolent purposes."[1]

Providence in Politics

The groundwork for the dominance of a single, uniting political influence had been laid with each successive world empire over the centuries: Assyrian, Babylonian, Medo-Persian, Greek, and Roman. (You can read about the succession of these empires after Assyria in the prophecy visions of Daniel 2 and 7.) By and large, each empire extended the borders of the previous one and expanded the number of provinces and peoples brought under its influence.

The unprecedented size of the Roman Empire was, therefore, the product of centuries, and God clearly had an eye to this end throughout the millennium preceding the birth of Christ. Rome at peace (*Pax Romana*, the period during which Christ was born) provided ideal circumstances for the spread of the message of God's coming into the world.

By virtue of His superintending governance over the governments of the world, God is the King of nations (Jeremiah 10:7). Into the hand of His Son He has bequeathed the governments of the world (Psalm 2). That is why Christ is called "the blessed and only Potentate, the King of kings, and Lord of lords" who will be fully manifested as such in God's time (I Timothy 6:15).[2] In that day, when He comes to take to Himself His great power to reign (Revelation 11:17), the universal proclamation will ring out, "The kingdoms of this world are become the kingdoms of our Lord, and of his Christ; and he shall reign for ever and ever" (Revelation 11:15). But that is another book. We are here concerned with past providences.

Providence in Commerce

In order to transport troops and transmit information more efficiently, the Roman Empire devised an unprecedented system of communication and transportation. That is the human side. The divine side is that God (through the free choices of men ignorant of Him and His purposes) directed the building of this system in order to facilitate the movement of *His* armies and ambassadors for the communication of *His* message.[3] The Romans constructed a brilliantly engineered network of roads, some of which survive to this day, which made accessible the farthest reaches of the known and conquered world. The Romans also put into place an efficient postal system, which eventually expedited the spread of God's correspondence to man through the revelation of the New Testament.

Providence in Language

A single universal language throughout the empire was the enduring legacy of Alexander the Great's conquest three centuries before the birth of Christ. The introduction and establishment of Greek as the common tongue throughout the known world likewise enormously facilitated the widespread and rapid communication of the gospel. But providence also made use of that linguistic unity in another respect.

God's Old Testament revelation was given in Hebrew—a language virutally limited to one important but very small nation. With the introduction and establishment of Greek as the lingua franca came another vital preparatory work on the part of God—the translation of God's Hebrew Old Testament revelation into a universally accessible language: Greek. This translation (called the Septuagint), produced over a period of about a century (250-150 B.C.), introduced the self-revelation of God to the world at large. It became the Bible of Christ and the apostles, the Bible of the writers of the New Testament, and the Old Testament of the early church.

Why was this significant? "The Septuagint had, in the providence of God, a great and honorable part to play in preparing the world for the Gospel."[4] It is not too much to say that "Greek Judaism, with the Septuagint, ploughed the furrows for the gospel seed in the Western world."[5] Because of its widespread presence throughout the known world,[6] the Septuagint "paved the way for later Christian missions" as "the Christian missionaries were able to discover a ready point of contact wherever there had already spread a knowledge of the Old Testament."[7]

Providence in Philosophy

Providence in *philosophy*? Judge for yourself. The Greek philosophical world had long debated a variety of ideas and ideals. When the apostle John, under the inspiration of the Holy Spirit, introduced the Messiah to the world as the *Word* (John 1:1-14), this concept was not entirely novel. The Greek term is *logos*, used four times in these verses to refer to Christ. This Spirit-inspired expression entered a providentially prepared philosophical context. A brief outline of the progression of thought on this seminal expression highlights God's providential preparation of even the philosophical world.[8]

The Greek concept of logos

Heraclitus (ca. 500 B.C.) was one of the first to use *logos* in a philosophical sense to describe a universal reason or order (as opposed to chaos, chance, and randomness) in the world. Anaxagoras (ca. 400 B.C.) described this *logos* as a sort of intermediary between God and man. Zeno and the Stoics (ca. 300 B.C.) took a more pantheistic turn, viewing the world's reason and orderliness (which they believed manifested itself as a vapor) as the *logos* (also described, interestingly, as "providence").

The Jewish concept of logos

The Septuagint employed *logos* to depict God's "word" as both the agent of creation (Psalm 33:7) and the controller of creation (Psalm 147). In general, God's "Word" throughout communicates divine revelation (cf. Hebrews 1:1-3).

Philo (ca. 20 B.C.), an Alexandrian Jew influenced by Greek philosophy, synthesized the Greek and Hebrew concepts of *logos*. He viewed the *logos* as an intermediary between God and the world and even described it as God's firstborn son, an ambassador, an advocate, a high priest—even though he apparently had no concept that the coming Messiah would be none other than God in human flesh, and certainly no inkling that this Word would, in fact, appear in his own lifetime.

In short, God was providentially at work plowing the soil of the philosophical musings of men who did not know Him in order to set the stage for the presentation of His Son as the very expression and communication—the *Word*—of God Himself.

What Does the Bible Say?

We've taken a brief survey of what the history books have to say about God's providence in preparing the world for His Son. Let's turn our attention to evidences more directly mentioned in the scriptural accounts of the Incarnation. Notice the implications of providence at work in the narration of the crucial events leading up to the birth of Messiah.

The Timing of Zacharias's Lot (Luke 1:9)

The burning of the incense was an unusual honor that few priests enjoyed since their duties were assigned by lot. In fact, "the offering of incense was considered the highest duty and could be exercised only once in a lifetime."[9] Zacharias might have been selected by lot early in his life and never again have had opportunity to perform for that ministry. But by the choice of Providence, "for the first, and for the last time in life the lot had marked him for incensing" at *this* particular time.[10] As we learned from our study of Esther, God providentially governs the "chances" of lots and their timing. The timing and location of the angelic announcement to Zacharias at the temple guaranteed a public announcement and widespread anticipation of the coming of Messiah's forerunner and, hence, of the coming of Messiah.

The Conception and Birth of John (Luke 1:5-7, 24-25, 57-66)

The case of Zacharias and Elisabeth will be examined in more detail in chapter 13, but the context of this study warrants a brief mention here. How long before the angel's temple appearance to Zacharias do you suppose this godly old couple had given up praying for a child?[11] Not only had Elisabeth been barren all her life but also "they both were now well stricken in years" (Luke 1:7). They obviously had long since ceased praying for a child. Did their prayers fail or, more importantly, had God failed to answer their prayer? Absolutely not. The answer, however, did not come in the timing they had hoped or in the way they had anticipated, but far beyond all their expectation. It is a happy "coincidence" that Zacharias means "the LORD remembers." Even his name was providentially appropriate. Zacharias may have forgotten the prayers he had offered in his early manhood, but God had not.

Mary and Joseph (Matthew 1)

A veil of silence has been drawn over the personal history and upbringing of Mary and Joseph. But think of the necessary attentive care of the providence of God silently at work in the most minute and personal details of this relationship: the birth and preservation of both Mary and Joseph, the bringing (and keeping) of those two together, and even the providential superintending of their lineage over the preceding centuries.

The Conception of Jesus (Matthew 1:18-25; Luke 1:26-38)

The timing of this event was crucial. It came *after* the betrothal so that it would not disqualify her for betrothal, but *before* the marriage so that the Child was clearly not Joseph's (Matthew 1:18). Has it ever occurred to you that God could have forewarned Joseph (by angel or dream), just as He had informed Mary ahead of time, that the birth of this child was coming? Instead, God permitted Joseph to discover Mary's pregnancy on his own before explaining it to him. Think of the pain to Joseph, who had no reasonable alternative but to suspect a devastating immoral betrayal. But think also of the pain to poor, pure Mary, who was naturally suspected, by the very one whom she would never betray, of having done something she would never do.

Why did God do it this way? Why could He not have told Mary *and* Joseph ahead of time? This arrangement was essential in order to providentially preserve the validity of the event and the unclouded identity of the Child. The announcement to Mary was obviously necessary to prepare her for what was about to happen to her, and why and how. At the same time, it was essential for Joseph to have no previous knowledge of Mary's pregnancy whatsoever. Imagine the suspicion that would have been easily aroused if both Mary *and* Joseph had prior knowledge of this. ("So, you *both* had a dream that God was sending this child? Right. How convenient.") Moreover, it was necessary for Joseph to decide to keep the matter quiet rather than drawing the attention of a public accusation and shame beyond all repair of the event's credibility.

The Ordering of the Census (Luke 2:1-6)

God used a pagan emperor's issuing of a census that inconvenienced a massive population in order to bring one special couple to a birthplace prophesied seven centuries earlier (Micah 5:2). Why did God not simply direct Joseph to take Mary down to Bethlehem for the birth, along with all the other revelation and direction He gave through dreams and angels? Why did God instead employ the free act of Caesar Augustus's census to relocate them?

The census decree magnifies God's providence in human affairs and decisions. Dreams and angelic appearances can be fabricated. Again, think of the suspicions that would naturally arise were Joseph to have claimed that God told him to go to Bethlehem for the birth of this child that was supposed to be the prophesied Messiah. ("Another dream, eh? To go to

Bethlehem? My, my, wasn't that a coincidence.") The key events of the Incarnation were supernaturally revealed and guided, but the Scripture-fulfilling details of its outworking were left to divine providence working mysteriously through the free acts of men, in order to preserve the integrity of the event. That way, no one could accuse Joseph of fabricating a "messiah" by simply moving to Bethlehem for the birth and alleging its fulfillment of Micah 5:2. The providential means employed to accomplish these events transcended human contrivance. "A mere Galilean peasant travels to Bethlehem ostensibly at the decree of the Roman emperor. Actually, it is in fulfillment of the divine King's plan."[12]

The Birth of Jesus (Luke 2:6-7)

God's providences come in all shapes and sizes. Sometimes, as we saw in Esther (chapter 8), they take the form of God's extra touches—exquisite but ultimately "unnecessary" brushstrokes to the overall canvas that give pleasure to the sovereign Artisan and evoke in the careful observer a deepened admiration for His skill. Because there was no room in the inn, Mary was compelled to lay the Bread of Life in a feeding trough in a town named "House of Bread" (Bethlehem).

The Shepherds (Luke 2:8-20)

The divinely ordained presence of shepherds at the birth of the Lamb of God (John 1:29), who would Himself become God's Good Shepherd (John 10) over His people Israel (Ezekiel 34:22-25; 37:24; Isaiah 40:11),[13] is not without significance. Indeed, these "shepherds watched the flocks destined for sacrificial services" in the temple nearby[14]—the very sacrifices that Christ came to fulfill. They became the first evangelists to spread abroad the good news revealed to them about the arrival and identity of the long-awaited Messiah.[15]

Simeon and Anna (Luke 2:25-38)

Often the presence of providence is wrapped in the subtlest details of the sacred text. God promised Simeon that he would see the promised Messiah before he died and then providentially led him "by the Spirit" into the temple at the very moment of the Child's dedication. Likewise, the subtly described arrival of godly Anna, "coming in that instant," was also providentially timed.

The Magi (Matthew 2:1-12)

Elements of providence connected with the magi include a number of factors: the providential preservation of the knowledge of God's prophecy in their distant Gentile society; the appearance of the star at the appropriate place and time to bring the magi to the Christ child; the fact that the star did not lead them directly to Bethlehem but allowed them to go first to Jerusalem, resulting in a public announcement of the event and the citation of the prophecy of Micah in the court of Herod; the dream warning them not to return to Herod so as to gain time and protection for the Child. (For a more thorough treatment of the arrival of the magi, see Appendix D.)

Herod's Massacre of the Infants (Matthew 2:13-23)

Sometimes what does *not* happen is as providentially significant as what *does* happen. Since Herod was so bent on destroying the Child, why did he *not* send spies after the magi to report His location, rather than trusting the magi to return? Providence. Not only did the sad and gruesome massacre of the infants in Bethlehem fulfill prophecy but it also led to the holy family's flight into and return from Egypt in providential fulfillment of another prophecy.[16] And note the eloquent statement of providential control over the wrath of man: "*Herod . . . put to death* all the male children. . . . *Now when Herod was dead,* behold, an angel of the Lord appeared in a dream to Joseph in Egypt, saying, Arise . . . for *those who sought the young Child's life are dead*" (Matthew 2:16, 19-20, NKJV, emphasis added).[17]

A Look in the Mirror

What ramifications does God's providential rule over nations and empires have for modern national and international circumstances? If God superintended all the affairs of politics and commerce, culture and philosophy in preparation for His Son's first coming into the world, we can be sure He is overseeing the preparation for His Son's second coming into the world. What personal lessons and applications can you draw from such examples of God's providence over the broadest aspects of "secular" society?

In chapter 1, I pointed out that embedded in the incarnation narrative is an astounding assertion. Luke 1:37 is immortalized in the words of the KJV: "For with God nothing shall be impossible." But the verse more literally reads, "For with God every saying is not impossible"—or as we would say, "with God no saying is impossible." This same word "saying" is translated "word" in Romans 10:17 ("Faith cometh by hearing, and hearing by the word of God") and refers to the specific words or utterances (*rhema*) of God contained in the Word (*logos*) of God.

Luke 1:37, then, is not so much a general assertion of God's omnipotence (that He can do anything). It is more specific than that. It is an assurance that He is fully able to and intent on performing every "saying"—every prophecy and promise He has ever uttered. If God has said it, He can do it and *will* do it—no matter how improbable it may seem or how impossible it may sound. Remember the context—the biological impossibility of the virgin birth! How does this angelic testimony about God's trustworthiness apply to His "sayings" to you in the Bible?

11

PROVIDENCE IN THE PASSION OF CHRIST

God's

providence

is powerful.

It is so powerful that it even brings good out of evil; making bad men and

fallen angels to serve God's designs, while they intend no such thing: giving

the greatest efficiency to causes apparently the most contemptible;

and infallibly

securing the

very best ends.

All conspiracies

and combinations

against providence

are vain.

—William S. Plumer

Providence in connection with a blessed event, such as the Incarnation of the Son of God, is easy to see and accept. But providence over the darkest deeds of human depravity? Providence over the most vicious and cruel acts ever perpetrated by man in the long history of human wickedness? Providence when all reason and sanity seem to be tearing apart at the seams, when evil and chaos seem to take over in a devilish coup, when all that is good and pure and full of hope comes crashing down? Providence over the Crucifixion of Christ?

We have already learned that God's providence reigns even in our darkest hours, hedges man's most depraved designs, and transforms freely chosen evil deeds into the steeds that bear the chariot of His sovereign strategies. There is no more profound illustration of this truth than the Crucifixion of Jesus Christ.

At the Crucifixion of Christ, hell itself seemed to break lose and ally with all the innate depravity of earthly powers to frustrate the plan of God. Afterwards, the early disciples cited Psalm 2 and its direct application to the events of the Crucifixion.

> *Why did the nations rage,*
> *And the people plot vain things?*
> *The kings of the earth took their stand,*
> *And the rulers were gathered together*
> *Against the LORD and against His Christ.*[1]

But the impious alliance succeeded in serving the sovereign designs previously purposed by the King they rejected. The psalm continues,

> *He who sits in the heavens shall laugh;*
> *The LORD shall hold them in derision. . . .*
> *[Saying] "Yet I have set my King*
> *On My holy hill of Zion."*[2]

The rebellion of man is the footman of God, and Satan's revolt is His bondslave. The Scripture is full of this truth by way of subtle illustration, indirect implication, and explicit assertion. In all the ghastly details of this highest crime of human insurrection and murder, no detail was attributable to chance, no event was an accident, no moment of time swerved outside the calm control of the providential purposes of the sovereign

God. "The LORD hath his way in the whirlwind and in the storm" (Nahum 1:3*b*).

What Does the Bible Say?

Let's first examine the testimony of Scripture regarding the necessary events leading up to and surrounding the centerpiece of Christ's redemptive work—the Crucifixion.

Preserving Providence Throughout the Life of Christ

Prior to the Crucifixion, Christ's enemies not only secretly plotted but also actively attempted to kill Him on a number of different occasions. From each of these attempts providence protected Him, until the bloody desire of man finally synchronized with the sovereign timing of God. You can trace the shadow of God's providentially protective hand chronologically throughout the life of His Son, until the arrival of that perfect timing. Then, ironically, God forced their hand to carry out their murderous plot *not* when *they* wanted to do it, but at just the time providentially designed by Him. Just as God did not send forth His Son until the fullness of time had arrived (Galatians 4:4), so God sacrificed His Son only when the fullness of His time had arrived.

I make a point here of attributing Christ's protection specifically to providence rather than to miracle. In none of these cases is His deliverance described in terms of miraculous intervention.[3] In fact, in most cases we are never even *told* how Christ escaped or was protected. God never split open the earth to swallow Christ's enemies, or sent fire from heaven to block their way from seizing Him; nor did He ever send legions of angels to rescue Him—though Christ could have asked for that (Matthew 26:53). The Father's chosen method of preservation was not spectacular miraculous intervention but secret providential protection by His mysterious working through common events. In all likelihood, an eyewitness could have offered some reasonable explanation for why the threat did not materialize—yet the only ultimate conclusion one could draw from the preponderance of the evidence, as in the story of Esther, is that it *had* to be God.

Deliverance from Herod's slaughter (Matthew 2:13-18)

God could have employed a variety of miraculous means to protect Christ right in the middle of Herod's murder and mayhem—fire from heaven or temporary blindness would have worked nicely. After all, He had utilized such miraculous protective means in the past for lesser individuals. Instead, God directed Joseph to employ a very mundane and nonmiraculous means to protect the Child: running away to Egypt.

Deliverance from the first attempt on His life at Nazareth (Luke 4:28-30)

The idea of casting the Christ over the cliff at Nazareth was not a passing idle thought, a suggestion being merely entertained, a recommendation being bandied about by his enemies while they contemplated its pros and cons. They physically caught hold of the Lord on the spot, thrust Him out of the synagogue, and carried Him up that hill with the full intent of lynching Him. I have seen the steep and jagged crag of Nazareth over which the Jews intended to hurl the Lord. He would not have survived without miraculous intervention (an arguably scriptural alternative, Psalm 91:11-12).[4] Instead we find the explanation, intriguing in its enigmatic simplicity, that Christ "passing through the midst of them went his way." How did that happen? What did that look like? We really do not know. We are informed simply that "by some unexplained means he made his way out."[5]

Deliverance from constant plotting on His life throughout His ministry

About a year after the Nazareth incident, when Christ went to Jerusalem for Passover (His second since His public ministry began), He healed a lame man at the Pool of Bethesda on the Sabbath. In response, the Jews "sought [lit., "were seeking"] to slay Him" (John 5:16). And when Christ asserted that God was His Father, "the Jews sought [lit., "were seeking"] the *more* to kill him" (John 5:18). Not long after, when Christ again healed a man on the Sabbath, curing his paralyzed hand, "the Pharisees went forth, and straightway took counsel [lit., "immediately began taking counsel"] with the Herodians against him, how they might destroy him" (Mark 3:6; Matthew 12:14; Luke 6:11).

As a result of these plots, Jesus temporarily moved His ministry north again to Galilee for the remainder of that year, for "the Jews sought [literally, "were seeking"] to kill him" (John 7:1). He returned, of course, for Passover the following year, but promptly retired once more to Galilee. When Christ came again to Jerusalem later that year for the Feast of Tabernacles, He engaged the Jews in an extended debate in which repeated mention is made of their intent, and attempts, to kill Him (John 7:19, 25, 30; 8:37, 40).

Exactly how far any of these plots progressed we are never told, except for two occasions when the Jews went so far as to threaten capital punishment on the spot (John 8:59; 10:31; cf. 11:8). What we do know is that for over half of His public ministry, animated discussions were ongoing and various strategies were posed and debated among His enemies as to how they could silence Him—effectively and permanently. John alone offers the only explanation for His providential protection; His hour had not yet come (John 7:30; 8:20; cf. 12:23, 27; 13:1; 17:1).

Deliverance from attempts to kill Him early in the Passion Week

On Monday[6] of His last week in Jerusalem as He taught in the temple, the chief priests, the scribes, and the leaders among the people were seeking how they might destroy Him (Luke 19:47-48; Mark 11:18). The next day, after He told a parable aimed at exposing the hypocrisy and unbelief of the Jewish leaders, they attempted to get their hands on Him immediately but were restrained by their fear of the people (Matthew 21:46; Mark 12:12; Luke 20:19). The phraseology "indicates that they not only desired to do so, but actively endeavored to discover means to arrest Jesus,"[7] as Luke adds, "in that very hour."

Deliverance into the hands of the Jews in God's time

The Jews had already decided to murder the Lord. At this point in their deliberations (apparently later that same Tuesday), they continued "seeking how to seize Him by stealth and kill Him" (Mark 14:1, NASB). *"But,"* they decided, *"not* on the feast day, lest there be an uproar among the people" (Matthew 26:1-5; Mark 14:1-2; cf. Luke 22:1-2). God, however, forced their hand to fulfill their wicked designs in *His* providential timing, not theirs. By divine design, the Passover Lamb of God would be taken and slain at the Passover, not sooner and not later. Commenting on the time juxtaposition of Matthew 26:1-5, William Hendriksen summarizes the silent tug of war between the Jewish leaders on one end and the invisible hand of providence on the other:

> "Not at the Festival," said the plotters. "At the Festival," said the Almighty; "after two days," echoed Jesus. His words and the words of the conspirators seem to have been spoken at the same time, for the context seems to imply that here, for once, the full temporal sense must be given to the opening word of verse 3, "Then." The divine decree always wins; in the interest of the kingdom, and to God's glory (Psalm 2:4; 33:10, 11).[8]

Deliverance to the hand of Pilate, whose power was from God (John 19:10-11)

"Speakest thou not unto me? knowest thou not that I have power to crucify thee, and have power to release thee?" Deflating this thinly veiled warning, Jesus bluntly informed Pilate that he had no independent authority over Him whatsoever—only the authority granted by God to do what He had already determined to be done. "Jesus is asserting that God is over all and that an earthly governor can act only as God permits him."[9] We can draw comfort and confidence in our day from Jesus' assertion regarding the providential parameters surrounding the power of the state arrayed against Him. Is it any less true today than it was then, any less true for us than for our Lord, any less true for the body than for the Head?[10]

Providential Fulfillment of Prophecy

The circumstances surrounding the last week of our Lord's life and ministry were crowded with fulfilled prophecies—the providence of God on display, working with majestic mystery through natural events and free human choices. Exploring the full range of providential activity involved in any one of these fulfillments could yield a separate chapter. The following list is partial and suggestive. The reference to the event itself is followed by the prophecy that it fulfilled.

- He entered Jerusalem on an ass (Matthew 21:1-7; John 12:12-16/Zechariah 9:9).

- He was spontaneously praised by children (Matthew 21:10-16/Psalm 8:2).

- He was later rejected by the people (John 12:36-42/Isaiah 53:1; Isaiah 6:10).

- He was betrayed by a friend (John 13:18/Psalm 41:9).

- He was sold for thirty pieces of silver, later used to buy Potter's Field (Matthew 27:3-10/Zechariah 11:12-13; Jeremiah 18:2; 19:2, 11; 32:6-9).

- He was deserted by His followers (Matthew 26:31; Mark 14:27/Zechariah 13:7).

- He was the object of undeserved hatred (John 15:25/Psalm 35:19; 69:4).

- His garments were parted and gambled for (John 19:23-24/Psalm 22:18).

- His body was pierced but unbroken (John 19:31-37/Psalm 34:20; Zechariah 12:10).

- He was numbered with transgressors in His death (Luke 22:37/Isaiah 53:12).

- He was appointed a place with the wicked but was, instead, associated "with the rich one" in His burial (Matthew 27:57-60/Isaiah 53:9).

This last example is a portrait of God's providence that deserves closer scrutiny.[11] Isaiah 53 delineates the progression of Messiah's trial (v. 7), death (v. 8), and burial (v. 9). "He made his grave with the wicked" is more literally rendered, "they appointed his grave [to be] with the wicked ones [plural]." In other words, it was their intent[12] to dishonor this one even further by casting His dead body into a common grave with the other criminals. "But" instead, He was associated "with the rich one [singular]" at His death.

Matthew alone records two significant facts that mark the explicit fulfillment of Isaiah 53:9 (Matthew 27:57-60). All the Gospel writers mention Joseph of Arimathea, but only Matthew records that he was "a *rich* man"; and only Matthew records that the tomb in which they laid Jesus was Joseph's "*own* new tomb." Given the necessarily hurried preparations for the feast day, a mass grave for all three crucifixion victims had certainly already been dug (probably in the accursed Valley of Hinnom).[13] In other words, the authorities had already appointed His grave to be with the wicked ones (that is, with the two malefactors crucified beside Him). But, through the sudden, surprising, and unforeseen intervention of the wealthy Joseph of Arimathea, Jesus was instead associated "with the rich one" at His interment, as a providential testimony to His distinctiveness (from "the wicked ones") and sinlessness.

Satan: Tool of Providence in the Crucifixion

I relish the word "tool" here because it certainly irks Satan to be described that way. Luther once remarked that "the best way to drive out the devil, if he will not yield to the texts of Scripture, is to jeer and flout him, for he cannot bear scorn." That is true of any arrogant, pompous, self-important pretender to a throne. That is why Thomas More observed, "The devil . . . the prowde spirit . . . cannot endure to be mocked."[14] So there is a peculiar satisfaction in seeing Satan, seemingly gaining the upper hand in his opposition to Christ, actually reduced to a pawn in the hand of our sovereign Savior at every turn. Every apparent satanic victory only played providentially into the hand of God.

Satan sought to hinder Jesus' redemptive mission (Matthew 16:21-23; Mark 8:31-33)

What means did Satan engage for this insidious ploy? Judas? The hateful Jewish leaders? No. He did it through Peter! Look at the context. Peter had just voiced his confession that Jesus was the Christ, the Son of the living God. In reply, Christ spoke highly of Peter's understanding as God-given and of Peter's important role in the work of the kingdom (Matthew 16:13-20). To prepare His followers for what was coming, Christ then predicted His approaching humiliation and death. Peter, perhaps fairly bursting with a sense of his newly conferred importance,

> took Jesus to himself, probably apart from the others, and "began to rebuke him," not from mere impulsiveness, but from deliberate conviction that Jesus was unduly discouraged, and with a new note of authority and officiousness [self-importance] towards him, perhaps of protection. . . . As much as to say that he and the other apostles would never let it happen to the Master.[15]

Peter *rebukes* "the Son of the living God." And do not miss the significance of the stunning, stinging reply of Christ. Only moments earlier He had blessed Peter for having been taught the truth of His identity from the Father. Now He suddenly identifies *Satan* as the source of Peter's protest regarding the Cross. Peter, taught by the Father, was still susceptible to satanic deception. So are we. Too often our own ideas and designs trample roughshod over our creed. Peter professed Jesus to be God, then *argued* with His words! We profess the *Lord* Jesus Christ, then disobey His Word and resist His leading. Let's be as hard on ourselves as we are on Peter.

Satan entered into Judas twice (Luke 22:3-6; John 13:2, 27)

Scripture records two explicit occasions on which Satan entered Judas: first on Tuesday, when he conferred with the chief priests and received a paltry sum of blood money from them (Luke 22:3-6; cf. John 13:2); then again on Wednesday night,[16] when he received the sop from Jesus' own hand at the Passover meal (John 13:27).

Judas's action is probably as complicated as it is mysterious. Several factors may account for his decision: spite, resentment, vengeance, self-preservation, mingled with his long-fed and deep-seated avaricious spirit.[17] Nothing in the record indicates that Judas consciously invited Satan to enter. Everything, in fact, argues against that assumption. Satan does not need to be invited; he needs merely not to be resisted. Judas's "yielding to selfish impulse opened the way to satanic control."[18] That habitually unchecked selfish impulse readily rose to the satanic suggestion, by which "Judas opened the door to Satan. He did not resist him, and Satan did not flee from him."[19] But even as Judas played willingly into the hands of Satan, Satan played unwittingly into the hands of providence.

Satan sought and obtained permission to sift Peter and the other disciples (Luke 22:31-32)

Despite our modern impatience with the "thee's" and thou's" of Scripture, the effort to eliminate this archaism necessarily sacrifices an element of accuracy and understanding. In modern English we use "you" for both singular and plural. The advantage of the older English in the Authorized Version is that you always know whether the pronoun (in Greek or Hebrew) is singular or plural. "Thee" and "thou" and "thy" *always* signify a singular pronoun in the original, whereas "you" and "ye" and "your" *always* indicate a plural.[20] Unfortunately, modern English versions erase that distinction by the use of "you" for both singular and plural. Many English readers are unaware of this distinction even when they read the KJV.

Peter was not the only one to be sifted by Satan. Luke 22:31 reads, "Simon, Simon, behold, Satan hath desired to have *you* [plural; that is, all of the disciples], that he may sift *you* [plural] as wheat." Jesus was informing and warning Peter—even in the face of Peter's promise of loyalty to the death—that Satan desired *all* of the disciples to test them to the uttermost. Moreover, the vocabulary and tense of the phrase "hath desired" indicate that Satan's desire had, in fact, *already* been granted.[21] Satan had sought and already obtained permission from God to test any and all of the disciples.

This appears to be a parallel of what Satan sought to do with Job—to test the depth and genuineness of the disciples' faith and (he hoped) prove them to be self-serving frauds who would, in a pinch, desert the Lord. "But," Jesus adds to Peter (Luke 22:32), "I have prayed for *thee* [singular; that is, "for thee, in particular, Peter"] that *thy* [singular] faith fail not: and when *thou* [singular] art converted [that is, turned around after this trial], strengthen *thy* [singular] brethren" who were also severely tried. (Remember Thomas?) Peter's faith *faltered*—as did Job's, if you read his whole story carefully—but it did not *fail*. And afterward, he was the stronger for it and able to strengthen his brethren. Again, Satan's most malevolent intentions served Christ's purpose and strengthened His cause.

Satan was given "power" over Christ (Luke 22:52-53)

"Be ye come out, as against a thief, with swords and staves? When I was daily with you in the temple, ye stretched forth no hands against me." Jesus then answers His own question and, in so doing, points out to the Jewish leaders who came to arrest Him that night that this was all by design. Implicit in His remark is the point that they were providentially prevented from lifting a hand against Him until the appointed time. Finally, "their [appointed] hour" had arrived, and not "their hour" only, but also the hour granted to "the power of darkness." The sense is "This is your hour of success allowed by God; and it coincides with that allowed to the power of darkness."[22] What sounds like a defeat, an abdication of control to Satan, is actually divine permission by the sovereign God for Satan to do his worst—only to prove how weak and powerless he really is when he goes up against God. The betrayal, arrest, trial, and execution of Christ constituted Satan's "moment of triumph" providentially allowed by God; but a moment was all He could spare.

Doesn't Satan realize when his actions are serving only to fulfill God's prophetic word? Almost certainly. Even though Satan is an angelic creation and not omniscient like God, he nevertheless possesses a shrewd knowledge of Scripture and is capable of using it quite craftily in an attempt to twist it to his own ends (as his tempting encounters with Eve and Christ handily illustrate). Then why does he pursue a path that he knows is fulfilling God's prophesied purposes?

Part of the reason is his incurable perversity and intractable rebellion against everything God purposes. He is, after all, the Satan ("adversary"). But perhaps another part of the reason may be that he still believes he can pull off a different conclusion. Ambition blinds and deludes those who fall under its mesmerizing sway; absolute and all-consuming ambition blinds and deludes absolutely. Satan seems so bewitched (ironic word, that) by his ambition to rival God and become "like the Most High" that he continues to entertain the fantasy that he can outsmart God at His own game.

Many people are the same way. They know that what they are doing is contrary to God's Word; they know the warnings that God's Word attaches to sinful practices. Yet they persist in sin because they think that somehow they can pull off a different conclusion, that God won't really hold them accountable, or that engaging in certain sins won't really lead to the dire consequences God's Word describes. To such Paul warns: Do not deceive yourself; God is not mocked. Whatever a man sows, he eventually reaps (Galatians 6:7-9).

Circumstantial Providences: God's Extra Touches

Twentieth-century southern writer and poet laureate Archibald Rutledge penned *Life's Extras*, a little volume devoted to observing and exulting in all the unnecessary beauty and pleasure that God has added to grace our life on this earth. After all, the world would be perfectly functional without the extravagant variety of color and pattern in flowers and birds, or the succulent sweetness He has lavished on a Carolina peach. Much of what God could have made merely utilitarian He has, in goodness, made beautiful and enjoyable.

As we learned from our study in Esther, many of the most profoundly providential details of the story are technically unnecessary to the ultimate outcome of events. These are God's extras, added for His own holy amusement and our worshipful wonder. Likewise, the canvas of the Crucifixion—the ultimate drama and theological apex of human history—is gilded with providential extras that enhance the final picture.[23]

Michelangelo spent four years creating—with the help of several assistants—what has come to be universally regarded as his greatest masterpiece, the Sistine Chapel ceiling. Since that time the ceiling has been increasingly in danger of being lost forever, slowly eaten away by centuries of grime, soot, and other pollutants (as well as numerous botched attempts at preserving it). Finally, a team of specialists spent the entire decade of the 1980s restoring the chapel ceiling. Working systematically and in minute proximity to the frescoed ceiling, the restorers became so familiar with the intricate details of the work that they "learned to recognize Michelangelo's own brush mark, just as if it were his handwriting."[24] In the same way, careful attention to the delicate details of the biblical narrative—whether in the life of Joseph, the story of Esther, the experiences of Job, or the ministry and mission of Christ—reveals the divine brush marks, the very handwriting of God on the events of human history.

To change the metaphor, no Shakespearean play can match the Holy Spirit's attention to imagery and irony, symbolism and foreshadowing, detail and drama, in the biblical account of Christ's crucifixion. Consider these features of the Passion Week. Were they pointless coincidences? Accidental details? Or were they providentially designed "extra touches" to draw attention to His presence and activity and to beautify the events of this pivotal week in human history?

Timing of the Crucifixion—providential symbolism (cf. I Corinthians 5:7)
God brought all things—including the murderous intentions of wicked men and demons—to a head at the most symbolically appropriate moment in the whole Jewish calendar year—Passover. Exodus 12, Isaiah 53, and many similar passages lingered for centuries, awaiting this picture-perfect fulfillment when "Christ our Passover" would be "sacrificed for us" as "the Lamb of God" whose blood would secure protection from death and deliverance from sin.

The colt and the Upper Room—providential training of the disciples (cf. Matthew 21:1-6; Mark 11:1-6; Luke 19:29-30; cf. also Mark 14:12-16; Luke 22:7-13)
Have you ever wondered why Christ insisted on making the arrangements for the colt and for the Upper Room through His disciples and in such an "unnecessarily" unusual way? Why did He not make the arrangements Himself, or at least accompany them? Why the peculiar directions about loosing the colt and then explaining (in only the vaguest terms) to the owner what they were doing? Why the mysterious direction about

following a man bearing a pitcher of water in order to find their meeting place for the Passover?

Christ would not always be with His disciples. In fact, He would shortly be leaving them. In preparation for His departure, Christ seemed to be using these situations to condition them to trust His word and follow His instructions implicitly in His absence, and to cultivate their perception of His providential leading. This would prove to be an invaluable spiritual sensitivity and skill in the early days of the church throughout the Book of Acts. It is no less so for us.

Caiaphas's counsel—providential prophecy (John 11:46-53; 18:39)

Desperate to figure out a course of action that would safely but effectively rid them of their adversary, the Jewish leadership debated what to do about Jesus. Caiaphas, the high priest, advised his comrades that it was "expedient . . . that one man should die for the people, and that the whole nation perish not." Wittingly, Caiaphas was speaking from a purely pragmatic, political standpoint—it was necessary to destroy Jesus in order to avoid a Jewish uprising and the certain Roman punishment on the nation that would follow. Unwittingly, however, Caiaphas was actually prophesying the profound theological truth "that Jesus should die for the nation"—as John explains under inspiration (John 11:51-52).[25]

"John does not mean that Caiaphas had no control over his words. . . . But God so overruled that, while Caiaphas meant one thing his words had another . . . deeper and more important meaning."[26] God providentially put into the mouth of one of His Son's most vicious enemies and murderers a prophetic pronouncement of exactly what His Son would accomplish through the very deed of wickedness they were scheming. In fact, God used this unlikeliest of spokesmen to enunciate what would become one of the New Testament's most profound doctrinal truths—the substitutionary death of Christ—in theologically precise language.[27]

The cock—providential cue (Matthew 26:74; Mark 14:72; Luke 22:60; John 18:27)

The cock crowing is yet another "unnecessary" detail, providentially painted into the picture. Why did Jesus not simply say (and providence ordain) instead, "Before morning" or "Before this is all over, you will deny Me three times"? The detail of the cock adds an unmistakable specificity to the pronouncement. The crowing of the cock surely jarred all of Peter's senses and carried a potent dramatic impact.

Herod's visit—providential "coincidence" (Luke 23:6-12)

As far as Herod was concerned, he was just taking a little vacation from Galilee, or was perhaps in Jerusalem on business. But God wanted him there and providentially directed his plans to place him there. We know that Herod had "desired" to see Jesus for a long time to satisfy his own personal but unbelieving curiosity. Had Herod not been in Jerusalem at the time, Pilate almost certainly would have delayed his decision pending a hearing before Herod in Galilee. But that would not have fit the divine timetable. Once again, providence makes the arrangements to expedite not only what God has determined but when.

Pilate's wife's dream—providential warning (Matthew 27:19)

This extra detail is the only reference we find to Pilate's wife. Her presence is not necessary to the outcome. But it does serve a providential purpose. Only a decade earlier, in A.D. 21, a measure was proposed in the Roman senate to prohibit the wife of a provincial magistrate from accompanying him in judicial hearings—an increasingly common practice that disturbed some people.[28] Because that proposal failed in the chambers of the pagan Roman legislature, Pilate's wife appears in this scene. Why should she receive this dream omen? Why should she enter the picture at all? Whatever its gracious personal purpose may have been, it served as both a providential warning to Pilate of the gravity of the situation before him and as one more providential echo of the innocence of this one who was being condemned to death.[29]

Exchange of Barabbas—providential parable (Matthew 27:26; Mark 15:15; Luke 23:25)

Just as Caiaphas's pragmatic pronouncement was an unwitting providential precursor to the doctrine of the substitutionary atonement, the exchange of Christ for Barabbas becomes a providential picture of the substitutionary nature of Christ's work and our salvation. The sinless Lamb of God dies literally *instead of*, *in the place of*, an admitted guilty sinner. And look at the crimes of which Barabbas is guilty: *rebellion* (the essence of all human sin against God) and *murder* (the first recorded sin after the Fall and the gravest sin one human can commit against another, the slaying of a fellow creature created in God's image). The rebel sinner goes free, while the submissive sinless one dies in his place. Even his name drips with symbolism: Barabbas, "son of Abba."[30] Barabbas stands as a timeless providential parable of precisely what Christ was accomplishing on the Cross—dying as the innocent substitute for rebellious sinners such as you and me.

Crown of thorns—providential irony (Matthew 27:29; Mark 15:17)

In a providentially permitted touch of cruelty, the Creator is crowned with the very curse He inflicted upon earth for man's rebellion (Genesis 3:17-18). This must have been a high point in Satan's gloating savagery. Yet it merely underscores the truth that He who wore the curse became a curse for us, who deserved the curse (Galatians 3:13).

Crucifixion—providential means (John 18:31-32)

The death of Christ by any means other than crucifixion would have marked the failure of explicit prophecy and undermined the reliability of God's Word. Once they attempted to hurl Him over the precipice at Nazareth (Luke 4). On at least two occasions the Jews went so far as to pick up rocks to stone Him (John 8:59; 10:31). And not long after Jesus' death the Jews did, in fact, execute Stephen by stoning (Acts 7).[31] But neither the spontaneous murder by His enraged enemies nor the standard Jewish method of capital punishment (stoning) would do for Jesus. Christ *must* be *crucified*.

Not only was this kind of death uniquely pictured in Old Testament prophecy (Deuteronomy 21:22-23; Psalm 22), but Christ also specifically and repeatedly predicted His death by this particular method (John 3:14; 8:28; 12:32-34). "Jesus' prophecy was that He would be crucified," notes Leon Morris, "and John now records its fulfilment. Caiaphas's determination to secure a crucifixion fulfils the divine purpose."[32] Clearly, the intent of the Jewish leadership in securing through Pilate this uniquely Roman form of punishment was to squelch any credibility for Jesus' messianic claim by attaching to Him the stigma of the Old Testament curse, "he that is hanged [on a tree] is accursed of God" (Deuteronomy 21:23) Ironically, the intent of God was to attach to Jesus the stigma of this same curse—not to disprove His messianic identity but to validate His messianic work, as Paul points out: "Christ hath redeemed us from the curse of the law, being made a curse for us; for it is written, Cursed is everyone that hangeth on a tree" (Galatians 3:13). Once again, the evil intentions of wicked men intersect with the sovereign designs of God to infallibly secure His purposes.

Pilate's superscription—providential proclamation (John 19:19-22)

A placard proclaiming the criminal's name and the charge against him was customarily carried by a herald leading the execution procession or worn around the victim's neck. At the place of crucifixion, it was then affixed above the individual's head as a public testimony and warning.[33] Putting all the Bible accounts together, we can ascertain that the full superscription written by Pilate to be posted over Christ on the cross read as follows: "This is Jesus the Nazarene, the King of the Jews." The official public testimony, penned by the pagan Pilate, was a tacit admission that this one called Jesus of Nazareth was being put to death for being the King of the Jews.

That Pilate appointed those explicit words to be written in the first place—not couched in the language of insinuation or accusation but in the straightforward form of a declaration—was in itself an extraordinary stroke of providence. It was as much a commentary on the Jews as it was on Jesus. Moreover, the Jews' visible irritation with the wording of Pilate's placard and their vigorous protest to Pilate himself—which he ignored with the elegantly dismissive retort, "What I have written I have written"—further magnifies God's hand over the smallest details of this affair. Whatever human considerations motivated Pilate to inscribe those words, "the Divine fact is that the superscription was written with the finger of God even though Pilate all unconsciously was His penman."[34]

PROVIDENCE IN THE PASSION OF CHRIST

Midnight at noonday—providential picture (Matthew 27:45; Mark 15:33; Luke 23:44-45a)

Since the Passover celebration fell on a full moon, these passages cannot possibly describe a solar eclipse but a supernatural phenomenon. The closest we have to an explanatory description is Luke's remark that "the sun was darkened"—literally "the sun failed," suggesting "that the cause [of the darkness] lay in the sun itself rather than an atmospheric obstruction to its rays."[35] Providence painted a vivid picture of the darkness of sin and of the separation from God that its judgment brings.[36] The sun was extinguished when the Sun of Righteousness (Malachi 4:2), the Light of the World (John 8:12), suffered and died. This was a stroke of sable from the divine brush on the living canvas that was both real and illustrative; for without Him, all is midnight.

Dramatic disturbances—providential pictures (Matthew 27:51-54)

At the moment of Christ's death, the temple veil separating the holy place from the holy of holies, representing the earthly dwelling place of God Himself, was torn open. And not merely torn, but ripped by the hand of God "from top to bottom." That veil was sixty feet high and woven from heavy material as thick as the palm of a man's hand.[37] What was the significance of this act of God?

By divine law, only one man (the high priest) was allowed past that veil only once a year (on the Day of Atonement) into the holiest place where the presence of God had dwelt. Through the object lesson of this divine arrangement the Holy Spirit was teaching Israel that access into the presence of God was strictly limited (Hebrews 9:6-9). That veil became a symbol of the physical body of Jesus Christ, so that when the body of Christ was "torn" through His death on the cross, the veil of the temple was simultaneously torn—signifying that we now have personal access, full and free, into the presence of God through the sacrifice of Christ (Hebrews 10:19-22).

At the same time, the earth quaked so violently that rocks split and tombs were left gaping. Three days later (after Jesus' resurrection, we are told), dead saints were raised from those tombs and appeared to many in

Jerusalem. These events were designed to demonstrate that Christ, by His death, entered the stronghold of him "that had the power of death, that is, the devil" (Hebrews 2:14) and bested him on his own turf. As the "firstfruits" of the resurrection (I Corinthians 15:20) and the firstborn from among the dead (Colossians 1:18; Revelation 1:5), Christ rose first, followed by a great host of resurrected saints.[38] He who was "the Resurrection, and the Life" (John 11:25) ransacked the realm of death, and made a show of it openly through dramatic disturbances that painted providential pictures.

Roman guard—providential witnesses (Matthew 27:62-66)

Why was it that Jesus' own disciples neither understood nor remembered His repeated prediction that He would rise the third day, yet His enemies did? God used the memory of His unbelieving enemies to *help* Him safeguard the legitimacy of the Resurrection! By placing the Roman guard, the Jews helped to prove that the disciples could not possibly have come and stolen the body—though they later absurdly tried to perpetrate that very lie (Matthew 28:11-15). But providence was at work not only in His enemies' memory of Christ's words; it was evident even in His disciples' amazing dullness regarding the same predictions.

The disciples' incomprehension—providential dullness? (Luke 9:21-22; 9:43-45; 18:31-34)

This one is worth exploring in more detail. The Gospel writers record three occasions on which the Lord predicted His approaching death and resurrection. After the second of these predictions, Luke alone adds some remarkable terminology. He recounts that the Lord's statement "was hid [concealed] from them," literally "in order that they should not perceive it" (Luke 9:45). *Was hidden?* By whom? *In order that they should not perceive it?* Why? The grammatical force of the terms unmistakably implies that "they were not allowed to understand the saying," indicating that "this ignorance of the disciples was specially ordered for them."[39]

After the third occasion on which Jesus explicitly spelled out His approaching death and resurrection, Luke alone again adds a remarkable assertion (Luke 18:34). He pens a threefold statement of the disciples' utter incomprehension of Christ's blunt and plain-spoken prediction: (1) they did not understand these things, (2) this saying was hidden from them, and (3) they did not know these things.

How could this be? Which word did they not understand? Who was hiding these clear predictions from their comprehension? Most commentators appeal to the parallel passages (Matthew 20:17-28; Mark 10:32-45) to support their explanation of this startling verse. The disciples, they say, were simply too distracted by the anticipation of their part in the glory of an earthly kingdom. Their preoccupation with the earthly and physical made them spiritually dense and insensitive to the grave truths that Christ was trying to impress upon them.

That explanation is not satisfying here for two reasons. In the first place, Luke himself does not include the context of the disciples' arguments over the kingdom to help explain their unusual response to Christ's words. In the second place, even that explanation docs not adequately account for the unmistakable force of Luke's three expressions of incomprehension piled on top of one another.

So how do we account for the disciples' failure to understand the Lord's unambiguous words? Luke himself, and Luke alone, later provides the key that unlocks what was going on here. In Luke 24 he records that, after His resurrection, Christ showed Himself to the disciples and said, "These are the words which I spake unto you, while I was yet with you, that all things must be fulfilled, which were written . . . concerning me." At that precise moment Christ lifted the veil from their eyes: "then *opened he* their understanding, that they might understand the scriptures" that "it behoved [was necessary for] Christ to suffer, and to rise from the dead the third day" (24:44-46).

How is it that Jesus' own disciples, who heard these predictions repeatedly, did not understand or remember them? The inspired terminology of the text indicates that the disciples failed to comprehend this truth because even while it was being revealed to them, it was simultaneously being "hidden from them." Hidden from them by whom? By the Lord Himself! Only the Lord, then, could remove that dullness and incomprehension—which is exactly what Luke says happened! Clearly, it was *Christ Himself* who was suspending their understanding even while He was revealing predictive truth to them. And it was Christ alone who could then open their understanding to finally comprehend the truth they had previously heard. The question is, why?

Why would the Lord reveal something so crucial to the disciples and at the same time "hide" it from them? Part of the answer lies in the fact that the disciples' "dulness was providential and it became a security to the church for the truth of the resurrection."[40] The words and deeds of Christ's enemies, who did remember, supply the rest of the answer.

The Lord revealed yet hid this from the disciples *to insure that they would do nothing to cast any doubt on the authenticity of the Resurrection.* Any confident anticipation of the Resurrection on their part would make the disappearance of the body look suspicious and contrived. In spite of Christ's repeated and unambiguous prediction that He would rise from the dead the third day, *none* of His followers actually expected or anticipated such an event. Consequently, "the theory that they believed [in the Resurrection] because they *expected* Him to rise again is against all the evidence."[41] By declaring His Resurrection to the disciples ahead of time, Christ was prestoking their faith so that when it did come to pass, they would remember His words and believe (cf. John 13:19; 14:29). By simultaneously hiding it from the disciples until its fulfillment, God prevented the disciples from acting in a manner that would compromise the integrity of the event.

Yet the clear meaning of the prediction was not "hidden" from the enemies of Christ. They understood and remembered. God employed the unbelief and hostility, as well as the understanding and memory, of His own enemies to *help establish and validate the authenticity of the Resurrection.* By securing the tomb and setting the guard (Matthew 27:62-66), and by having to concoct such an implausible alibi (Matthew 28:11-15), God's fiercest enemies helped Him authenticate the very truths they themselves rejected. "Surely the wrath of man shall praise thee" (Psalm 76:10)! With all the precautions taken by His enemies to keep Him in the grave, there could be no other explanation than that He really had risen from the dead. It was a divine masterstroke.

This episode of "providential dullness" underscores a very practical and pertinent truth for us. God Himself holds the gift of comprehending even what He plainly reveals in the Word. He is free to hide from us, for His own reasons, even the most obvious of biblical truths. Without His illumination, we are prone to error, to insensitivity, to dullness. We must consciously seek and rely on God's grace to help us never become confident in our own ability to decipher eternal, spiritual, God-given truth.

Sovereign Superintendence over the Crucifixion

Finally, note these direct assertions of God's unswerving providential control over every aspect of the Crucifixion.

- John 19:11—"Jesus answered, Thou couldest have no power at all against me, *except it were given thee from above. . . .*"

- Acts 2:23—"Him, *being delivered by the determinate counsel and foreknowledge of God*, ye have taken, and by wicked hands have crucified and slain."

- Acts 3:17-18—"And now, brethren, I [know] that through ignorance ye did it, as did also your rulers. But *those things which God before had shewed by the mouth of all His prophets, that Christ should suffer*, he hath so fulfilled."

- Acts 4:27-28—"For of a truth against thy holy child Jesus, whom thou hast anointed, both Herod, and Pontius Pilate, with the Gentiles, and the people of Israel, were gathered together, *for to do whatsoever thy hand and thy counsel determined before to be done.*"

G. C. Berkouwer summarizes the thrust of these remarkable passages:

> The interlacing of Divine and human activity is revealed pre-eminently in the history of Christ's suffering. Satan and men act out their part. . . . Christ experiences Divine abandonment in the crucible created by human enterprise—in the opposition against Him and the delivering of Him to

the death of the cross. God acts *in* men's acts: in Pilate's sentence, in Judas' betrayal, yea, in everything that men do with Christ. God's activity embraces all these and leads them along His mysterious way.[42]

John Piper distills this same truth more concisely: "People lift their hand to rebel against the Most High only to find that their rebellion is unwitting service in the wonderful designs of God. . . . The hardened disobedience of men's hearts leads not to the frustration of God's plans, but to their fruition."[43]

A Look in the Mirror

The invisible hand of providence was behind the events of the Crucifixion, guiding and restraining, directing and permitting. Men and demons, in carrying out their own will, could do only that which would carry out His will.

> The death of Christ was not an accident; it was a major part of the divine plan to redeem sinful mankind. The fact that God knew what was going to happen did not remove the responsibility of those human beings who freely violated the law of God to kill an innocent Person, who turned out to be the great King. God's purpose was redemption; man's purpose was murder. The two purposes intersect at the cross, and the result is salvation for all who will believe![44]

If God can so sovereignly control such combined, focused chaos and hatred, is it possible that He could for a moment lose control over the affairs of your life?

One writer relates two poignant incidents that put a human face, a personal touch, on the relevance for our own suffering of Christ's providential suffering.

> My blind friend Peter shares how humiliated he was when, as a teenager, he fell after striking his head on a low branch. Sprawled on the ground in front of his friends, he felt hurt and embarrassed. His confidence in God was shaken: *You don't understand what it's like to be blind, God. To not know where the next blow might come from!* But Jesus does . . . (Luke 22:63-64).

Another friend, Gloria, fell into deep anguish over the dismal prognosis of her daughter's illness. Little Laura had already suffered enough from the degenerative nerve disorder she had been born with, and now the doctors' forecast included more suffering and impending death. One night after leaving her daughter's bedside, she spat, 'God it's not right. You've never had to watch one of your children die!' As soon as the words escaped, she clasped her hand over her mouth. He did watch his child die. His one and only Son.[45]

Any parent understands that personal suffering is more endurable than helplessly watching one's own child suffer. More profoundly than we know, God understands that experience—not theoretically because He is an all-knowing God, but experientially because He is also man. In the God-Man was combined the personal suffering and the watching God. But God was not a helpless onlooker, and that adds an immeasurable depth of meaning to the experience. His own suffering *could* have been avoided, but it wasn't; it was voluntary. And it was for you.

> God suffered in Christ. He knows what it is like to experience pain. He has travelled down the road of pain, abandonment, suffering and death. . . . God is not like some alleged hero with feet of clay, who demands that others suffer, while remaining aloof from the world of pain himself. He has passed through the shadow of suffering himself . . . and, by doing so, transfigures the sufferings of his people.[46]

His Word assures us that He is as providentially and lovingly in control of our circumstances as He was when His own Son undeservedly suffered unspeakable horrors.

> *This is my Father's world,*
> *O let me ne'er forget*
> *That though the wrong seems oft so strong,*
> *God is the Ruler yet.*[47]

Has God's providence over Christ's crucifixion, then, no practical application to your experiences?

12

PROVIDENCE IN THE CHURCH

Faith in God's providence, instead of repressing our energies, excites us to diligence. We labor as if all depended upon us, and then fall back upon the Lord with the calm faith which knows that all depends upon him.

—C. H. Spurgeon

You may have noticed that, with the exception of a few key verses here and there, most of our time throughout this study has been spent in the Old Testament. Even the last two chapters on the Incarnation and the Crucifixion focused extensively on the links between the Old and New Testaments. One might be tempted to wonder, therefore, whether providence is still a valid principle in the church age. Is providence still God's *modus operandi,* His primary method of operation?

What Does the Bible Say?

To answer this question, we will take a survey trip through the narrative of the early church. By this time, our eyes and ears should be trained to recognize providence when we see its telltale brushstrokes or hear its "still small voice." Let's survey the teaching of the Book of Acts regarding the activities of providence, expressed below in practical terms of broad truths and timeless principles. Once again, the force of these lessons will be multiplied if you read this chapter with your Bible open, investigating the record of these incidents for yourself.

God may intervene directly in the affairs of His church and in the individual lives of His people (Acts 5:1-11; cf. I Corinthians 11:30).[1]

Who struck Ananias and Sapphira? Peter didn't do it. Peter didn't even ask God to do it, though he did predict (in language clearly suggestive of direct providential intervention) that God would do to Sapphira what He had done to her husband (Acts 5:9). Jesus Christ, the Lord who is actively building His church (just as He said He would, Matthew 16:18), stepped invisibly and providentially into the proceedings. What effect would it have on our churches—and on our own lives—if Christ governed His church as actively and directly today? There is no biblical reason that He could not similarly step providentially into the proceedings of the church today. This passage is designed to provide ample warning against presumptuously daring to test the reality of the Holy Spirit's knowledge and presence in His church.[2]

God is free to alter circumstances in ways that are humanly impossible (Acts 5:17-24).

Arrested and imprisoned by the Jewish authorities, the apostles were promptly released by an angel and instructed to return to the temple to continue the very activity for which they had just been arrested. God frequently employs angels as the agents of His providence. God's deliverances or interventions may rarely be as dramatic in our experience as they were in the crucial days of the church's infancy. Nevertheless, His ability to alter our circumstances—even when it seems humanly hopeless and impossible—is still quite intact. Church history is filled with testimonies to this truth.

John Paton, nineteenth-century missionary to the New Hebrides, experienced God's providential intervention on more than one occasion. "Missi," urged Nowar, the converted island chief, "sit down beside me and pray to our Jehovah God, for if He does not send deliverance now, we are all dead men." Paton was no stranger to harrowing experiences with the savage cannibals on the Pacific island of Tanna. In 1862, as he recounts in his autobiography, he faced perhaps his closest brush with seemingly certain death at the hands of hostile islanders.

> We prayed as one can only pray when in the jaws of death and on the brink of eternity. We felt that God was near and omnipotent to do what seemed best in His sight. When the Savages were about three hundred yards off, at the foot of a hill leading up to the village, Nowar touched my knee, saying, "Missi, Jehovah is hearing! They are standing still." . . . We saw a messenger or herald running along the approaching multitude, delivering some tidings as he passed, and then disappearing into the bush. To our amazement, the host began to turn, and slowly marched back in great silence, and entered the remote bush at the head of the island. Nowar and his people were in ecstasies, crying out, "Jehovah has heard Missi's prayer! Jehovah has protected us and turned them away back."[3]

Rosalind Goforth, wife of the famous missionary to China, Jonathan Goforth, records their narrow escape from a Chinese mob during the Boxer Rebellion in the early 1900s. I have included this lengthy account because it is a riveting read and vividly illustrates God's providential protection through an instructive variety of subtle means. Hoping to escape the growing hostilities of the Chinese, the missionaries packed up their belongings on several wagons.

> After prayer, we all got on our carts and, one by one, passed out into the densely crowded street. As we approached the city gate we could see that the road was black with crowds awaiting us. . . . My husband turned pale as he pointed to a group of several hundred men, fully armed, awaiting us. They waited till all the carts had passed through the gate, then hurled down upon us a shower of stones, at the same time rushing forward and maiming or killing some of the animals. My husband jumped down from the cart and cried to them, "Take everything, but don't kill." His only answer was a blow. The confusion that followed was so great it would be impossible to describe the escape of each one in detail. Each one later had his or her own testimony of that mighty and merciful deliverance. But I must give the details of my husband's experience.

One man struck him a blow on the neck with a great sword wielded with two hands. "Somehow" the blunt edge of the sword struck his neck; the blow left a wide mark almost around his neck, but did no further harm. Had the sharp edge struck his neck he would certainly have been beheaded! His thick helmet was cut almost to pieces, one blow cutting through the leather lining *just over the temple*, but without even scratching the skin!

Again he was felled to the ground, with a fearful sword cut, which entered the bone of the skull behind and almost cleft it in two. As he fell he seemed to hear distinctly a voice saying, "Fear not, they are praying for you." Rising from his blow, he was again struck down by a club. As he was falling almost unconscious to the ground he saw a horse coming at full speed toward him; when he became conscious again he found the horse had tripped and fallen (on level ground) so near that its tail almost touched him. The animal, kicking furiously, had served as a barrier between him and his assailants. While he was dazed and not knowing what to do, a man came up as if to strike, but whispered, "Leave the carts." By that time the onlookers began to rush forward to get the loot, but the attacking party felt the things were theirs, so desisted in their attack upon us in order to secure their booty.

A word as to myself and the children. Several fierce men with swords jumped on my cart. One struck at the baby, but I parried the blow with a pillow, and the little fellow only received a slight scratch on the forehead. Then they dropped their swords and began tearing at our goods at the back of the cart. Heavy boxes were dragged over us, and everything was taken. Just then a dreadful-looking man tried to reach us from the back of the cart with his sword, missing by an inch. I thought he would come to the front and continue the attack, but he did not. I had seen Mr. Goforth sink to the ground covered with blood twice, and given him up for dead. Just then Paul [their son], who had been in the last cart, jumped in, wild with delight at what he seemed to think was great fun, for he had run through the thick of the fight, dodging sword thrusts from all sides, and had succeeded in reaching me without a scratch. . . . Paul seemed to feel no fear, but said, "Mother, what does this put you in mind of? It puts me in mind of the Henty books!"[4]

The Goforths' escape is only one more of the numberless testimonies of God's people throughout the history of His church that have known God's providential protection and deliverance in the face of humanly impossible circumstances.

God may preserve or deliver His people through aid even from our enemies (5:33-40).

We have seen more than once before the strange and unexpected tools God sometimes uses. When the Jews' enemies wrote King Darius of Persia in hopes of securing a royal decree to force them to stop rebuilding the temple (Ezra 5), God used their correspondence to accomplish exactly the opposite effect. Darius wrote back (Ezra 6) commanding them not to hinder the Jews, to send their tax revenues directly to Judah for the project, and to give them anything else they requested to assist in the building!

Here in Acts 5, the Sanhedrin—the Jewish "supreme court"—is poised to pass a sentence of execution on Peter and the other apostles. Their reaction to the bold and convicting testimony of these men is expressed in the phrase "cut to the heart" (Acts 5:33). The verb's literal translation is simpler and more colorful—they were "sawn through."[5] The word figuratively pictures these men as enraged by what they heard. Notice the reaction when the same term is used in Acts 7:54—"When they heard these things [from Stephen], they were cut to the heart [lit., "sawn through"], and they gnashed on him with their teeth." We might say they "came unglued," or (if you will pardon the pun on being "sawn" in two) they were "beside themselves" with rage!

It is at this crucial point that Gamaliel, a ranking Pharisee on the council (5:34), urges caution (5:35) and counsels restraint in their decision (5:38-39). His words do not evidence any sympathy or inclination toward Christianity; his advice appears to be primarily pragmatic. Nevertheless, "Gamaliel's pragmatic moderation works to the apostles' benefit," demonstrating that "God can raise up unlikely defenders for His people."[6]

Sometimes such providential persuasion takes the form of a change of heart resulting in conscious aid from those who were enemies. In the mid-1800s, Baptist preacher I. B. Kimbrough's fundraising travels on behalf of Carson and Newman College (Tennessee) once took him through a secluded forest where two armed brigands accosted him and demanded all his money. Dismounting from his horse, Kimbrough divided his money into two separate piles. The smaller pile, he informed them, was his personal cash which they were free to have. "That larger pile," he continued, "is God's money, and I dare you to touch it. I collected it for the young preachers of the state who are struggling for an education at Carson and Newman College." The thieves, taken aback by the man's demeanor, asked about the college and about Kimbrough's work. Cowed by the sobering threat, the bandits agreed not to take any of the money. Instead, before they parted from Kimbrough, each robber contributed five dollars for the college.[7]

On other occasions, the evil decisions and worst intentions of the enemies of God's truth serve only to further His work. William Tyndale (1494-1536) was greatly used by God to multiply the understandability and accessibility of the Bible to the common man by translating the New Testament from Greek into English. The problem was that such translations were, at the time, illegal in England (and virtually everywhere else, for that matter) without the express, official permission of the king and the church authorities. Neither was kindly disposed to Tyndale's efforts. The punishment for proceeding without that permission was imprisonment and, in many cases, execution. In order to give the people access to God's Word in their own language, however, Tyndale proceeded. He exiled himself from his native England to Germany for the work of translating and printing. The illegal books were then smuggled into England under a variety of ingenious disguises—in the false bottoms of cargo barrels containing wheat or secreted into bags of flour or cornmeal.[8] Tyndale was aided in this endeavor by merchants who carried the contraband into England. Whenever the Testaments were discovered by government or church officials in England, they were seized and publicly burned;[9] anyone convicted of distributing or even possessing them faced severe punishment as well.

Arthur Packington,[10] a London merchant, overheard that Bishop Tunstall of London desired to buy as many Testaments as possible for burning, hoping in that way to exhaust the supply and stamp out the enterprise. Because of his connections, Packington knew the whereabouts of those who purchased and distributed the Testaments in England and offered his services to Bishop Tunstall, assuring him that he could procure the bulk of them. Tunstall was delighted. What he didn't know, however, was that Packington was a friend of Tyndale and sympathetic to his endeavor.

"The bishop thinking he had God by the toe, when indeed he had (as after he thought) the Devil by the fist," eagerly agreed to reimburse Packington for whatever costs he incurred. Packington promptly contacted Tyndale, who was in debt, with the news that he knew someone who was prepared to buy all the present printing of New Testaments (as well as other "notorious" books authored by Tyndale). "Who?" asked Tyndale.[11] "The bishop of London," replied Packington. "O that is because he will burn them!" Tyndale exclaimed with alarm. "Indeed," replied Packington with a wink and a nod. Some say Packington offered—at Bishop Tunstall's expense, of course—up to four times the actual cost per Testament.[12] The advantages of the proposition dawned on Tyndale. He could use the surplus not only to get out of debt but also to produce even *more* New Testament translations. Moreover, Tunstall's large-scale burning of God's Word would arouse an even greater outcry among the people. "And so forward went the bargain, the bishop had the books, Packington had the thanks, and Tyndale had the money." Thinking he was destroying Tyndale's work, Tunstall was actually financing and furthering it exponentially. This surely must have been one of those occasions when "He that sitteth in the heavens" laughed (Psalm 2:1-4).

But the story—and the truth it illustrates—does not end there. Tyndale was later condemned as a heretic and burned at the stake. He died praying, "Lord, open the king of England's eyes." After Tyndale's death, John Rogers (under the alias of Thomas Matthews) picked up the pen that fell from Tyndale's hand. He finished translating the Old Testament from Hebrew into English and presented it to a printer in England. The printer sought the church's sanction for publication and Archbishop

Cranmer, in turn, asked Secretary of State Thomas Cromwell to seek the king's permission. Though an enemy of Tyndale's Bible publishing venture, Henry VIII officially broke from the Catholic Church near the end of Tyndale's life (yet another example of Psalm 76:10, especially given the immorality that motivated his break with Rome).[13] Under these changed circumstances, the king reasoned that an official English translation might prove useful from a political standpoint—a means of further undermining Rome's authority over the English church. Perusing the translation and satisfied that he saw no evidence of Tyndale's hand in it, the king granted his permission for publication. Providentially, he somehow missed seeing the elaborately decorative initials "WT" in huge print at the end of Malachi.[14] Consequently, the "Matthews Bible" as it was known—which was largely the work of the hunted and martyred William Tyndale—was published in England in 1537, one year after Tyndale's death.

Two years later, Miles Coverdale's revision of the Matthews Bible (commissioned by Secretary of State Cromwell) was published as the "Great" Bible (because of its enormous size). By royal decree, every church was to purchase one and keep it chained in the church with free access to anyone who wanted to read it. In fact, each church was required to provide a reader for anyone who was illiterate. On the title page of the Great Bible, listed among the names of the authorizing bishops, appeared the name of a Bishop Cuthbert. His full name was Bishop Cuthbert *Tunstall*. Less than three years after Tyndale's martyrdom, this same bishop who had done all in his power to destroy Tyndale's work unwittingly put his stamp of approval on what was, in significant measure, an updated edition of Tyndale's work that he had sought to burn out of existence only a few years earlier. Smiling all the while, God makes even the most destructive stratagems of the enemies of His Word His tools.

God may choose not to intervene even in behalf of His choicest servants (Acts 7:54-60).

Despite the dramatic examples of deliverance we have seen, God does not always choose to intervene. Just as John the Baptist before him and James after him, Stephen met what we humanly call "an untimely demise." But martyrdom is no less providential than deliverance, and the martyrdom of these men was as providentially superintended by God as was the martyrdom of His own Son. Such deaths are neither a failure on God's part nor a victory on Satan's. They are part of the outworking of God's all-wise and always good purposes. Remember, God both *exercises and withholds* His sustaining, preserving providence.

On January 8, 1956, five young men maneuvered their small airplane for a landing on a narrow gravel strip beside a river deep in the jungles of Ecuador. Most of them were newly married, some of them had small children, but all of them had sacrificially devoted their lives to Christian missions. They had already had some previous contact with the Auca Indians they were going to visit. The prospects seemed promising, the indicators all positive.

Roger Youderian, Ed McCulley, Nate Saint, Jim Elliott, and Pete Fleming stepped out of the plane, only to be savagely attacked and murdered by the very Indians they had come to evangelize. Could God have directed them differently? Yes. Could God have protected them? Certainly. Did they commit some act of indiscretion that put them outside the realm of God's protective providence? Impossible. You cannot escape God's providential power and oversight any more than you can escape His presence or knowledge (Psalm 139:1-12). What, then, is the explanation for this "tragedy?"

You have probably heard that "the safest place to be is in the center of God's will." A veteran missionary to Colombia, South America, once explained how experience and personal Bible study led him to modify that saying. "The most fulfilling, joyful, and peaceful place to be is in the center of God's will," he concluded. "But it is not necessarily the safest." This is not heresy—unless we measure orthodoxy by conformity to cliché rather than to Scripture. This is biblical realism. Citing the examples of Paul and Jesus, he continued,

> It seems to me that the Bible is full of examples of God's people often—
> not occasionally—being placed in unsafe, uncomfortable, and dangerous

situations. . . . Most prayers in Scripture focus not on the personal safety and benefit of believers but on the power, majesty, testimony, and victory of God over his—and our—enemies. . . . The Lord calls us to obedience in spite of the 'costs'—not to personal comfort and safety![15]

God's perfect will may not be the "safest" place by any normal human definition—but it is the place of supreme peace and confidence in His providential oversight over all our circumstances.

Our death is as much a matter of providence as our life. It may seem tragic or ignominious or accidental. But God's providence rules over tragedy, ignominy, and, yes, even accidents. Moreover, we must labor to think God's thoughts, to maintain God's perspective. John the Baptist's end was not the end of John the Baptist. James's end was not the end of James. Stephen's end was not the end of Stephen. The two witnesses in Revelation (11:3-12), so mightily used by God, seem invincible. They are. They will be overcome and slain by the enraged populace, their dead bodies left on display for the gloating mobs who will send one another gifts in celebration of their apparent triumph over these troublesome, meddlesome prophets. But they will be raised up in full view of those who destroyed them—a sign that will not bode well for God's enemies. And Roger, Ed, Nate, Jim, and Pete? Their end was not the end of them either, or—as we will see—of their ministry.

God is capable of working in people we would never expect, even through events that seem to us tragic, senseless, and counterproductive to the cause of Christ (Acts 7:58–8:3).

Try putting yourself in the position of a first-time reader of Acts. Given the first glimpse you get of Saul, he is probably the last person in whom you would ever expect God to be working. Here he is, a consenting witness to the death of Stephen. Were any believers praying for him? (Other than praying for God's judgment on him, I mean.) Perhaps, though we are never told (with the exception of Stephen's dying request that the sin of his martyrdom not be laid to their charge, Acts 7:60). Did any believers suspect God might be working in that man's self-righteous, hostile, gospel-hating heart? You have no idea what God is doing in the hearts and lives of people around you—often in people you might least expect.

God uses persecution and affliction to accomplish His purposes for and through us (8:3-4).

Historically, persecution has been the wind of God's providence to scatter His people and, with them, the seed of the Word. Nothing in the text indicates that the disciples had been ignoring the commission; quite the contrary. "What is plain is that the devil (who lurks behind all persecution of the church) over-reached himself. His attack had the opposite effect to what he intended. Instead of smothering the gospel, persecution succeeded only in spreading it"[16]—like the sudden slamming down of a large object on a fire merely blows the fire in all directions. Divine permission of persecution was God's providential way of effecting the broader fulfillment of His commission.

God may direct us to minister in unpromising places and unlikely situations, with apparently minimal potential, for His own purposes (8:26-40).

God providentially directed the Spirit-led Philip and a Spirit-prepared Ethiopian to intersect in an unlikely spot and under unusual circumstances. This was no ordinary individual; he served as royal treasurer in the court of the queen of Ethiopia.[17] Think of the exponential extension of the gospel well into the African continent through this single "coincidental" meeting out in the middle of nowhere. And think of the valid arguments Philip could have offered against such a missionary venture. Why leave a thriving and promising work in Samaria, where he was clearly needed and being used by God (8:5-25)? Why go into such a sparsely populated area (8:26)? But Philip was obedient to the leading of God.

Incidentally, do you know what the Ethiopian was reading when Philip found him? Of all passages, he was reading Isaiah 53—that poignant prophecy of the Servant of Jehovah suffering for the sins of His people. That in itself was providential. But he was not reading it in the Hebrew Old Testament; indeed, it is all but certain that he would not have been able to even if he'd had access to a Hebrew Bible. He was read-ing the Septuagint, that all-important translation of the Hebrew Old Tes-tament into Greek that we talked about in chapter 10. The Greek text quoted in Acts 8:32-33 as the passage he was reading is identical to the Greek in the Septuagint text, though slightly different from the Hebrew text. By virtue of God's directing and dispersing of that Greek transla-tion, the eunuch's providential preparation was decades, even centuries, in the making.

God may intervene in the lives and affairs of people in spectacular, unexpected, extraordinary ways if He chooses (9:1-8).

The Lord Jesus' confrontation with Saul of Tarsus was most unusual, if not unique in the history of Christian conversions. But it demonstrates an important and timeless truth. God is free and fully able to break into time and space to intervene in people's lives. On the road to Damascus was not the first time He had ever done so, nor would it be the last.

Let's return to Ecuador for a moment. You have already read about the death of the five young missionaries by the Auca Indians in 1956. But you may not have heard the rest of the story. Thirty-three years later, in January 1989, Olive Fleming Liefeld (martyr Pete Fleming's widow, now remarried) returned to Ecuador with her husband, Walter, and daughter Holly, and journeyed by canoe back to the very spot where her first hus-band was murdered. Accompanying the Liefelds was Rachel Saint (martyr Nate Saint's sister), who had continued laboring there among the Indians of Ecuador and served as their interpreter.

Their party was led by two Indian guides, Kimo and his wife, Dawa. Kimo had been one of the murderers of the five missionaries. Dawa had watched the massacre from the edge of the jungle. Both had since been converted. In the course of recounting the events of that day thirty-three years earlier, Dawa and Kimo related that after the missionaries had been killed, all the natives heard singing. *Singing?*

"Who was singing? The five men?"

"No," Dawa replied, "their dead bodies were lying on the beach."

Who *was* singing, then?

Dawa pointed behind us, then swept her arm over the trees as she spoke. Something had happened over the jungles. . . . Rachel [serving as their interpreter], herself confounded, then proceeded to tell us a story that we could hardly comprehend, let alone believe. "After the men were killed, Dawa in the woods and Kimo on the beach heard singing," Rachel said. "As they looked up over the tops of the trees they saw a large group of people. They were all singing, and it looked as if there were a hundred flashlights." Flashlights? Rachel explained, "This is the only word for 'bright light' that they know. But they said it was very bright and flashing. Then suddenly it disappeared." A host of people singing? Flashing lights? What had Kimo and Dawa seen? What did the people look like? Were they talking about angels? . . . Kimo and Dawa had not made up the story. We guessed that most likely they had been terrified by the vision, and therefore did not talk about it when first questioned about the killings. Perhaps it took years of Bible teaching for them to understand what they had seen. Clearly, however, it had a profound impact on their eventual conversion to Christianity. When Pete and the other men died that Sunday in 1956, no one thought that God would choose the gory sight of their martyrdom to display his power—his "light"—to the Aucas. God was working in ways Pete had never anticipated. [18]

God is free to intervene in the lives and affairs of men in spectacular, unexpected, extraordinary ways if He chooses. That is not to say that we look for the spectacular. Few people have had Damascus Road experiences or Ecuadorian visions. The fact that God is free to reveal Himself or to accomplish His purposes in unexpected ways does not, in itself, legitimize all that is reportedly spectacular and extraordinary. We ought not to be gullible. But we, of all people, should not be surprised when He chooses to do the extraordinary—in any age.

God can intervene in humanly hopeless, dangerous, and even life-threatening situations (12:1-19).

Peter faced a genuine and fatal threat from Herod. Indeed, the untimely demise of his worthy predecessor in persecution (vv. 1-2) probably did not give Peter much cause to expect a different end for himself.

Without twisting the text, this passage breaks nicely into a series of nearly alliterated points. Notice:

- The power of the threat (12:1)—Herod had the power to execute his threat (no pun intended) and was clearly determined to do so.

- The precedent of death (12:2)—Herod had already killed James.

- The imprisonment of Peter (12:3-4)—with a view to his execution, Peter was placed under heavy guard.

- The prayers of the church (12:5)—illustrating "the world and the church, arrayed against one another, each wielding an appropriate weapon."[19]

- The precise timing of God (12:6)—deliverance came the night before Peter was to be executed, not a day sooner.

- The providential deliverance of God (12:7-17)—the deliverance came in the form of an angel, though Peter thought he was dreaming.

- The perturbation of Herod and penalty on the soldiers (12:18-19).

It is important to point out that, contrary to the common assumption, the narrative never specifies exactly what the church was praying for. "Well," someone impatiently objects, "of course they were praying for Peter to be released from prison." Were they? "Isn't it obvious?" No. Read Acts 12:5 carefully. The only precedent we have for the church's prayer under similar circumstances is in Acts 4:23-30. There, in the face of recent imprisonment, persecution, and renewed threats, the church made only one request. And it wasn't for deliverance from prison or persecution; it was for boldness in the face of both (4:29). In Acts 12, therefore, given what had just recently happened to James (12:1-3), it certainly must have appeared that Peter's time had now come. After all, if we assume they prayed for Peter's deliverance, we must also assume they had prayed for James's deliverance as well. It seems more likely that in Acts 12:5 they were praying for Peter's stability of faith and boldness of testimony in the face of what appeared to be certain martyrdom.[20] Against all human hope and expectation, and perhaps "exceedingly abundantly above all" that they asked or thought (Ephesians 3:20), God—and with an elegant and timely ease—did the apparently impossible.

William Bartram is an unfamiliar name to most people. Son of the famous early American botanist John Bartram, William was a naturalist who explored the virgin frontier of southeastern North America in the 1700s and early 1800s. His journal, *Travels of William Bartram*, is a fascinating and delightful account of his adventures. As you can imagine, the untamed wilderness of that region of America in those days made for some riveting experiences. Bartram recounts walking through the woods on one occasion when,

> on a sudden, an Indian appeared crossing the path at a considerable distance before me. On perceiving that he was armed with a rifle, the first sight of him startled me and I endeavored to elude his sight by stopping my pace and keeping large trees between us. But he espied me, and turning short about, sat spurs to his horse and came up on a full gallop. I never before this was afraid at the sight of an Indian, but at this time I must own that my spirits were very much agitated; I saw at once that, being unarmed, I was in his power. And having now but a few moments to prepare, I resigned myself entirely to the will of the Almighty, trusting to His mercies for my preservation. My mind then became tranquil and I resolved to meet my foe with resolution and cheerful confidence. The intrepid Seminole stopped suddenly 3 or 4 yards before me and silently viewed me, his countenance angry and fierce, shifting his rifle from shoulder to shoulder and looking about instantly on all sides. I advanced towards him with an air of confidence and offered him my hand, hailing him "brother"; at this he hastily jerked back his arm, with a look of malice, rage and disdain; when again looking at me more attentively he spurred up to me, and with dignity in his look and action, gave me his hand. . . . I believe his design was to kill me [but] we shook hands and parted in a friendly manner; and he informed me of the course and distance to a trading house where I found he had been extremely ill-treated the day before. . . . The trading company received me and treated me with great civility. On relating [this incident], the chief replied, "My friend, consider yourself a fortunate man; that fellow is one of the greatest villains on earth, a noted murderer and outlawed by his countrymen. Last evening we took his gun, broke it in pieces, and gave him a severe drubbing; he made his escape, carrying off a

new rifle, with which, he said, going off, he would kill the first white man he met."[21]

God can use human disagreements as the catalyst for diversifying the ministry and more effectively accomplishing His purposes (Acts 15:36-41).

This passage records a surprising but very human incident. Who would have guessed that such strife would erupt between the great apostle Paul and the "son of consolation," Barnabas? The word translated "contention" is the root from which we get "paroxysm" (a fit, convulsion, or sudden violent emotion or reaction). It is a strong word that graphically portrays Paul and Barnabas as being provoked with one another and arguing heatedly over (don't miss this) a very spiritual subject—namely, who should, and should not, accompany them on their next missionary journey. Paul was as yet unwilling to entrust the shared responsibilities of such a journey to John Mark, who had deserted them on their previous journey. Barnabas, as John Mark's cousin (Colossians 4:10; another wrinkle that, understandably, must have fueled Barnabas's disagreement to some degree), felt it important to give the young man a second chance.

This Spirit-inspired window into the flesh-and-blood reality of life in the early church should be at least as encouraging as it is shocking. Shocking because we do not expect to see such behavior in normally Spirit-filled men; it reminds us that the flesh is still very much alive even in the great and godly. Encouraging because it removes them from the pedestals we erect for them in our imagination and reminds us that they were no less human than we are and, therefore, no more spiritual than we can be by the grace of God. In this passage the Holy Spirit discreetly displays the humanness of these apostles to demonstrate, among other things, that "true devotion to a great cause does not guarantee infallibility of judgment nor imperturbability of temper."[22]

The subsequent history of the early church as it unfolds in the New Testament also renders this an instructive episode. The disagreement between these two may have closed the chapter on the "working partnership of Paul and Barnabas, but it did not end their friendship."[23] There is no reason to "think that Paul and Barnabas went off shaking their fists at one another. They were good and great men. They certainly agreed to disagree and continued praying for one another"[24] Paul continued to hold Barnabas in high esteem (I Corinthians 9:6) and, ironically, even ended up working closely with Mark as well (Colossians 4:10). All this illustrates a vital truth for the important battles of our day: "it is not so much our differences of opinion that doth us the mischief; (for we may as soon expect all the clocks in the town to strike together, as to see all good people of a mind in every thing on this side of heaven) but the mismanagement of that difference."[25]

God is not the author of confusion or contention. But just as we have seen that He can use sin and evil intent, so He can turn these experiences to His purposes as well. The point is not who was right, Paul or Barnabas.[26] (Even the text does not comment on that.) The point is that what Satan sought to incite and inflame for the purpose of division, God turned to His purpose of multiplication. In other words, "the event was providentially overruled for good."[27] Because of this argument, the missionary work was doubled. Again, it is not disagreement that hinders God's use of us, but ill will.[28]

God may close the door on seemingly logical or needful ministries, only to redirect later into the paths of His choosing (Acts 16:6-10).

We are not told what means the Holy Spirit used to "forbid" Paul and Silas from preaching the Word in Asia, or to foil their attempts to go into Bithynia. Was it circumstantial leading, perhaps (weather or illness)? Or was it rather a strong inner compulsion? Still less do we know the divine reasons or motives for this direction—or rather, lack of direction, for "it is remarkable that in both cases [16:6 and 7] the guidance was negative only, keeping the missionaries from a false move but not pointing out where they should go."[29] Finally that positive direction came (16:8-9). But in the mean time, it surely did not seem to make sense and must have been somewhat frustrating. Take a look at a map. Given where Paul's party found themselves, Asia and Bithynia were the most logical next steps; and surely the inhabitants of those regions needed the gospel too. But it was not God's timing. Sometimes God's providential leading is, for a season, negative as He closes doors without immediately opening any others. But the *when* is as intrinsically a part of God's will as the *what* and the *where*.

God may allow us to suffer wrongfully in order to bring us into contact with certain sinners (16:16-34).

Welcome to the Life of Joseph 102. First the Holy Spirit barred Paul and Silas's attempts to enter Asia and Bithynia. Then He clearly directed them to go to Macedonia. And where did they end up? In jail. Surely this could not have been God's leading or intent, could it? They might have wondered this themselves, if they hadn't been through this so many times before.

Trials and difficulties do not contradict God's leading. God providentially permitted the wrongful twelve-year imprisonment of a tinker-turned-preacher who had a wife and family (including a blind daughter) to care for. But out of that prison cell in Bedford Jail was born John Bunyan's *Pilgrim's Progress,* a literary creation without peer that has blessed and instructed untold millions of saints since that time. In the case of Paul and Silas, this was another "providential relocation"—God's way of bringing them into contact with another prepared individual, the Philippian jailer (and who knows how many others through his circle of influence).

God is in sovereign control of the elements; natural disasters are His tools to shape His purposes (27-28).

"The LORD hath his way in the whirlwind and in the storm, and the clouds are the dust of his feet" when He rides, as on His trusty and familiar steed, upon the wings of the wind (Nahum 1:3). Consider some of the providential effects of the storm recorded at the end of Acts: (1) Paul's faith and ministry were magnified before the other prisoners and soldiers onboard the ship; (2) Paul's life was preserved; (3) God created an unusual opportunity to display His goodness and mercy to all;

(4) Paul was able to minister to people he would never have met otherwise—the Malta islanders and even a government official named Publius.

If you have never read the *Journal of John Wesley,* you owe it to yourself and to your faith to do so. A fascinating record of this greathearted small man, Wesley's diary is packed with examples of remarkable providences in his life and ministry. Not the least delightful aspect of this journal is Wesley's penchant for wry understatement. Once, having boarded a ferry during a storm, Wesley describes how

> many stood looking after us on the riverside; [when we reached] the middle of the river, in an instant the side of the boat was under water and the horses and men rolling one over another. We expected the boat to sink every moment, but I did not doubt of being able to swim ashore. The boatmen . . . quickly recovered and rowed for life. And soon after, our horses leaping overboard, the boat was lightened, and we all came unhurt to land. They wondered what was the matter I did not rise (for I lay alone in the bottom of the boat), and I wondered too, till upon examination I found that a large iron crow[bar], which the boatmen sometimes used, was (none knew how) run through the string of my boot and was pinning me down that I could not stir. If the boat had sunk, I should have been safe enough from swimming any further. The same day and, as near as we could judge, the same hour, the boat in which my brother was crossing the Severn . . . was carried away by the wind and in the utmost danger of splitting upon the rocks. But the same God, when all human hope was past, delivered them as well as us.[30]

Remember John Paton, missionary to the New Hebrides? One night hostile natives set fire to the church beside his house, then waited nearby to kill those inside when they attempted to come out to fight the fire. Running out, Paton was surrounded by several savages with clubs.

> I heard a shout—"Kill him! Kill him!" . . . I said, "Dare to strike me and my Jehovah God will punish you. . . . We love you all; and for doing you good only you want to kill us. But our God is here now to protect us and to punish you." They yelled in rage and urged each other to strike the first blow, but the Invisible One restrained them. I stood invulnerable beneath His invisible shield. . . . At this dread moment occurred an incident, which

my readers may explain as they like, but which I trace directly to the interposition of my God. A rushing and roaring sound came from the South. . . . Every head was instinctively turned in that direction, and they knew from previous hard experience that it was one of their awful tornadoes of wind and rain. Now, mark, the wind bore the flames *away* from our dwelling-house; had it come from the opposite direction, no power on earth could have saved us from being all consumed! . . . The stars in their courses were fighting against Sisera! The mighty roaring of the wind, the black cloud pouring down unceasing torrents, and the whole surroundings, awed those savages into silence. Some began to withdraw from the scene, all lowered their weapons of war, and several, terror-struck, exclaimed, "This is Jehovah's rain! Truly their Jehovah God is fighting for them and helping them. Let us away!" A panic seized upon them; they threw away their remaining torches; in a few moments they had all disappeared in the bush; and I was left alone praising God for His marvelous works. . . . Truly our Jesus has all power, not less in the elements of nature than in the savage hearts of the Tannese.[31]

God preserves the life of His servants till their work is done (Acts 9:20-25; 9:26-30; 14:1-6; 14:19-20; 21:30-32; 23:12-22; 25:1-6; 27:39-44; 28:1-5).

Paul, of course, experienced much persecution, including intense verbal opposition (Acts 13:45), expulsions (Acts 13:50), imprisonments (Acts 16:23), and beatings (Acts 16:23; 21:32). Beyond these many persecutions, however, Luke records seven specific and distinct attempts on Paul's life by the Jews, and two "natural" but very real threats to Paul's life. Paul truly was "in deaths oft" (II Corinthians 11:23), but unto God the Lord belong escapes from death (Psalm 68:20). Notice the variety of means and methods God providentially employed to protect Paul, despite repeated attempts on his life.

- **In Damascus** (Acts 9:23-25)
  Circumstances: Just days or weeks after his conversion.
  Escape: Disciples sneaked him over wall in a basket at night to escape ambush.

- **In Jerusalem** (9:29-30)

  Circumstances: First trip to Jerusalem after conversion.

  Escape: Disciples conducted him to Caesarea for his trip to Tarsus.

- **In Iconium** (14:5-6)

  Circumstances: First missionary journey.

  Escape: Fled to Lystra.

- **In Lystra** (14:19-20)

  Circumstances: Actually stoned and assumed dead.

  Escape: Revived, returned to the city, and departed next day for Derbe.

- **In Jerusalem** (21:30-32)

  Circumstances: Seized by mob in the temple.

  Escape: Rescued by timely arrival of Roman soldiers.

- **In Jerusalem** (23:12 ff.)

  Circumstances: Conspiracy of over forty men who swore not to eat or drink until they killed Paul in ambush. Note God's assurance to Paul the night before (Acts 23:11).

  Escape: Paul's nephew discovered the conspiracy (sound familiar?) and revealed it to the Roman commander, who moved Paul suddenly that night to Caesarea under heavy guard.

- **Between Caesarea and Jerusalem** (25:1 ff.)

  Circumstances: High priest and others requested "a favor" of the newly appointed Festus, upon his arrival in Jerusalem on his third day in office, to summon Paul up to Jerusalem, while they waited in ambush along the road.

  Escape: Festus refused and commanded instead that they go with him to Caesarea if they wished to testify against him, which they did ten days later. During the hearing, however, Festus, "willing to do the Jews a favor," asked Paul if he was willing to go to Jerusalem to be tried; instead, Paul appealed to Caesar in Rome.

PROVIDENCE IN THE CHURCH

- **On the Mediterranean Sea** (27:42-44)
  Circumstances: Storm and shipwreck on way to Rome. Although this is different from the premeditated attempts by the Jews to kill Paul, it nonetheless represents another near brush with death from which God delivered Paul.
  Escape: Through Paul's testimony and God's work in the heart of Julius, the centurion—for the sake of saving Paul—prevented the soldiers' intention of killing all the prisoners (cf. Acts 27:3, 20-26, 30-32, 33-36).

- **On Malta** (28:1-6)
  Circumstances: Bitten by venomous serpent while placing wood on fire.
  Escape: "He shook the beast off . . . and felt no harm." The natives of the island, familiar with the local wildlife, fully expected him to die or at least swell. God plainly, providentially protected him.

The life and ministry of Paul demonstrates dramatically the oft-repeated truth that God's servant is immortal till his work on earth is done. Countless others have experienced the reality of this principle since then.

"They encircled us in a deadly ring, and one kept urging another to strike the first blow or fire the first shot," wrote John Paton in 1862. With weapons in their hands, death in their eyes, and threats on their lips, the savages surrounded the missionary and his native friends. Paton recounts,

> My heart rose up to the Lord Jesus; I saw Him watching all the scene. My peace came back to me like a wave from God. I realized that I was immortal till my Master's work with me was done. The assurance came to me, as if a voice out of Heaven had spoken, that not a musket would be fired to wound us, not a club prevail to strike us, not a spear leave the hand in which it was held vibrating to be thrown, not an arrow leave the bow, nor a killing stone the fingers, without the permission of Jesus Christ, whose is all power in Heaven and on Earth. He rules all nature, animate and inanimate, and restrains even the Savage of the South Seas.[32]

A Look in the Mirror

God did protect Paton and the others then, and many other times throughout his ministry. Paton's autobiography is a study in the earthly immortality of God's faithful servants.

No person or power can injure us or halt our ministry outside of God's sovereign control. Far from breeding an arrogant attitude of presumption, this truth should foster a deep-seated humility at our own unworthiness and fragility and, at the same time, an equally deep-rooted confidence in the absolute power and authority of the King, whom we serve. We can possess the same underlying confidence in God's sovereign control over our circumstances.

Chastisement, imprisonments and prison releases, unlooked-for aid through our enemies, deliverance from death, allowance of death, persecution, unusual ministry opportunities, closing and opening doors to ministry, disagreements, even things as down-to-earth as storms and snake bites—this is the stuff life is made of for the believer. Can any believer possibly conclude that God's providence, sketched in the record of the early church, has no relevant, practical application to his or her life and ministry?

13

PROVIDENCE AND PRAYER

My brethren, prayer is an essential part of the providence of God; so essential, that you will always find that when God delivers his people, his people have been praying for that deliverance. They tell us that prayer does not affect the Most High, and cannot alter his purposes. We never thought it did; but prayer is a part of the purpose and plan, and a most effective wheel in the machinery of providence. The Lord sets his people praying, and then he blesses them.

—C. H. Spurgeon

Many years ago, a Christian man in our church (I'll call him "Jake") came forward at the end of a service to confess that he had not prayed in years. After reading a particular Calvinist author, Jake had come to the conclusion that prayer to a sovereign God who already knew the end from the beginning was pointless.

Charles Spurgeon—himself a staunch Calvinist—was certainly not of that persuasion, as the quotation at the beginning of this chapter illustrates. Calvinist theologian Charles Hodge likewise asserted that "a prayerless man is of necessity, and thoroughly, irreligious" and "spiritually dead."[1] In fact, so far from discouraging prayer, Hodge insists that God is

> roused into action by prayer, in a way analogous to that in which the energies of a man are called into action by the entreaties of his fellow-men.
> This is the doctrine of the Bible; it is perfectly consistent with reason, and

is confirmed by the whole history of the world, and especially of the Church. . . . Once [we] admit the doctrine of theism, that is of the existence of a personal God, and of His constant control over all things out of Himself, [then] all ground for doubt as to the efficacy of prayer is removed, and it remains to us, as it has been to the people of God in all ages, the great source of spiritual joy and strength, of security for the present and confidence for the future.[2]

So the point of the illustration about Jake is not that Calvinism causes people not to pray! One could arguably come to the same conclusion Jake did simply from reading certain Bible passages that emphasize God's sovereignty. The breakdown comes in our understanding and application of truth—when we carry truth to a practical conclusion that may seem logical but is, in fact, unbiblical.[3] That is why this subject is worth pursuing in the context of our discussion of providence—to be certain that our practical *application* of this blessed truth, as much as our understanding of it, is governed by Scripture, and that what we believe about providence from the Bible actually guides our practice in the vital exercise of prayer.[4]

If we believe that "God continuously preserves and maintains the existence of every part of His creation, from the smallest to the greatest, according to His sovereign pleasure" and that "God graciously guides and governs all events, including the free acts of men and their external circumstances, and directs all things to their appointed ends for His glory," then why—and what—should we pray? That is the question this chapter seeks to answer.

What Does the Bible Say?

If the Bible teaches God's providential control over all things, then, why *should* we pray? The short answer is *because God commands us to pray*.[5] Repeatedly. As obvious as it may sound, this really is a test of our belief that *God* is the sovereign—not our own understanding. When a child obeys only those parental instructions that make sense to his seven-year-old mind, he is being neither obedient nor wise but rebellious and foolish. ("Why should I brush my teeth? They're just going to get dirty again."

"Why shouldn't I be able to play in the street as long as I watch out for cars?") When we are willing to submit to and practice only what immediately makes sense to us, and ignore what doesn't (even when it is clearly commanded), we have substituted *ourselves*—our finite mind—as the sovereign. So the first reason we pray is that the true Sovereign says so.

But that is just the short and obvious answer. As with children, short obvious answers are not always entirely satisfying. Some issues revealed in Scripture include little additional explanation apart from the assurance that what God does and requires we may not understand now but will understand eventually (John 13:7). In the case of prayer, however, we have a bit more to go on.

I should clarify from the outset that this chapter on prayer is concerned specifically with intercession or petitionary prayer. Clearly, the doctrine of God's sovereign providence supplies us with ample and endless causes for prayers of worship, praise, and adoration. Nor does providence stifle prayer in its most basic and intimate sense of frank conversation with God. The apparent discrepancy with which we are concerned here is how the command to ask God to do or not do certain things, either for others or ourselves, is to be reconciled with the doctrine of providence. We pray because we are commanded to, but "how we understand God's action in the world will determine how and when and why and for what we pray."[6]

Prayer Glorifies God for His Providence

One Sunday evening a well-known London pastor effectively secured his congregation's attention with an intriguing introduction. His opening words that night were as follows:

> One book charmed us all in the days of our youth. Is there a boy alive who has not read it? "Robinson Crusoe" was a wealth of wonders to me; I could have read it over a score of times, and never have wearied. I am not ashamed to confess that I can read it now with fresh delight. Robinson and his man Friday, though mere inventions of fiction, are wonderfully real to the most of us. But why am I running on in this way on a Sabbath evening?

Is not this talk altogether out of order? I hope not. A passage in that book comes vividly before my recollection tonight as I read my text; and in it I find something more than an excuse. Robinson Crusoe has been wrecked. He is left in the desert island all alone. His case is a very pitiable one. He goes to his bed and he is smitten with a fever. This fever lasts upon him long, and he has no one to wait upon him—none even to bring him a drink of cold water. He is ready to perish. He had been accustomed to sin, and had all the vices of a sailor; but his hard case brought him to think. He opens a Bible which he finds in his chest, and he lights upon this passage, *"Call upon me in the day of trouble: I will deliver thee, and thou shalt glorify me."*[7]

This sermon, titled "Robinson Crusoe's Text" on Psalm 50:15, underscores the overarching purpose of all prayer—namely, the glory of God. The pastor, Charles Spurgeon, describes the arrangement as a "delightful partnership" in which each party has a share.

Here are the shares. First, here is your share: "Call upon me in the day of trouble." Secondly, here is God's share: "I will deliver thee." Again, you take a share—for you shall be delivered. And then again it is the Lord's turn—"Thou shalt glorify me." Here is a compact, a covenant that God enters into with you who pray to Him and whom He helps. He says, "You shall have the deliverance, but I must have the glory. . . ." He must have all the honour from first to last.[8]

Far from being self-centered, such prayer is "radically God-centered" because in making such a prayer, "I acknowledge that at the center of my life there is a gaping hole of emptiness" that only God can fill, needs that God alone can meet.[9] As a result, my entirely God-dependent prayer results in His getting all the glory—not by default or assumption, but by virtue of my purposeful and public petition to Him and His obvious reply.

So how is God glorified by prayer? Prayer is the open admission that without Christ we can do nothing. And prayer is the turning away from ourselves to God in the confidence that he will provide the help we need. Prayer humbles us as needy, and exalts God as wealthy. . . . Prayer is the essential activity of waiting on God: acknowledging our helplessness and his power, calling upon him for help, seeking his counsel. So it is evident why prayer is so often commanded by God. . . . Prayer is the antidote for the disease of self-confidence that opposes God's goal of getting glory by working for those who wait for him.[10]

In other words, prayer draws deliberate attention—both personally and publicly—to what providence effects and to the fact that it is God who does it, not us and not chance.[11] And prayer offered in Christ's name—that is, on the basis of His authority and merit alone rather than out of any right or merit we may suppose we possess in ourselves—draws attention to His providential activity on our behalf for the Father's glory: "And whatever ye shall ask in my name, that will I do, that the Father may be glorified in the Son" (John 14:13). But how do we correlate prayer with the settled certainties of God's providential activity?

An Example—Prayer and Promise (Luke 1)

A godly couple prayed for children—for even *one* child—for years . . . and years. Nothing happened. The spring of youth tumbled into summer, summer eased into the autumn of middle age, and middle age crept subtly into winter with its telltale frost on their hoary heads. Somewhere along the line, for obvious reasons, they ceased praying for a child. Do even the most believing saints in their sixties or seventies continue praying for children? "They had waited together these many years, till in the evening of life the flower of hope had closed its fragrant cup; and still the two sat together in the twilight, content to wait in loneliness, till night would close around them."[12]

Hard as it may have been to accept, it eventually became apparent to them that God, for some reason, had determined to leave them childless. Whatever quiet suspicions it raised and whatever subtle social liabilities it created,[13] it did not embitter this couple nor deter them from "walking in all the commandments and ordinances of the Lord blameless[ly]" (Luke 1:6). Even though "they were both righteous before God," they had been denied what they longed for. In their youth the wife was barren. When we meet them in the opening verses of the Gospel of Luke, both of them are now well-advanced in age.[14] Nevertheless they were, within the year, blessed with the miracle of the birth of a son named John.[15] Their names were Zacharias and Elisabeth.

The importance of prayer here is obvious, but where does the connection to providence come in? To appreciate fully the theological irony of this account, we have to travel back momentarily nearly three-quarters of a millennium. The life and ministry of John was prophesied centuries in advance. The opening verses of Isaiah 40 foretell the necessary appearance and crucial preparatory ministry of Messiah's forerunner—verses that John would come to recognize and assert as explicit references to himself and to his mission (John 1:23). Three centuries later, another prophet described the appearance of this messianic precursor (Malachi 3:1; 4:5-6) in words that the angel Gabriel expressly ascribed to John (Luke 1:17).

In other words, the life and ministry of John the Baptist—so deeply interwoven with the appearance of Messiah Himself—were settled facts, sealed by prophecy and secured by providence. Remarkably, however, Gabriel's announcement ties the coming birth of this prophesied figure directly to the *prayers* of Zacharias! "Fear not, Zacharias, *for thy prayer is heard*; and thy wife Elisabeth shall bear thee a son, and thou shalt call his name John" (Luke 1:13).[16]

How many times had this godly couple prayed for a child? And *how long* had it been *since* this now *aged* couple had breathed that prayer? Ten, fifteen, twenty years, perhaps? Though the immediate answer from heaven for years was silence, Gabriel assured Zacharias that his prayer had always been heard.[17] God memorialized this vital lesson by providentially embedding it in the very meaning of Zacharias's own name, which means "Jehovah remembers." They had long before ceased praying for what was now plainly biologically impossible. In that sense, they had long since forgotten these prayers and forsaken these hopes. But God had heard and remembered, because God *hears* and *remembers*.

The larger point is the inexplicable but essential connection between providence and prayer.[18] Would John have been born providentially if Zacharias had not prayed? Logic is quick to answer, "Of course; it was prophesied." Why, then, does the inspired account emphasize Zacharias's prayer? Indeed, why does it mention his prayer at all? Because prayer is, as Spurgeon noted, "a most effective wheel in the machinery of providence." Prayer is one of the providential means through which God accomplishes His settled purposes. But why? We have already suggested one reason—it underscores our awareness of His involvement and highlights His glory. But I think there is yet more to it.

Prayer Adjusts Us to God's Purposes

Not just any kind of prayer adjusts us to God's purposes. Some people pray in an effort to get God to adjust Himself to their purposes. But we are talking about the place of petitionary prayer in connection with the providences of a sovereign God. God has some rather strong feelings on the kinds of things we ought to pray. And He has wrapped up His intentions for our prayers in some intriguing imperatives.

An Exhortation—Prayer and Prophecy (Isaiah 62)

Isaiah 62:6 furnishes an intriguing study with startling results. I would like to walk you through the process of this discovery so that you can see for yourself the reasoning behind the conclusion. Let me encourage you not to be put off by the details of the investigative process, for the angels are in the details. And once more, before you continue, let me urge you to take a few minutes to read three chapters in your Bible—Isaiah 60-62. This will greatly facilitate your ability to follow the discussion and enhance your confidence in the conclusions of this study.

The text

Isaiah 62:6 reads, "Ye that make mention of the Lord, keep not silence." The interpretation and application that these words immediately suggest seems to be an encouragement to preach boldly about the Lord, or to maintain a strong verbal testimony. Obviously these are good and biblical exhortations.

For the phrase "ye who make mention of the Lord," one translation offers the following alternative: "You who remember the Lord." Yet another translation reads, "You who call on the Lord, give yourselves no rest." The Hebrew verb is the word "remember" but it is actually the causative form of the verb.[19] Simply put, it means "cause to remember," "put in remembrance," or "remind."[20] (Why wrestle through all these grammatical details? Simply because we want to have the most accurate understanding possible of precisely what the Holy Spirit was intending to communicate when He breathed out these particular words and forms through Isaiah's pen.)

The Hebrew construction indicates that the verse has reference to causing the Lord to remember—that is, reminding the Lord, or putting the Lord in remembrance.[21] The curious phrase "keep not silent" is more literally rendered "no rest to you" or "no cessation to you." This terminology is essentially parallel to the New Testament command to "pray without ceasing," but with a specific focus and request in mind.

Literally, then, Isaiah 62:6 reads, "You who remind the LORD, no rest to you," or "You who remind the Lord, allow yourselves no rest." What does *that* mean? So far we've focused on only half of the sentence. Read the next verse for the rest of the sentence: "And give Him no rest, till He establish, and till He make Jerusalem a praise in the earth." The "Him" in verse 7 clearly refers back to "the LORD" in verse 6. Give God no rest? Not only are these "watchmen" to pray without ceasing or resting, they are also charged to give no rest to the Lord to whom they pray. What a remarkable mandate! And what a peculiar request—"until He make Jerusalem a praise in the earth"!

What we might initially have thought was an exhortation to preach turns out instead to be an exhortation to *pray*, and an astonishing one at that. To feel the full impact of this charge and its relevance to the discussion of providence, we must step back and look at the broader context in which this command is couched.

The context

In the chapters leading up to this passage, the Lord has been detailing all the abundance of wealth and blessing He is going to heap upon Israel. The magnitude of it is astounding. It begins in Isaiah 60 with the imagery of dawn, when the glory of God will rise and shine upon Israel, scattering the darkness of night like the sun at daybreak (vv. 1-2). The result? Israel will become (if you will excuse the irony of the metaphor) the mecca of all nations: "And the Gentiles shall come to thy light, and kings to the brightness of thy rising" (vv. 3-4). God will gather the wealth of the nations into Israel (vv. 5-9), the sons of foreigners to build up Jerusalem (v. 10), the kings of the nations and their armies to serve Israel (vv. 10-12), and even the prized flora of other nations to beautify the land (v. 13). Their former enemies will bow at their feet (v. 14) and their once desolate land will become the garden spot of the world (v. 15). The best of the world's resources and riches will be theirs (vv. 16-17), along with the peace and presence of their God (vv. 18 20). Isaiah 61:1-9 details even further their central and exalted position among all the nations of the world.

Why all this to Israel? It is necessary to underscore that none of this has anything to do with Israel's superiority or righteousness or merit. God's election of Israel as His special people was an act of sovereign grace and free mercy in the first place (Deuteronomy 7:7-9; Malachi 1:2-3). This unprecedented blessing will be a divine act of sovereign grace and free mercy as well. God emphasizes repeatedly that He will perform these things out of loyalty to His own covenant promises and prophetic words to Israel and out of His determination to glorify Himself in the place He has chosen to dwell, to reign, and to manifest His presence on earth (note 60:7, 9, 10, 13, 15, 16, 21; 61:3, 9). Isaiah, overwhelmed at this future prospect, exults in God's gracious salvation (61:10-11).

There is some debate over who is speaking when chapter 62 opens. Is it a continuing reflection of Isaiah's own excitement over these divine promises to his nation, or does the speaker shift back to the Lord?[22] For the purpose of our discussion it makes little difference whether it is the prophet or the Lord Himself who issues the exhortation in 62:6b-7; the message is the same. After laying out in stunning detail what He promises to do for Israel, God issues an equally stunning command to them to become co-laborers with Him, through their prayers, in bringing about what He has already promised to perform! This is an exhortation to pray without ceasing for the fulfillment of these prophecies and, through prayer, to give God not a moment's rest until He fulfills what He has said He would do. But why would God require that men unceasingly remind Him to fulfill what He Himself has already sovereignly purposed and faithfully promised to perform? And more to the point, what does it have to do with *us*?

New Testament parallels?

The preceding discussion may seem pertinent for Old Testament Israel, but what does it have to do with New Testament Christians? Is Isaiah 62:6-7 an exclusive exhortation for Israel alone, or does the principle have application to the church? More importantly, are there any parallel exhortations in the New Testament? Let's look briefly at two examples, beginning with a less familiar passage that will give sharper focus and definition to the more familiar.

In his second epistle, Peter describes in graphic detail the final fiery destruction of the present heavens and earth and the future creation of a new heavens and earth. In light of the coming destruction of everything material in this present world, he exhorts us to reconsider our values and priorities.

> Seeing then that all these things shall be dissolved, what manner of persons ought ye to be in all holy conversation [manner of life] and godliness, looking for and hasting unto the coming of the day of God, wherein the heavens, being on fire, shall be dissolved, and the elements shall melt with fervent heat?

What exactly does it mean to "haste unto" the coming of the day of God? Some think it refers to being "eager" for the coming of that day.[23] But the normal sense of the verb in the overwhelming number of occurrences is "to hurry [to do something]" or "to hasten [something] along."[24] If Peter has in mind this more common meaning, he is saying that we are to be both eagerly anticipating and hastening, or hurrying, the coming of that day. This is the sense adopted by a majority of translations.[25] Even in the original AV 1611 ("Looking for and hasting vnto the comming of the day of God") a marginal note reads, "Or, hasting the comming."[26] If we accept the predominant usage of the verb and adopt the reading preferred by most translations and allowed by virtually all,

> Peter would be urging his readers as God's chosen people to be His instruments in furthering the divine purpose. This participle then is not just an indication of their pious attitude but also a call for aggressive Christian action. . . . Certainly aggressive evangelism and believing intercession, supported by the holy lives of His saints, are divinely appointed means of furthering God's purpose and program.[27]

But how can we hurry the coming of that day? Isn't God's timing settled?[28] These questions are similar to those we raised regarding God's prophetic promises in Isaiah 60-62. The providential timing of His coming in II Peter 3:12 is as known to an omniscient God as the providential fulfillment of His promises in Isaiah 60-62 is certain for an omnipotent God. Yet in both, man is graciously allowed—indeed, commanded—to participate. That leads to a second New Testament passage.

Have you ever thought about the meaning of a phrase you have probably prayed countless times? Why did Jesus instruct His disciples to pray, "Thy kingdom come" (Matthew 6:10)?[29] Isn't it going to come whether we pray this or not? Hasn't God breathed out a great deal of prophetic material assuring us that His kingdom will arrive in His time? Certainly there is a personal application of this prayer, that God's rule would be more fully realized in us individually and in all His people. But the word "come" signals that something much bigger is in view, "the kingdom of glory which shall one day be set up"[30] when God's name will be universally revered and His "will [shall] be done on earth as it is in heaven." Sincere prayer for promised providences is a mysterious yet divinely ordained means for hastening the coming of the day of God. "The Church may be said to bring the day nearer when it prays, 'Thy kingdom come.'"[31]

"Hallowed be Thy name. Thy kingdom come. Thy will be done in earth as it is in heaven." These petitions are not insignificant rote requests, mere matters of protocol for formal religious occasions. They are patterns of the kinds of divine concerns on which our praying should focus. These are petitions of massive theological and eschatological scope, prayers that in a breath encompass the whole breadth, the grand sweep, of God's revealed purpose for the earth. Mean them when you pray them! Desire them when you pray them! Expect them when you pray them, for they are requests that will be infallibly fulfilled. John breathed the spirit of this prayer. After seeing, in vision form, the fulfillment of this very request—the coming kingdom of God—he exclaimed, "Even so, come Lord Jesus" (Revelation 22:20).

Christ proceeded to put a very practical edge on the blade of this prayerful practice. A little later in this same context of Matthew 6, He exhorted His followers not to worry about the most basic necessities of life—food and clothing—because the Father knows we need these things and He will supply them (Matthew 6:25-32). Instead, Jesus put His finger on the point where our prayerful concern ought to concentrate: "But seek ye first the kingdom of God, and his righteousness; and all these [necessary but lesser] things shall be added unto you" (Matthew 6:33).

Do you see the connection back to the prayer instruction Jesus had given earlier? Seeking God's kingdom does not mean that we are to *look* for it as though it were hidden somewhere but that we are to *pursue* it, specifically in prayer. Seeking God's kingdom is "to pursue the things already prayed for in the first three petitions of the Lord's Prayer (6:9-10)."[32] Rather than being consumed with our personal material needs in prayer, we are to make God's kingdom and righteousness the central focus of our prayers. When we do that, we hasten the coming of the day of God. But in addition, something very important happens to us in the mean time.

The effects of providence-focused praying

Let me try to tie together in a single package the principles underlying these remarkable exhortations God has given His people in both the Old and New Testaments. Why does God command His people to remind Him without ceasing, without giving Him a moment's rest, to perform what He has already promised and to pray for the arrival of events and conditions that He has already sworn He will bring to pass? There are at least three reasons that God has purposed for His people to pray for what He has already assured us His providence will perform. Each reason leads naturally into the next, like a tributary feeding into a stream, the stream into a river, and the river into the ocean of God's eternal purpose.

First, such prayer is a divinely determined means for effecting His purposes. Why would God's people be exhorted to remind an omniscient God to do anything, let alone to remind Him ceaselessly? He does not need to be reminded as though He might otherwise forget, nor begged as though he might otherwise not perform what He has already promised. "We have here the language of accommodation, for God really needs no reminding; but He does graciously involve others, through prayer, in the fulfillment of His great purposes."[33] Another writer describes it as "hold[ing] God to His promises, knowing that is what He desires. God's people should pray for things even when they know God has promised them."[34] "What is the matter of God's promises," wrote the reflective Matthew Henry, "must be the matter of our prayers."[35]

Why? Because as R. C. Sproul reminds us, "The responsibility for secondary causes that serve as means to the divine ends is still ours."[36] Prayer has no magical or persuasive power over God in and of itself. Rather, "petitionary prayer is effective in accomplishing things because God has chosen to involve us in the establishment of his purposes."[37] Terrance Tiessen explains the phenomenon this way:

> Prayer is one of the means that God has determined to use in the accomplishment of his will. In his eternal purpose God has included all of the events of human history, but he does not act alone, as though he were the only agent in the world. He has given to his children the privilege of participating in his program for establishing his kingdom on earth. One of the most significant means of our involvement is through petitionary prayer. . . . Although God could work without us, he delights to answer the prayers of his children and to be glorified by their thanksgiving when he does so. . . . so that our prayers are a necessary—though not sufficient—"cause" of the ultimate outcome.[38]

How God providentially moves His people to pray that He will providentially effect what He has already promised to perform is part of the mystery of providence as it relates to prayer. As we will see, however, Daniel is an outstanding example of this phenomenon of being a co-laborer, through prayer, with God.

Second, such prayer is a divinely determined means for focusing our attention on God and His purposes. Kingdom-centered praying "is the believer's ratification of God's will; it brings him into active cooperation with God in the furthering of God's will."[39] But why is this important to God? Does He *need* our prayers, our "ratification," our cooperation, to help Him accomplish His purposes? No, the Bible is quite clear that He is independent, omnipotent, and sovereign—and yet, as we noted above, He often chooses not to act alone but in response to our petitions and in concert with our prayers.

So why does He care to involve us, through prayer, in His providential activities? Not because such prayer is necessary to focus God's attention on what He needs to do, but because *it focuses our attention on what He wants to do.*[40] "In prayer we do not seek to change God's mind. We seek to discern his will and to pray accordingly, believing that there are some things that God has determined to do in answer to prayer."[41] It is in focusing our attention on what God desires and purposes that an even deeper work takes place.

Third, such prayer is a divinely determined instrument for changing us. Our hope as humans is to live a happy, unruffled, unencumbered, largely pain-free life, and to be able to "get things done" that we believe we are called to do or need to accomplish. But God has something different in mind. *God's* goal for us is not health, convenience, financial independence, smooth circumstances, or even being able to accomplish worthy, ministry-related objectives. If it were, Christ would have sent Mary to help Martha (Luke 10:38-42). If it were, there would be no car breakdowns for believers, no handicapped Christians, no believing parents with sick children, no Christian children who have to care for ailing parents. These would not be hard things for an omnipotent God to arrange—if that were His primary aim. But it isn't.

God's fundamental goal for believers is not to protect us from harm or suffering, to make us comfortable, or to benefit from our service. You can biblically sum up God's primary aim for your whole life in one un-comfortable word: *change*. Ironic as it may sound, *change* is the one *constant* that God purposes for every believer, regardless of circum-stances—whether you are in ministry or in a secular job, married or single, healthy or handicapped, chronically ill or terminally diseased. God's immediate and ongoing purpose for every Christian in time and on earth is to *change* us, to make us like Himself, to conform us to the image of His Son. Romans 8:28-29 is a key passage revealing this divine pur-pose—a passage, interestingly enough, that is tied immediately to the context of prayer (note Romans 8:26-27).

This kind of change is what the Bible calls "sanctification." Whole books are written on the subject. But what, specifically, does sanctifica-tion have to do with prayer and providence? When we purpose to partici-pate with God through prayer, that "effective wheel in the machinery of providence," we focus our prayerful attention on God's work and on dis-cerning His will from His Word so that His goals become ours, His pas-sions become ours, His desires and ambitions and loves and values become ours—then *we are becoming like Him*. We ourselves are shaped into God's likeness by such praying. In the end, that is what Isaiah 62:6-7, II Peter 3:10-14, and Matthew 6:9-10 and 25-33 are all about.

Yes, we are invited and encouraged to make all our requests known to God, to unfold our heart's desires freely and frankly to Him. But a biblically informed view of providence should guide what and how we pray. And a biblically informed understanding that there are specific ob-jects—present promises and future events that are certain—that God in-tends to govern our prayers will guarantee that He is unmistakably glorified and that we, as prayer participants with Him, are changed in the process. All this may sound ideal and theoretical and unattainable, so let's look at a specific biblical example of these very principles.

An Illustration—Prayer in the Face of Prophesied Providences (Daniel 9)

In the providence of God, a devout young man named Daniel was torn away from his homeland in 605 B.C. by the conquering Babylonians under Nebuchadnezzar. That episode, by the way, introduces another lesson in the textbook of providence: God often allows the righteous to suffer certain consequences along with the wicked. Daniel was a righteous exception in a nation of rebels whom God was chastening with the rod of Babylon; yet he was carted away into captivity along with those who had forsaken the Lord and His law. It was a great mercy both to the nation Israel and to the future church that he was, or both would have lost the historical and prophetic treasure that is the Book of Daniel. Moreover, Israel would have lost the one man we know whose prayers participated with God's purposes to effect the promised deliverance from captivity.

We pick up Daniel's story in chapter 9. This is a remarkable passage of Scripture on several levels: (1) it suggests that Daniel, a statesman in a foreign land, was a diligent student of God's Word; (2) it furnishes a strong argument by example for a literal approach to interpreting prophecy, for Daniel's response to his study of Jeremiah's prophecy demonstrates an instinctive literalism on his part; (3) it reveals the selflessness of a man lost in the purposes of God since he prays for what he must realize he is too old to benefit from personally; (4) it exemplifies a proper view of self not merely as an individual but as part of a community of God's people; and (5) it illustrates the marriage between providence and prayer.

The events of Daniel 9 unfold some sixty-eight years after Daniel was exiled. The year is 538 B.C. and Daniel, then in his seventies at least, had remained an astute and diligent student of the Scriptures. From his study of Jeremiah's prophecy (Daniel 9:2) he discerned that the captivity of Judah in Babylon was to end after seventy years.[42]

Realizing that the prophecy had only a short time before it would run its course,[43] he could have sat back, watched, and waited in excited anticipation over what God would surely do to fulfill His Word (however unlikely it may have appeared at the time). That would have been a logical, justifiable, and even believing reaction to the prophecy. What he did instead was something quite extraordinary. He began confessing the sins of the nation and praying that God would mercifully, graciously, faithfully fulfill all that He had already promised through Jeremiah.

Daniel believed that his sovereign and omnipotent God ruled the affairs of all the nations according to His will.[44] That is precisely why he prayed—he was obeying an exhortation embedded in Jeremiah's prophecy that echoes the one we saw in Isaiah 62:6-7. The first part of the prophecy sounds quite sovereign and straightforward—God *will* bring His people back to their land after a set and specific amount of time.

> For thus saith the LORD, That after seventy years be accomplished at Babylon I will visit you, and perform my good word toward you, in causing you to return to this place. For I know the thoughts that I think toward you, saith the LORD, thoughts of peace, and not of evil, to give you an expected end (Jeremiah 29:10-11).

But the passage does not end there. Woven seamlessly into the certainty of the divine purpose is the necessity of human response and responsibility.

> Then shall ye call upon me, and ye shall go and pray unto me, and I will hearken unto you. And ye shall seek me, and find me, when ye shall search for me with all your heart. And I will be found of you, saith the LORD: and I will turn away your captivity, and I will gather you from all the nations, and from all the places whither I have driven you, saith the LORD; and I will bring you again into the place whence I caused you to be carried away captive (Jeremiah 29:12-14).

The language regarding the future prayer of God's people is virtually as certain as the language regarding the prophecy of God's future actions.[45] One might be tempted to ask whether God would have kept His prophetic promises if no one had prayed—a moot question born of theological speculation. The prophesied praying by godly Israelites was as providentially certain as the prophesied restoration by God. A more pertinent question is this: Do you think Daniel's discovery and understanding of Jeremiah's prophecy near the end of that seventy-year period was mere coincidence? And did Daniel pray—does any person pray—out of the goodness of his own heart and the natural Godward inclination of his soul? Or did God providentially superintend Daniel's sanctification over the years, direct and enlighten Daniel's study at just the right time, and even move Daniel to the necessary confession and prayer described in Jeremiah's prophecy?

The reasons Daniel prayed in the face of such a certain prophecy illustrate the same three effects of providence-focused prayer covered in our previous discussion. First, Daniel's prayerful response to the prophecy shows that he recognized the link between God's responsibility to perform His promises and man's responsibility to pray that God would do so. Into His prophetic promise to deliver Israel after seventy years God tucked an exhortation ("And ye shall *seek* me and find me"). Daniel grasped the divine Word in obedient faith and immediate personal practice. Echoing the same expression he read in Jeremiah, Daniel resolutely set his face "to *seek*" God in prayer (Daniel 9:3).[46]

Second, Daniel was habitually preoccupied with God's purposes and desires for Israel. "His custom of praying three times a day with his windows open to Jerusalem still in desolation [Daniel 6:10] revealed his own heart for the things of God and his concern for the city of Jerusalem."[47]

Finally (and consequently), because Daniel shared God's priorities and vision for Israel, his heart beat at one with God's. By focusing so exclusively on God's Word, God's purposes, and God's concerns, Daniel was made more like God. That is abundantly evident in the passion and emphasis of his prayer in chapter 9.[48] Through the instrument of prayer, Daniel participated in God's prophesied purpose to bring the nation back to her land in seventy years.

> [Daniel] grounded his petitions in the Word of God. . . . By faith he accepted the revelation given to Jeremiah and, using it as his basis, began to pray accordingly. . . . Having learned God's will from the Scriptures, Daniel could pray with assurance and power for its accomplishment. Daniel practiced Bible-based praying.[49]

Prayer Checks Our Presumption on Providence

Let's shift from the big picture of a biblical philosophy of prayer to a narrower everyday concern—prayerfully discerning God's will through providential circumstances. Again, a biblical example will move all this from the theoretical realm to the flesh-and-blood arena of real life.

Some years ago Garry Friesen's *Decision Making and the Will of God* created a stir in Christian circles. According to Friesen, God does not have a specific will for individual Christians in a variety of major areas. Rather, believers should learn to make wise decisions based on scriptural principles and providential circumstances. "At no point in Scripture," he argued, "do we read of a believer asking, 'What is God's individual will for me in this matter?'"[50] In his Foreword to Friesen's book, Haddon Robinson suggested that the question "How can I know the will of God?" might even be a pagan question; he compared it to military leaders in the ancient world who consulted their heathen oracles for just such guidance in battle—"guidance" that often proved either ambiguously enigmatical or downright disastrous.[51] A notable biblical example undercuts both of these assertions. The passage is curiously absent from any discussion in Friesen's book.[52] But it furnishes an exemplary pattern for praying through the circumstantial providences of God.

Shortly after David's official coronation, the Philistines "came and spread themselves in the valley of Rephaim" (II Samuel 5:18). David asked God whether he should confront them in battle. God assured him that he should and that He would deliver them into his hand, and David achieved a sweeping victory over the Philistines (II Samuel 5:19-21). The *very next verse* records that "the Philistines came up yet again, and spread themselves in the valley of Rephaim"—the wording duplicates verse 18 *verbatim*.

David had faced these circumstances before. Wouldn't it be logical to assume that God's will would be the same? David assumed nothing. (*That*, by the way, is wise decision making.) In the face of identical providential circumstances, David essentially asked the Lord once again, "What is your will for me in this matter?"—and received quite a different answer. He was not to confront the enemy head on; that was not "God's will" this time. Instead, David was to circle around behind them, hide his strike force behind a mulberry grove, and hold his attack until he heard "the sound of a going in the tops of the mulberry trees." That supernatural sound in the trees above and in front of them was the audible signal of the Lord's presence to fight for them.

The point for the purpose of our discussion is simple. Seemingly providential circumstances alone are not trustworthy. We do not look at our surroundings for signs of direction without prayer to God for guidance, even in situations we think we can figure out because we have faced them before. Following the assumed providences of God without prayer to God is, quite ironically, the opposite of faith. It is somewhat like adoring creation while ignoring the Creator. Basing decisions on providential circumstances without prayer is to forsake a living relationship with the God of providence and to fall back on a rabbit's foot religion that looks to signs and omens for direction. Providences can be misunderstood, circumstances misread, and our own hearts misled. When it comes to seeking God's direction and making wise and right decisions, apparently providential circumstances are not a substitute for God.

How can we discern God's will amid seemingly providential circumstances? Puritan John Flavel offers sound advice for discerning God's leading through personal providences in your life.

> If therefore in doubtful cases you would discover God's will, govern yourselves in your search after it by the following rules:
>
> Get the true fear of God upon your hearts. Be really afraid of offending Him. God will not hide His mind from such a soul. "The secret of the Lord is with them that fear him; and he will show them his covenant" (Ps. 25:14).
>
> Study the Word more, and the concerns and interests of the world less. The Word is a light to your feet (Ps. 119:105), that is, it has a discovering and directing usefulness as to all duties to be done and dangers to be avoided. . . . Treasure up its rules in your hearts, and you will walk safely. "Thy Word have I hid in mine heart that I might not sin against thee" (Ps. 119:11).
>
> Reduce what you know into practice, and you shall know what is your duty to practice. "If any man will do his will he shall know of the doctrine"

(John 7:17). "A good understanding have all they that do his commandments" (Ps. 111:10).

Pray for illumination and direction in the way that you should go. Beg the Lord to guide you in straits and that He would not permit you to fall into sin. This was the practice of Ezra . . . (Ezra 8:21).

And this being done, follow Providence so far as it agrees with the Word and no further. There is no use to be made of Providence against the Word, but in subservience to it. . . . Providence in concurrence with the Word may give some encouragement to us in our way; but no testimony of Providence is to be accepted against the Word.[53]

One Last Look in the Mirror

A correct view of providence never makes one presumptuous when it comes to prayer. A biblical doctrine of providence invigorates the prayer life and motivates one to pray with a deep rooted confidence in the God of providence.

What kinds of concerns most characterize your prayers, either for yourself or for others? Material needs? Bodily afflictions? Again, there is nothing wrong with such requests. The fact that your heavenly Father already knows all your needs in these areas (Matthew 6:32) should not prevent you from making all your requests known to God by prayer and supplication in everything (Philippians 4:6). God desires for you to call to Him with your needs in the day of trouble so that He can deliver you and you can glorify Him (Psalm 50:15). But material concerns ought not preoccupy our prayers, for "after all these things do the Gentiles seek" (Matthew 6:32).

Study the prayers of the apostle Paul and you will discover a preoccupation with God's larger purposes.[54] Every petition is tied to God's greater goals. Study his prayer *requests* and you will find the same God-centered preoccupation, even when those requests involve the mundane.[55]

Discipline your spirit to pray with thought, to filter your requests through the sieve of God's larger purposes as He has revealed them in His

Word. "The Spirit rides most triumphantly in his own chariot" someone has said, and you cannot do better than to pray God's own words back to Him. You have probably heard it said that "prayer changes things." Above all, genuine, God-focused, Bible-centered prayer changes *people*—notably the one doing that kind of praying. Learning to pray that way is learning to think God's thoughts. God is after our "complete and entire and absolute identification with the Lord Jesus Christ, and there is nothing in which this identification is realized more than in prayer. . . . The idea of prayer is not in order to get answers from God; prayer is perfect and complete oneness with God."[56]

How much of your praying, for yourself and for others, focuses on God's goals and promises and prophecies? How much of your praying is driven by the desire to see God's name hallowed, God's kingdom established, God's will done throughout the earth? If that sounds impractical or overly broad or hyper-pious, you have not tried it. Anyone who begins thoughtfully to pray that way soon finds the Spirit's searchlight turned inward, driving him to examine whether in his own heart he shares God's passions, believes God's Word, hallows God's name, bows to God's rule, and submits to God's will. And it is that process of prayerfully adopting God's chief causes and concerns as our own that shapes our souls increasingly into the image of His Son.

May your understanding of God's providence from His Word enable you to rest in the reign of God and motivate you to confident and God-centered prayer. And may your praying to the God of providence drive you deeper again into His Word to know His mind.

EPILOGUE

This has been a book about God, His character and His ways, as He has revealed Himself in His own Word. We have dipped into the doctrine of divine providence in every major historical segment in the Bible—from Joseph in the patriarchal era of Genesis, to Pharaoh and his royal colleagues in the era of the exodus, the conquest, and the judges, to the monarchy, exile and restoration, to the life and ministry of Christ, to the early church. We have considered numerous examples of providence extracted from church history as well.

Still, I am struck most by how much has been left unexamined, unaddressed, unsaid. In many respects this is a primer, an unfinished book that you, the reader, may continue to write as you progress in your own investigation of God's providence in your Bible and your personal discovery of His providence in your life. There are other topics, too, that bear further investigation than has been possible to include in this volume.

For some readers I trust this book, by directing your attention to God's own words, may have guided you toward helpful answers to long-lingering questions. For others who may have read this in the midst of present difficulties and dark providences, I hope that some part of this book, through its focus upon the assurances of God's words, has ministered stability to your soul in your present need. For many others, God may well have intended these truths to shore up some aspect of your faith for ministry to others or for your own future providential testing known only to His mind. For additional inspiration, let me encourage your perusal of George Herbert's poem "Providence" (Appendix A) and a collection of sayings on providence called "Pearls of Providence" (Appendix B).

This book has necessarily left unanswered many questions, both general and specific, theological and personal. Let me encourage you to give some thoughtful application to "Personalizing Providence" (Appendix C)—a list of principles drawn from John Flavel's *Mystery of Providence,* which will give focus and direction to your personal application of the truth of God's providence in your own life. Appendix D ("The Arrival of the Magi") provides additional information or insight into specific topics raised elsewhere in the book. As to any lingering general or theological questions, you may find some of them addressed in "Salvation: Divine Determination or Human Responsibility?" (Appendix E).

One of my guiding purposes in writing this book has been to collect and introduce to the readers material that many are not likely to encounter otherwise, the reflections and conclusions of men and women much wiser and more gifted. I trust there has been enough freshness of approach and originality of thought to make this study both engaging and informative. Admittedly, however, nothing here is entirely *new*. Creativity and novelty are prized in the arts, but in theology they are dangerous. Michelangelo wrote that "even the greatest artist has no idea that is not already buried deep within the marble." For the faithful student of Scripture the process is somewhat the reverse—chipping your way into the stone of Scripture to discover the form and thought of God communicated there. In that sense, then, no theologian has any biblically valid idea that is not already buried within the Scripture—awaiting the discovery of the searching, hungering soul. May God make you one of those whose hunger for God's Word is filled, and whose feeding on the words of God carries you beyond the sacred page to seek, and to see, the Lord.

APPENDIX A

Excerpts of George Herbert's poem "Providence" have already been cited (see Prologue and Interlude). Many of the other stanzas illustrate various specific aspects of God's providence throughout nature and contain thoughts worthy of meditation. Here is the entire poem.

PROVIDENCE

O sacred Providence, who from end to end
Strongly and sweetly movest, shall I write,
And not of thee, through whom my
    fingers bend
To hold my quill? shall they not do
    thee right?

Of all the creatures both in sea and land
Only to Man thou hast made known thy
    ways,
And put the pen alone into his hand,
And made him Secretary of thy praise.

Beasts fain would sing; birds ditty to
    their notes;
Trees would be tuning on their native lute
To thy renown: but all their hands and
    throats
Are brought to Man, while they are lame
    and mute.

Man is the world's high priest: he doth
    present
The sacrifice for all; while they below
Unto the service mutter an assent,
Such as springs use that fall, and winds
    that blow.

He that to praise and laud thee doth
    refrain,
Doth not refrain unto himself alone,
But robs a thousand who would praise
    thee fain,
And doth commit a world of sin in one.

The beasts say, Eat me: but, if beasts
    must teach,
The tongue is yours to eat, but mine
    to praise.
The trees say, Pull me: but the hand
    you stretch,
Is mine to write, as it is yours to raise.

Wherefore, most sacred Spirit, I here
    present
For me and all my fellows praise to thee:
And just it is that I should pay the rent,
Because the benefit accrues to me.

We all acknowledge both thy power
    and love
To be exact, transcendent, and divine;
Who dost so strongly and so sweetly move,
While all things have their will, yet none
    but thine.

NOT BY CHANCE

For either thy command or thy permission
Lay hands on all: they are thy right and left.
The first puts on with speed and
  expedition;
The other curbs sin's stealing pace and
  theft.

Nothing escapes them both; all must
  appear,
And be disposed, and dressed, and tuned
  by thee,
Who sweetly temper'st all. If we could
  hear
Thy skill and art, what music would it be!

Thou art in small things great, not small
  in any:
Thy even praise can neither rise, nor fall.
Thou art in all things one, in each thing
  many:
For thou art infinite in one and all.

Tempests are calm to thee; they know
  thy hand,
And hold it fast, as children do their
  fathers,
Which cry and follow. Thou hast made
  poor sand
Check the proud sea, ev'n when it swells
  and gathers.

Thy cupboard serves the world: the meat
  is set,
Where all may reach: no beast but knows
  his feed.
Birds teach us hawking; fishes have their
  net:
The great prey on the less, they on some
  weed.

Nothing engendered doth prevent his
  meat:
Flies have their table spread, ere they
  appear.
Some creatures have in winter what to eat;
Others do sleep, and envy not their cheer.

How finely dost thou times and seasons
  spin,
And make a twist checkered with night
  and day!
Which as it lengthens winds, and winds
  us in,
As bowls go on, but turning all the way.

Each creature hath a wisdom for his good.
The pigeons feed their tender offspring,
  crying,
When they are callow; but withdraw their
  food
When they are fledge, that need may teach
  them flying.

Bees work for man; and yet they never
  bruise
Their master's flower, but leave it, having
  done,
As fair as ever, and as fit to use;
So both the flower doth stay, and honey
  run.

Sheep eat the grass, and dung the ground
  for more:
Trees after bearing drop their leaves for
  soil:
Springs vent their streams, and by expense
  get store:
Clouds cool by heat, and baths by cooling
  boil.

238

Who hath the virtue to express the rare
And curious virtues both of herbs and
    stones?
Is there an herb for that? O that thy care
Would show a root, that gives expressions!

And if an herb hath power, what have the
    stars?
A rose, besides his beauty, is a cure.
Doubtless our plagues and plenty, peace
    and wars
Are there much surer than our art is sure.

Thou hast hid metals: man may take them
    thence;
But at his peril: when he digs the place,
He makes a grave; as if the thing had sense,
And threatened man, that he should fill
    the space.

Ev'n poisons praise thee. Should a thing
    be lost?
Should creatures want for want of heed
    their due?
Since where are poisons, antidotes are
    most:
The help stands close, and keeps the fear
    in view.

The sea, which seems to stop the traveller,
Is by a ship the speedier passage made.
The winds, who think they rule the
    mariner,
Are ruled by him, and taught to serve his
    trade.

And as thy house is full, so I adore
Thy curious art in marshalling thy goods.
The hills with health abound; the vales
    with store;
The South with marble; North with furs
    and woods.

Hard things are glorious; easy things
    good cheap.
The common all men have; that which
    is rare
Men therefore seek to have, and care
    to keep.
The healthy frosts with summer-fruits
    compare.

Light without wind is glass: warm without
    weight
Is wool and fur: cool without closeness,
    shade:
Speed without pains, a horse: tall without
    height,
A servile hawk: low without loss, a spade.

All countries have enough to serve their
    need:
If they seek fine things, thou dost make
    them run
For their offence; and then dost turn their
    speed
To be commerce and trade from sun to
    sun.

Nothing wears clothes, but Man; nothing
    doth need
But he to wear them. Nothing useth fire,
But Man alone, to show his heav'nly breed:
And only he hath fuel in desire.

NOT BY CHANCE

When th' earth was dry, thou mad'st a sea
of wet:
When that lay gathered, thou didst broach
the mountains:
When yet some places could no moisture
get,
The winds grew gard'ners, and the clouds
good fountains.

Rain, do not hurt my flowers; but gently
spend
Your honey drops: press not to smell
them here:
When they are ripe, their odour will
ascend,
And at your lodging with their thanks
appear.

How harsh are thorns to pears! and yet
they make
A better hedge, and need less reparation.
How smooth are silks compared with a
stake,
Or with a stone! yet make no good
foundation.

Sometimes thou dost divide thy gifts to
man,
Sometimes unite. The Indian nut alone
Is clothing, meat and trencher, drink
and can,
Boat, cable, sail and needle, all in one.

Most herbs that grow in brooks, are hot
and dry.
Cold fruits warm kernels help against
the wind.
The lemon's juice and rind cure mutually.
The whey of milk doth loose, the milk
doth bind.

Thy creatures leap not, but express a feast,
Where all the guests sit close, and nothing
wants.
Frogs marry fish and flesh; bats, bird and
beast;
Sponges, nonsense and sense; mines, th'
earth and plants.

To show thou art not bound, as if thy lot
Were worse than ours, sometimes thou
shiftest hands.
Most things move th' under-jaw; the
crocodile not.
Most things sleep lying; th' elephant leans
or stands.

But who hath praise enough? nay, who
hath any?
None can express thy works, but he that
knows them:
And none can know thy works, which are
so many,
And so complete, but only he that owes
them.

All things that are, though they have
sev'ral ways,
Yet in their being join with one advice
To honor thee: and so I give thee praise
In all my other hymns, but in this twice.

Each thing that is, although in use and
name
It go for one, hath many ways in store
To honour thee; and so each hymn thy
fame
Extolleth many ways, yet this one more.

APPENDIX B

Pearls of Providence
In addition to those quotations at the beginning of each chapter, this collection of quotations also shows various aspects of God's providence.

[Providence] teaches that an infinitely wise, good and powerful God is everywhere present, controlling all events great and small, necessary and free, in a way perfectly consistent with the nature of His creatures and with His own infinite excellence, so that everything is ordered by His will and is made to subserve His wise and benevolent design.
—Charles Hodge, *Systematic Theology,* vol. 2, pt. 1, ch. XI, sect. 2.

The best commentary on Providence is the Bible.
—William S. Plumer, *Jehovah-Jireh: A Treatise on Divine Providence,* p. 140

To the believer the "amazing coincidences" of history are but manifestations of God's intervention for His omniscient, benevolent purposes. . . . But it is no less true that when God does not deliver His people, He is still at work for their good. God has a purpose in His granting as well as in His withholding.
—Edward Panosian, *The Providence of God in History,* pp. 13-14

A God without dominion, without providence and final causes, is nothing but fate and nature.
—Sir Isaac Newton, quoted by Plumer, p. 8

The doctrine of the providence of God leaves no room for fate, blind or otherwise. God is not blind; neither is He capricious. For Him there are no accidents. . . . If one molecule flies wild by chance, then God is not sovereign. If God is not sovereign, then God is not God. God and chance simply cannot coexist.
—R. C. Sproul, *The Invisible Hand,* p. 156

NOT BY CHANCE

Our indiscretion sometimes serves us well,
When our deep plots do fail: And that should teach us
There's a divinity that shapes our ends,
Rough-hew them how we will.

—Shakespeare, Hamlet, Act V, Scene 2

We can all see God in exceptional things, but it requires the growth of spiritual discipline to see God in every detail. Never believe that the so-called random events of life are anything less than God's appointed order. Be ready to discover His divine designs anywhere and everywhere.

—Oswald Chambers, My Utmost for His Highest

"God reigns" is a logical sequence from "God is." To deny God's providence is as atheistical as to deny His existence.

—Plumer, p. 10

If we understand the providence of God and love the God of providence, we are able to worship Him with the sacrifice of praise He inherently deserves when things occur that bring pain, sorrow and affliction into our lives. This understanding of providence is vital to all who would worship God. It is a worship of faith that is rooted in trust.

—Sproul, p. 11

I adore and kiss the providence of my Lord, who knoweth well what is most expedient for me, and for you, and your children.

—Samuel Rutherford, quoted by Plumer, p. 8

If we will not be candid and diligent students of God's word and providence, we must live and die without wisdom.

—Plumer, p. 131

APPENDIX C

Personalizing Providence

This appendix features a synopsis of chapters 8-11 and 13 in John Flavel's *The Mystery of Providence*. Flavel's expansions on these points is worth the effort of reading. Each point below warrants time for thought, meditation, and personal application. The last section is a sober appeal for believers to keep a journal of God's providences in their own lives.

The duty of meditation on providence

[It is] the duty of the people of God to meditate upon these performances of Providence for them, at all times, but especially in times of difficulty and trouble:

- Because God has expressly commanded it.
- Because neglect of it is everywhere in Scripture condemned as a sin.
- [Because] without due observation of the works of Providence no praise can be rendered to God for any of them.
- [Because] without this we lose the usefulness and benefit of all the works of God for us or others.
- [Because] it is a vile slighting of God not to observe what He manifests of Himself in His providences.
- [Because] men can never order their addresses to God in prayer, suitable to their conditions, without due observation of His providences.

Advantages of meditating on providence

By this means you may maintain sweet and conscious communion with God from day to day.

A great part of the pleasure and delight of the Christian life is made out of the observations of Providence.

Consider what an effectual means the due observation of Providence will be to overpower and suppress the natural atheism in your hearts.

The remembering and recording of the performances of Providence will be a singular support to faith in future difficulties.

The remembrance of former providences will minister to your souls continual matter of praise and thanksgiving.

The due observation of Providence will endear Jesus Christ every day more and more to your souls.

The due observations of Providence have a marvellous efficacy to melt the heart, and make it thaw and submit before the Lord.

Due observation of Providence will both beget and secure inward tranquillity in your minds amid the vicissitudes and [upheavals] of things in this unstable vain world.

Due observations of the ways of God in His providences towards us have an excellent usefulness and aptitude to advance and improve holiness in our hearts and lives.

The consideration and study of Providence will be of singular use to us in a dying hour.

Practical implications of providence

If God performs all things for you:

- God is to be owned by you in all that befalls you in this world, whether it is in a way of success and comfort or of trouble and affliction.

- how great is His condescension to and care over you.

- see how obliged you are to perform all duties and services for God.

- do not distrust Him when new or great difficulties arise.

- seek God by prayer for everything, and never undertake any design without Him.

- then it is our great interest and concern in all things to study to please Him, upon whom we depend for all things.

How to meditate on the providence of God

Labour to get as full and thorough a recognition as you are able of the providences of God concerning you from first to last.

In all your observations of Providence have a special respect to that Word of God which is fulfilled and made good to you by them.

APPENDIX C

In all your reviews and observations of Providence, be sure that you eye God as the author and orderer of them all (Proverbs 3:6).

Work up your hearts to those frames, and exercise those affections which the particular providences of God that concern you call for (Ecclesiastes 7:14).

If Providence delays the performance of any mercy to you that you have long waited and prayed for, yet see that you do not despond, nor grow weary of waiting upon God for that reason.

Do not pry too curiously into the secrets of Providence, nor allow your shallow reason arrogantly to judge and censure its design.

Advantages of recording our experiences of providence

I cannot but judge it the concern of Christians that have time and ability for such a work, to keep written memorials or journals of Providence by them, for their own and others' use and benefit. For want of collecting and communicating such observations, not only ourselves, but the Church of God is greatly impoverished. . . .

If Christians in reading the Scriptures would judiciously collect and record the providences they shall meet with there, and but add those that have fallen out in their own time and experience, O what a precious treasure would these make! . . .

Providence carries our lives, liberties and concerns in its hand every moment. Your bread is in its cupboard, your money in its purse, your safety in its enfolding arms; and surely it is the least part of what you owe to record the favors you receive at its hands.

Do not trust your slippery memories with such a multitude of remarkable passages of Providence as you have, and shall meet with in your way to heaven. . . . Written memorials secure us against that hazard [of forgetting God's providences], and besides, make them useful to others when we are gone, so that you do not carry away all your treasure to heaven with you, but leave these choice legacies to your surviving friends. . . .

Take heed of clasping up those rich treasures in a book, and thinking it enough to have noted them there; but have frequent recourse to them, as oft as new needs, fears or difficulties arise and assault you.

APPENDIX D

The Arrival of the Magi

The Christmas after I became a Christian I set up the family manger scene as usual. The lifeless figures we had all seen for years before our conversion out of Roman Catholicism took on fresh meaning and an unaccustomed reality. Naturally, I arranged all the shapes beside the stable. Then I heard that the wise men were not present at the birth of Jesus or even at the stable; actually, I was told, they probably did not arrive until a year or two later! I promptly rearranged the scene, placing the wise men on the far side of the room. Admittedly, my response was partly facetious; but it was also partly sincere. In my young and eager Christian desire, I wanted to reflect the biblical account as accurately as I could.

Arguments for a late arrival

Conventional wisdom is of the opinion that the wise men, or "magi," did not appear on the scene until a considerable time after the birth of Christ. Matthew includes their arrival as part of his account of the birth of Christ. That, of course, does not necessarily mean that they came soon after the birth. Matthew never says specifically when they arrived. So we have to search the details of the text for clues and implications.

For instance, it is often pointed out that Matthew uses the term "young child" (*paidion*), rather than the normal word for "infant" (*brephos*), when he refers to the child that the wise men saw (Matthew 2:8, 9, 11, 13, 14). It is also true that the holy family was in a "house" when the magi arrived, not a "stable" (Matthew 2:11). Finally, Herod's decision to murder male children up to two years old (Matthew 2:16), based on his interrogation of the wise men regarding the star's appearance (Matthew 2:7), suggests to many that the magi may have arrived as much as two years later.

These are legitimate observations and it may be that the magi actually did arrive quite some time after the birth of Jesus. Obviously, we are not dealing with a fundamental doctrine of the faith. Nevertheless, any student of the Bible worth his Strong's *Concordance* should be curious to discover as much as he can about the events recorded for us in the Bible. There are, therefore, several offsetting considerations that should also be taken into account.

Did the wise men find a "babe" or a "young child"?

It is true that Matthew describes Jesus as a "young child" (*paidion*) rather than a "babe" (*brephos*) when the magi arrived. (In fact, Matthew never uses the latter word at all in his book.) Luke, on the other hand, refers to Christ as a "babe" (*brephos*) in the record of the angelic announcement to the shepherds and in the record of the shepherds' visit—both on the very night of the child's birth (Luke 2:12, 16). However, Luke also uses the word *paidion* to describe Jesus when He is just over one month old, at the temple presentation after Mary's forty-day purification period (Luke 2:27). Finally, Luke's use of the same word to refer to the *eight-day-old* John the Baptist (Luke 1:59) shows that the word *paidion* is chronologically relative. That is, while *paidion* may be used to describe a young boy or a toddler, it may also be used to describe a one-week-old infant. Matthew's use of *paidion* in the account of the magi's visit, therefore, does not in any way prove that Christ was past the infant stage by the time of their arrival.

How did they get into a "house"?

The fact that the magi found the Christ child in a "house" rather than in the stable also fails to prove a late visit. The text does not tell us how or when they managed to move into a house. Therefore, any explanation necessarily rests on some degree of speculation. The family obviously did not live in the stable for the duration of their stay in Bethlehem. The stable was an immediate necessity because of Mary's imminent delivery and the lack of any other available quarters; but it was only a temporary necessity.

Now picture the shepherds' reaction. After witnessing the majestic angelic announcement of the birth of the Savior, they arrive to worship and find Him *in a feeding trough in a stable?* Their long-awaited *Messiah?* The scene is quaint and even commonplace to us two thousand Christmases later. But could those shepherds possibly have bowed the knee in homage to their Sovereign in a dingy stable and not have been incredulous at the incongruity? Is it feasible that not one of those shepherds would have invited them to some lodging more worthy of a newborn babe, let alone a King? It is almost unthinkable that the shepherds, who knew through the angelic announcement who this infant was, would not have offered the holy family immediate shelter in one of their own homes nearby. Indeed, it seems probable that they had suitable quarters at least by the next day or so.

Conceivably, then, the magi could easily have arrived in Jerusalem soon after and followed the star to the house of whatever shepherd or friend had gladly opened his door to the angelically heralded Christ child. This scenario is admittedly speculative, but it is no more speculative than the assumption that "house" necessarily indicates a considerable lapse of time. On the contrary, the above explanation seems to present a much more feasible and realistic alternative.

What about Herod's calculations and the star?

Herod's inquiry of the magi and his subsequent destruction of male children two years old and under may seem on the surface to infer a late visit. But this inference is based on an assumption. One must assume that the star did not appear in the east until Christ was actually born—as though there were some necessary connection between the appearance of the star and the day of Christ's birth. There was certainly a supernatural connection between the star and the birth. But the sole purpose of the star indicated in the text was *not* to mark the *day* of Christ's birth but *to lead the magi to Christ* (Matthew 2:9).

It seems more reasonable, therefore, to posit that the star providentially appeared *before* Christ's birth. How long before? Long enough to give those for whom it was intended time to make the journey. It may well have appeared at the time of Mary's conception. Given the characteristic way in which God providentially orchestrates events to accomplish His purposes in perfect timing, this presents a much more likely alternative. Herod's calculations, in this case, would have been based on the star's appearance—with a safe margin for error added—but not on the actual age of the infant.

APPENDIX D

What are we to do with the shepherds' proclamation of Messiah's birth?

Finally, there is at least one positive argument that lends further support to an early visit of the magi. According to Luke 2:17, the shepherds immediately spread abroad the news of the birth of the Messiah, for whom the Jewish world had long been waiting with great anticipation. Similarly, Anna was widely circulating the news about the birth of this Messiah at the temple presentation of Jesus (Luke 2:38).

But Matthew 2:3 and following describes Herod's surprise and alarm at the arrival of these strange foreigners and the news they brought. Given Herod's notoriety for murderous paranoia, it is unrealistic to suppose that news of Messiah's birth was sweeping throughout the countryside, and yet the visit and message of the magi a year or so later came as a complete surprise to Herod. The magi, therefore, must have arrived very shortly after Christ's birth, before the news and rumors had reached the monarch's ears. In fact, it seems most likely that their arrival must have been before the rumors from the countryside were confirmed by those who witnessed the temple presentation and the prophetic proclamations of Simeon and Anna, as well as all those to whom they spread the news.

Conclusion

How soon after the birth of Christ did the magi arrive? No one knows for certain. Given the above considerations, however, it seems likely that the visit occurred sometime within the first month after Messiah's birth, with Herod's infanticide following on the heels of the temple presentation. What difference does it make? None, doctrinally speaking. But, in my opinion, an early arrival not only better fits the available data but magnifies God's providence even more. God does not run things reactively. He is the Maestro of providential orchestration, of split-second timing, of perfect point and counterpoint.

The story of the magi is included in Matthew's account of what has become a part of the traditional Christmas narrative, and there is good warrant for regarding it as such. Incidentally, I no longer place the wise men on the opposite side of the room; there is really no biblical reason not to leave them somewhere near the manger scene. God includes them in the Christmas story for very important reasons, and so should we.

APPENDIX E

Salvation: Divine Determination or Human Responsibility?

Through the centuries this battle has raged like a theological holy war. Crusaders for both sides have attacked their doctrinal enemies too often with an unholy zeal. Brothers have parted, churches have split, fellowships have divided, denominations have formed, and labels have been devised (some descriptive, some defamatory) as a result of this question and its practical ramifications.

After all these centuries, the debate remains at an impasse. How is it to be resolved? One cannot argue the superiority of the men on either side of the issue. Both positions have had their share of good, godly, able advocates (as well as the other kind). Nor can either side claim a monopoly on clear and unequivocal Scripture. Each side of the debate has its favorite proof texts that allegedly undermine the other's position. Likewise, each side is baffled by certain passages and squirms at the prick of certain scriptural thorns in their theological flesh. Yet both sides have their own answers to such problem passages—answers that often involve some subtle adjustment of the wording, some rational redefinition of the terms, some leap of logic, however large or small, to make all the passages fit more comfortably within the logical confines of their systematic theology.

What, then, is the solution? A genuine impasse is, by nature and definition, unresolvable. If we insist on devising a complete answer to every question and fitting every verse into a system that we find logically comfortable and easily explicable, the impasse will always remain. Our only choice will be to side with one view or the other—accepting all the strengths and rationalizing all the weaknesses of whatever position we choose. But there is another startlingly uncomplicated alternative. It may sound simplistic; in fact, it is merely simple. Let the Bible say what it says—plainly, unadorned by logic and rationalization, without removing its teeth, without tinkering with the terminology—even if you cannot fully understand or explain it. There, it seems, is the rub.

The Limitations of Logic

Shakespeare's *Henry V* opens with an apology to the audience for imposing upon their imagination because of the limitations of the theater. "Can this cockpit [this small stage] hold the vasty fields of France?" the narrator asks rhetorically. The task of theology, properly approached, faces this same limitation. Can any systematic theology, however thick or multi-volumed, adequately display the immeasurable vistas of an infinite and eternal God? "But pardon, gentles all," the bard continues, "the flat unraiséd spirit that hath dared, on this unworthy scaffold, to bring forth so great an object." Necessary and helpful as they are, the constructs of systematic theology and human reason are an insufficient scaffold for the presentation of so great an object as the thoughts and actions of the unfathomable Godhead.

Where biblical theology leaves off, with its explicit focus on what has been revealed, systematic theology often attempts to carry the investigation further through logic and deduction. Sound systematic theology takes the statements of biblical revelation and applies logic, both to organize the data into a kind of theological textbook and to deduce answers not directly addressed in Scripture.

Logic is, of course, a God-given tool, essential for understanding human and divine communication. Drawing logical inferences from Scripture is perfectly legitimate and, indeed, necessary. Jesus (e.g., Matthew 22:31-32), Paul (e.g., Romans 9-11), and others (e.g., James 2:20-26) exemplify this method in their handling of Scripture. At the same time, Paul flatly declares when an apparently logical path leads to a theological cul-de-sac (e.g., Romans 9:18-20). Everyone admits that there are limits to logic—at least in theory.

The assertion that human logic has limitations, however, does not mean merely that logic can carry us along only so far and then stops. There are numerous false turns down which apparent logic can take us and still be logical. In other words, it is possible for something to be both "logical" and wrong. If a deduction is based on a false premise, a seemingly reasonable assumption, or an inadequate or inaccurate knowledge of the facts, that deduction may appear to be perfectly logical and yet be dead wrong. Paul is the most vocal in drawing the line between legitimate logical conclusions and deductions that are as wrong as they are reasonable. Each "God forbid" from the pen of Paul warns the reader against arriving at some apparently logical but erroneous, even damnable, conclusion. We are not at liberty to draw inferences that contradict other explicit statements of Scripture. And we must be tentative about defending apparently logical inferences that carry us beyond explicit statements of Scripture.

One of the challenges to logic is the paradox. Someone has defined a paradox as truth standing on its head to get attention. A paradox is not a contradiction but an apparent contradiction—truth presented in terms of polarities. God is three persons yet one being. Jesus is fully God and fully man. These are not contradictions but paradoxes. It is just as heretical to say that the truth lies somewhere between the two poles as is it to deny either pole of the truth. Within the confines of human logic, the finite categories in which we are accustomed to think, they appear to conflict. Yet, we are willing to suspend our logic in deference to what God says is so, in the face of biblical revelation that clearly asserts the reality of apparently contradictory truths.

This suspension of logic, this acting on the basis of what God says is so (rather than on our own understanding of what seems to make sense or our perception of what seems to be the case) has a very common name: faith—taking God at His word. This is not to say that faith is illogical. Belief in apparently illogical propositions (such as the Trinity or the twofold nature of Christ) is an entirely logical human response to propositions that God affirms are true. Faith acknowledges that revelation may transcend the limitations of human logic.

Logic is a persuasive thing. Paradoxical as it may sound, logic can also be an intoxicating influence, clouding our ability to walk the narrow path between explicit biblical statement and the tenuous extensions of apparent logic that branch off from that path in both directions. At some point in the debate over virtually every major Bible doctrine, two roads diverge in the theological wood. It is vital to learn to detect where reason veers off from the road of explicit biblical statement. Once you step off the edge of the cliff of clear revelation, trusting in the power of logic to levitate your position, the fact is you are still standing out in thin air with nothing under you.

Getting to the Point

Few dispute the limitations of logic and the necessity of simple faith when it comes to theological issues that clearly transcend our comprehension (such as the nature of the God-Man). Once the debate shifts to the mechanics of salvation, however, we are strangely less inclined to accept by faith paradoxical affirmations as equally true. We insist on hammering out a comprehensive, logical, systematic theology that can answer questions that the Bible, frankly, leaves unanswered.

Is it not illogical to suppose that we can fully understand and explain the doings of a God we readily admit is utterly beyond our comprehension? Is it not unreasonable to insist on theologically psychoanalyzing the works of a God whose infinite nature we freely acknowledge bursts all the boundaries of finite understanding?

The answer to the question raised in the title of this essay—"Is salvation a matter of divine determination or human responsibility?"—is not divine determination *or* human responsibility. The only thoroughly biblical answer is yes. Scripturally, it is not an "either-or" but a "both-and" proposition. Why is this so hard?

For one thing, it is logically unsatisfactory and apparently contradictory. Our insatiable appetite for order and answers makes it difficult to admit—not just in theory but in our practice and in our theology—that God's ways are not our ways, and leave it at that. "For as the heavens are higher than the earth, so are my ways higher than your ways, and my thoughts than your thoughts" (Isaiah 55:9). We don't mind applying this principle in a general, hypothetical way to God's wisdom or methods. But we balk when it interferes with our theological system, our obsession with pigeonholing every Bible fact into a neat, orderly arrangement that leaves no questions unanswered.

But God's point in Isaiah 55:9 is essentially that He is not logical. That does not mean He is illogical. It means He transcends our logic. He is *supra*logical. His thinking, His design, His way, His "theology" is infinitely above our intellect, beyond the grasp of our comprehension, out of the reach of our clever rationalizations. Someone has expressed it cleverly and succinctly: God is *theo*-logical. Man is *anthropo*-logical. The extent of our logic is inherently deficient and inadequate, primarily because our information and comprehension is so limited. Like a two-dimensional square compared to a three-dimensional cube (or to four-dimensional reality), we are merely a finite reflection of an infinite God in this respect.

C. S. Lewis offers a superb illustration of our limitations from the field of geometry. If you are operating in a one-dimensional realm, he explains, you can draw a straight line. Move into two-dimensions and you can draw a square—which consists of four straight lines. In a three-dimensional world you can construct a cube which, in turn, is made of six squares.

> Do you see the point? . . . In other words, as you advance to more real and more complicated levels, you do not leave behind you the things you found on the simpler levels: you still have them, but combined in new ways—*in ways you could not imagine if you knew only the simpler levels.*[1]

"Those things which are revealed belong unto us and to our children forever" but "the secret things belong unto the Lord" (Deuteronomy 29:29). So why do we insist that profound and eternal issues must make complete sense to us? We betray our folly when we presume to discover His secret things and proceed to press them into the limited dimensional realm of a humanly devised systematic theology. Easier to fit the ocean into a test tube, or gather all the mountains into a petri dish, than to press the thoughts and methods of an infinite God into the Lilliputian cage of human logic. If the Bible contains no clear answer or explanation to a given question, isn't it foolish to plug our limited logic into problem passages in order to manufacture "truths"—and then call them biblical and argue over them?

We serve a precise God. Virtually every major biblical doctrine demands knife-edge precision as we work our way back and forth balanced on the tightwire stretched between two unambiguous and equally valid poles of truth. One footfall too far, one step—however reasonable—beyond the biblical data in either direction, topples one toward heresy. The effort to reconcile the issues of election and free will, of divine determination and human responsibility, is no different. It is a "quest [that] stands upon the edge of a knife."[2] There is little room to stray.

The key to not overstepping the boundary is not easy but it is relatively simple. Learn to see and accept where the Bible draws a line. Distinguish between express statements of Scripture and logical leaps—extensions that may make sense but do not enjoy the "luxury" of explicit biblical affirmation. Trace the branches to the limbs to the trunk of the tree of biblical revelation; but where the trunk disappears below the surface of the ground (into the realm of the unrevealed "secret things"), it is both idle and dangerous to dig with the spade of human logic. It may make for interesting speculative debates. But it does not make for sound theology.

It is no accident that Paul concludes what is arguably his most logically and theologically profound (and, consequently, his most difficult and debated) passage with this exclamation: "O the depth of the riches both of the wisdom and knowledge of God! how *unsearchable* are his judgments, and his ways *past finding out!*" (Romans 11:33).

Terms of the Debate

In the debate over the mechanics of soteriology, problems arise when we fail to observe and consistently maintain precise, scripturally accurate definitions for the terms involved. We ought not be gun-shy about explicitly biblical terms. Are believers actually elected (chosen) by God? There is no question about that (II Thessalonians 2:13). Were believers actually chosen (elected) by God even before He ever created the world? Yes

(Ephesians 1:4). Did God predestinate all whom He foreknew to be conformed to the image of His Son? Without question (Romans 8:28-29).

On the other side, if divine election is a fact, are we still responsible to communicate the message of the gospel? Of course (Matthew 28:18-20). Are individuals responsible to respond to the gospel in order to be saved? Certainly (John 3:16, 36). Are we incapable of responding to the gospel without the previous drawing of God? Jesus said so (John 6:44). Are those who fail to respond to the gospel accountable for their damnation? Undoubtedly (II Thessalonians 1:7-9).

Do these truths wreak havoc on our logical systems of theology or undercut our pet explanations of God's actions and our responsibility? Probably. How could it be otherwise? We are time-bound, earth-bound creatures wrestling with eternal truths about an infinite God. We are in the realm of the secret things. Why, then, are we afraid to say, "I don't really comprehend this, but God says it. I don't understand how this command fits with this truth, but I'll believe the truth and obey the command, and leave the understanding to God." There is something, after all, to the old bumper sticker mentality that "God said it. I believe it. That settles it"—although it might be better turned, "God says it. That settles it. So I believe it."

The moment we insist—in order for a passage to fit the context of our theological system—that "world" does not really mean "world" but "world of the elect," or that if God elects some to believe then He obviously must elect others to damnation, or that election "according to foreknowledge" must refer to God's foreknowledge of who would respond,[3] we have just stepped off the foundation of explicit biblical statement and into the realm of systematic theological logic. "But it must be this way," someone protests, "or it just doesn't make sense." Make sense to whom?

Several illustrations have been suggested in an attempt to resolve the tension. Some pose the analogy of a railroad track. Two distinct tracks run parallel into the distance where, to the naked eye, the tracks appear to run together and become one; yet they remain distinct and parallel. Others note that every coin has two sides. You may examine one side fully and carefully, then turn the coin over and inspect the other side in great detail. But, hold it at whatever angle you will, you will never be able to see completely or focus fully on both sides at once. Many biblical truths fit such analogies. The question of divine determination and human responsibility in salvation is no different, giving rise to a popular soteriologically specific illustration: an individual voluntarily enters a banquet hall under a banner that reads, "Whosoever will, let him come"; upon entering, however, he looks over the inside doorway and reads a different banner: "Chosen in Christ before the foundation of the world." How does this work? I don't know, and neither does anyone else. But there are passages that address this very dynamic of polarity in the context of soteriology.

Examples of Textual Tension

Many of the standard proof texts have been badly battered and buffeted from centuries of debate. We all have our rational ripostes to those texts at the ready, hands hovering over our theological holsters. In His wisdom, however, God has given to us a surprising and gratifying array of verses that incorporate, within a single verse, both facets of the theological debate. Note the Spirit-inspired juxtaposition of divine will (**bold**) and human responsibility (*italics*) in the verses below. Most are self-explanatory. Some merit an additional observation.

Matthew 11:20-28. "Then began he to upbraid the cities wherein most of his mighty works were done, because they repented not. . . . At that time Jesus answered and said, I thank thee, O Father, Lord of heaven and earth, because **thou hast hid these things** from the wise and prudent, **and hast revealed them** unto babes. Even so, Father: for so it seemed good in thy sight. All things are delivered unto me of my Father: and no man knoweth the Son, but the Father; **neither knoweth any man the Father, save the Son, and he to whomsoever the Son will reveal him.** *Come unto me, all ye that labour and are heavy laden,* and I will give you rest."

Luke 22:22. "And truly the Son of man goeth, **as it was determined**: but *woe unto that man by whom he is betrayed!*"

Matthew 23:37. "O Jerusalem, Jerusalem . . . **how often would I have gathered** thy children together, even as a hen gathereth her chickens under her wings, and *ye would not!*"

John 6:37. "**All that the Father giveth me shall come** [ηκω, to arrive] to me; and *him that cometh* [ερχομαι, to come] to me I will in no wise cast out." This is quite startling. To argue that the explicit change in verbs is capricious or insignificant is to dismiss the deliberate word choice of the Son of God and the superintending inspiration of the Holy Spirit. All those whom the Father gives to the Son will arrive; whoever comes voluntarily will not be cast out.

John 6:44, 45, 64-65. "**No man can come to me except the Father . . . draw him.** . . . Every man therefore that hath heard, and hath learned of the Father, *cometh* unto me. . . . But there are *some of you that believe not.* . . . Therefore said I unto you that **no man can come unto me, except it were given unto him of my Father**." And yet Jesus only a little earlier said, "*Ye will not come unto me* [lit., "*You are not willing to come to me*"], that ye might have life" (John 5:40).

Acts 13:48.[4] "**And as many as were ordained to eternal life** *believed*"—an inscrutable echo of Jesus' words from the preceding passages in John 6.

Acts 16:14. "And a certain woman named Lydia, . . . heard us: **whose heart the Lord opened**, [so] that *she attended unto the things which were spoken of* [by] *Paul*." The latter phrase literally reads, "**whose heart the Lord opened** *to heed the things spoken by Paul*."

I Corinthians 3:6. "*I have planted, Apollos watered*; but **God gave the increase**." The same principle applies to both evangelistic ministry and the individual experience of salvation.

I Thessalonians 1:3-4. "Remembering without ceasing *your work of faith, and labour of love, and patience of hope* in our Lord Jesus Christ, in the sight of God and our Father; knowing, brethren beloved, **your election of God**." How could Paul possibly "know" their election? By observing their response to the Word. Note verse 6, "And *ye became followers* of us, and of the Lord." In other words, Paul's "knowledge of their election was an intuitive conviction based upon known and observed facts."[5]

APPENDIX E

II Thessalonians 2:13-14. "But we are bound to give thanks always to God for you, brethren beloved of the Lord, because **God hath from the beginning chosen you to salvation** THROUGH **sanctification of the Spirit** AND *belief of the truth*: whereunto he called you by our gospel, to the obtaining of the glory of our Lord Jesus Christ." This remarkable passage juxtaposes the two poles of the soteriological paradox. "The salvation of believers rests on the divine choice, not on human effort";[6] yet there are "two aspects or sides of the element in which the divine choice realizes itself—the divine or objective aspect, sanctification by the Spirit; and the human or subjective aspect, believing reception of the truth."[7]

Do any of these, as they stand, do damage to the neat logic of our theological system? Let them. To do otherwise—to redefine the words, to tinker with the terminology, to run the verses through the sieve of a theological system—is to make human logic the line by which we gauge whether God's explicit statements are completely true and plumb as they stand or whether they need a little adjustment here, a little refinement there. We dare not construct a system of theology that helps the Holy Spirit by refining or redefining the words He selected or by interposing words He chose to omit so as to tweak out of it, ever so gently, a slightly modified meaning that better fits the system.

Noteworthy Remarks

Some theologians, willing to set aside the stringent logical demands of a theological system (even their own), have understood the limitations of logic, the need for balance, and the necessity of sticking with the explicit statements of Scripture. Reflecting on the John 6 passages cited above, Scottish Presbyterian David Brown remarked:

> Pity that, in the attempts to reconcile these [the divine drawing and the human coming], so much vain and unsavory controversy has been spent, and that one of them is so often sacrificed to the other; for then they are not what Jesus says they are, but rather a caricature of them. The link of connection between divine and human operation will probably never be reached on earth—if even in heaven. Let us then implicitly receive and reverently hold both; remembering, however, that the divine in this case

ever precedes, and is the cause of, the human—the 'drawing' on God's part of the 'coming' on ours; while yet our coming is as purely spontaneous, and the result of rational considerations presenting themselves to our minds, as if there were no supernatural operation in the matter at all.[8]

The theological balance is beautiful, allowing every passage to say precisely and fully what it says—no more and no less.

No one could doubt the fervent evangelistic tenor of the ministry of Charles Haddon Spurgeon, a staunch Baptist Calvinist. In a sermon on Esther, he observes that "the divine will is accomplished, and yet men are perfectly free agents." Logic rebels. How can that be? Spurgeon answers the objection:

> "I cannot understand it," says one. My dear friend, I am compelled to say the same—I do not understand it either. . . . Certain of my brethren deny free agency, and so get out of the difficulty; others assert that there is no predestination, and so cut the knot. As I do not wish to get out of the difficulty, and have no wish to shut my eyes to any part of the truth, I believe both predestination and free agency to be facts. How they can be made to agree I do not know, or care to know; I am satisfied to know anything which God chooses to reveal to me, and equally content not to know what he does not reveal. . . . Believe these two truths and you will see them in practical agreement in daily life, though you will not be able to devise a theory for harmonizing them on paper.[9]

The scriptural poise is perfect, permitting paradoxical truths to stand in tension to one another without subjecting the declarations of an infinite God to the scrutiny of my finite understanding.

This approach is not novel. We have all sung John Newton's words about this mysterious balance many times:

> **'Twas grace that taught my heart to fear,** and grace
>   my fears relieved;
> How precious did that grace appear the hour *I first*
>   *believed.*

Daniel Whittle captures the balance even more explicitly in this well-known hymn:

> I know not how *this saving faith* **to me He did impart,**
> Nor how *believing in His Word* wrought peace within
>   my heart.
> I know not how **the Spirit moves,** convincing men of sin,
> Revealing Jesus through the Word, **creating** *faith in Him.*

Earlier in this essay I used the analogy of a tensioned tightwire of truth stretched between two paradoxical poles. Here is another someone has suggested. Theology is structured like an arch. One side does not make an arch. It takes the tension of both sides pressing against each other in opposite directions to hold the keystone in place. In the final analysis, does the arch hold up the keystone, or does the keystone hold up the arch? Yes.

Drawing Conclusions

Carefully consider the following questions and, more importantly, the explicit wording of the accompanying references. Is election sovereign and unconditional or is it activated in accordance with human response? The answer is yes (II Thessalonians 2:13). Does salvation involve effectual grace or the exercise of free will? Yes (I Thessalonians 2:13). Did Christ die for the sins of the world or for the elect? Yes (John 1:29; 3:16; 10:11). Will the elect be certainly, sovereignly, and graciously converted or are we obligated to proclaim the gospel to all men? Yes (John 6:37; Matthew 28:18-20). Are the events of human history orchestrated by divine decree or is there a genuine element of human responsibility which affects circumstances? Yes (Acts 2:23).

Does all this sit well with our natural curiosity and human logic? The answer is no. So what? The bottom line, the final court of appeal, must be the explicit statement of Scripture—not our satisfaction that all bases have been covered and all questions answered, not our sense of logical harmony, and not our theological comfort with where the chips seem to fall. Can the emphasis on one side of the truth be blown out of proportion, leading to the abuse of the other side? Certainly. What, then, is the solution? Side with the half of the truth with which we are more comfortable? But that is to deny the other half of the truth. Should we insist that the "real" truth must lie somewhere in the middle? But that is to deny both halves, both poles of the truth in the fullness of their scriptural presentation. May we not, must we not, fully hold both truths in balanced tension?

The profound insight of Charles Simeon on the paradoxical terminology of Scripture is equally convicting to all sides of the debate and deserves both sober reflection and personal application.

> The author is disposed to think that the Scripture system is of a broader and more comprehensive character than some very dogmatic theologians are inclined to avow; and that, as wheels in a complicated machine may move in opposite directions and yet subserve one common end, so may truths apparently opposite be perfectly reconcilable with each other and equally subserve the purposes of God in the accomplishment of man's salvation. The author feels it impossible to avow too distinctly that it is an invariable rule with him to endeavor to give every portion of the Word of God its full and proper force, without considering what scheme it favors, or whose system it is likely to advance. Of this he is sure, that there is not a decided Calvinist or Arminian in the world who equally approves of the whole of Scripture . . . who, if he had been in the company of St. Paul whilst he was writing his Epistles, would not have recommended him to alter one or other of his expressions.

> But the author would not wish one of them altered; he finds as much satisfaction in one class of passages as in another; and employs the one, he believes, as freely as the other. Where the inspired Writers speak in unqualified terms, he thinks himself at liberty to do the same; judging that they needed no instruction from him how to propagate the truth. He is content to sit as a learner at the feet of the holy Apostles, and has no ambition to teach them how they ought to have spoken. I love the simplicity of the Scriptures; and I wish to receive and inculcate every truth precisely in the way, and to the extent, that it is set forth in the inspired Volume. Were this the habit of all divines, there would soon be an end of most of the controversies that have agitated and divided the Church of Christ. My endeavour is to bring out of Scripture what is there, and not to thrust in what I think

might be there. I have a great jealousy on this head; never to speak more or less than I believe to be the mind of the Spirit in the passage I am expounding.[10]

This is not theological schizophrenia; this is respect for the biblical text in the form in which it was inspired (we are verbal inspirationists, are we not?) over respect for a humanly devised system of arranging it. Some have emphasized the biblical assertion of God's election to the neglect of evangelism and the necessity of a personal profession of faith. Logical? Perhaps, but dead wrong. Is the solution, then, to throw out or redefine the explicit biblical assertion of election? Is not the solution to insist that the same God who sovereignly elects also sovereignly commands us to evangelize? And that the gospel we are commanded to declare demands obedience and personal profession?[11] We must hold both simultaneously, since both are explicitly asserted. Rightly and biblically understood, election does not hinder evangelism; it encourages it by insuring that some *will* respond.

Again, some become so protective of human freedom and responsibility that the very thought of election is regarded as a heretical threat to an evangelistic ministry. Logical, maybe, but wrong. The comfort, encouragement and humbling wonder of election—identified by Paul in Ephesians 1 as one of the "spiritual blessings" for which we are to bless God—is forfeited. We diminish God's glory when we forget that it was solely God's initiative that secured and effected our salvation.[12] Is the solution, then, to rationalize away the explicit "whosoever wills" of the Bible and reject real free will as a farce? Is not the only genuinely biblical solution to acknowledge the explicit revelation that God chose before the foundation of the world and calls all men everywhere to repent and to believe and obey the gospel? Each of us is responsible to compel our logic to bow submissively at the altar of divine revelation. Rightly and biblically understood, free will does not contradict divine election; God's Spirit effectually *persuades* the elect to become *voluntary* participants in His saving grace. David Brown captured this tension in his quotation already cited above.

Our ultimate allegiance must not be to human logic or systems of theology. Our consciences and our theology must be held captive by the explicit statements of the Word of God—whether or not it answers all our questions, whether or not the results appear to fit together logically. The truth of Isaiah 55:8-9 must be free to govern our theology as much as it governs our acceptance of circumstances.

The Lord's interrogation of Job dramatically demonstrates the deficiency of our knowledge of God and His ways. With our wealth of translations, commentaries, and theologies, there is a tendency to think that we can systematize God, explain all His past actions, pigeonhole His present doings, and predict His future plans in minute detail. There is, to be sure, a foundational body of truth in the Scriptures of which we can be certain. Nevertheless, even when we speak what we know is true and right and in accordance with clear revelation, we must confess with Job that we are speaking of things we do not understand, things too wonderful for us to know (Job 42:3).

In short, we do not know as much as we think we know, and only an infinitesimal fraction of what there is to know. This does not deny our possession of absolute, objective truth. But it is a candid acknowledgment that there is a vast amount of truth about God to which we do not have access and which we are simply not big enough to comprehend. The secret things still belong to the Lord.

In the difficult questions of theology that have been debated for centuries by wise and godly men in the church, our attitude should be humbly instructed by the response of Job to God. We must acknowledge and remember our smallness (40:4), our ignorance (42:3), and God's undiluted freedom to do what He pleases, when and how He chooses (42:2)—and to reveal it in whatever way He sees fit. Accepting all of God's Word as it stands and waiting till we see Him to have all our questions answered is the essence of theological humility (42:5-6).

May God help us to discern the often thin line between scriptural statement and human logic, to herald the former with confidence, to hold the latter with deference, and to be governed in creed and conduct by the whole counsel of God.

NOTES

Chapter 1

[1] Charles and Jean Hurlburt were my wife's uncle and aunt. See "When Seemingly Senseless Tragedy Strikes," *Frontline* 5, no. 3 (1995) (also available at magazine's website at www.f-b-f.org).

[2] John Newton, *Out of the Depths: An Autobiography* (Chicago: Moody Press, n.d.), Letters VII-VIII, pp. 64-79.

[3] Cf. R. C. Sproul, *The Invisible Hand* (Dallas: Word Publishing, 1996), pp. 118-19; Edward M. Panosian, "The Providence of God in History" in Edward M. Panosian, David A. Fisher, and Mark Sidwell, *The Providence of God in History* (Greenville, S.C.: Bob Jones University Press, 1996), pp. 14-15.

[4] See "Trusting Amidst Medical Crises," *Frontline* 6, no. 3 (1996) (also available at the magazine's website at www.f-b-f.org).

[5] Panosian, p. 17.

[6] One of the lesser-known but riveting accounts of this story is *Unfolding Destinies* (Grand Rapids: Discovery House, 1998) by Olive Fleming Liefeld, wife of martyred missionary Pete Fleming.

[7] William S. Plumer, *Jehovah-Jireh: A Treatise on Providence* (1865; reprint, Harrisonburg, Va.: Sprinkle Publications, 1993), p. 10.

[8] For twenty-five years Abraham has clung tenaciously to nothing but the naked word of God alone. Scripture records seven distinct occasions on which God promised Abraham a child: (1) Gen. 12:1-3 (when Abraham is 75); (2) Gen. 12:7 (after Abraham surveys the land); (3) Gen. 13:14-17 (after Lot's departure); (4) Gen. 15:4-6 (after the rescue of Lot); (5) Gen. 15:18 (with a solemn covenant); (6) Gen. 17:1-8, 15-19, 21 (when Abraham is 99), and (7) Gen. 18:9-14.

[9] God's wise providence in allowing these deprivations as well as His goodness in bestowing their ordinary functions mirrors his ability to meet any emergency Moses might have suggested" (Walter C. Kaiser Jr., "Deuteronomy" in *Expositor's Bible Commentary*, vol. 2 [Grand Rapids: Zondervan, 1990], p. 328). One also wonders if God's words do not suggest a veiled threat to Moses. Moses has received a mouth and, with it, the capacity to speak from the creating hand of a gracious God. Rather than submitting that instrument and capacity to the Creator's calling, however, Moses repeatedly attempts to excuse his disobedience. The attentive reader can sense God's rising displeasure with

Moses' respectful but entrenched insubordination to Him, culminating in the explicit reference to God's anger in 4:14. Is God hinting in 4:11 that just as He was the one who gave Moses the ability to speak, He is the one who can remove it as well? The principle at least is valid elsewhere that the one who refuses to use his gifts in the service of the King will lose those gifts, and their rewards, to others who are faithfully submitted (Matt. 13:12; Luke 19:26).

[10]For one of the most thorough and thoughtful attempts to answer the question of why, see Joni Eareckson Tada and Steven Estes, *When God Weeps: Why Our Sufferings Matter to the Almighty* (Grand Rapids: Zondervan, 1997), chapters 7-9. Tada pens this portion of the book from the authority of painful personal experience coupled with a profoundly Bible-centered orientation. This book lacks the meticulous thoroughness and theological dignity of Puritan John Flavel's *Mystery of Providence*. It falls short of the thorough and systematic arrangement of biblical material in Jerry Bridges's *Trusting God*. Yet it is more focused than both of these on the relation of providence to suffering. For those of us who have, as yet, suffered little, it confronts with the reality of suffering around us and cajoles us to cultivate a more thoughtful empathy toward others. For all readers, it issues a call to avert our myopic gaze from ourselves and our circumstances to the presence and purposes of a sovereign and loving God in our midst. For an analysis of this book as a whole, see the author's review in *Biblical Viewpoint* (April 1999): 97-101.

[11]*Deuteronomy* (Nashville: Broadman & Holman, 1994), p. 424.

[12]*The Book of Deuteronomy* (Grand Rapids: William B. Eerdmans, 1976), pp. 388-89.

[13]"There are favourable or smiling providences and there are what appear to be dark, cross or frowning providences. If, as we believe, a frowning providence comes from the hand of the same Father as a smiling providence how can we reconcile these things?" (John J. Murray, *Behind a Frowning Providence* [Carlisle, Pa.: Banner of Truth Trust, 1990, p. 11). Despite his confidence in this truth, that becomes one of Job's central questions.

[14]Derek Kidner, *Psalms 1-72: An Introduction and Commentary*, vol. 14a of Tyndale Old Testament Commentaries (Downers Grove, Ill.: Inter-Varsity Press, 1973), p. 243.

[15]Derek Kidner, *A Time to Mourn and a Time to Dance: The Message of Ecclesiastes* (Downers Grove, Ill.: Inter-Varsity Press, 1976), p. 68.

[16]Kidner.

[17]You have probably noticed by now the word "LORD" in all uppercase letters. For those who may not be aware, there are several names and titles for God in the Old Testament. "LORD" is the consistent translational device to designate when the personal, covenant name of the one true God—Jehovah, or

Yahweh—appears in the Hebrew. It is the name derived from the verb "I AM," which God has taken as His eternal designation (see Exod. 3:13-15) and which denotes several facets of His character (self-existence, changelessness, all-sufficiency). So this Isaiah passage, for instance, is not arguing merely that there is only one true God who may go by many names (Allah, Buddha, Jesus, etc.). It is specifying that the God named Yahweh, the God of the Jews, is that one and only true God.

[18]"The commonest question is whether I really 'believe in the Devil.' Now, if by 'the Devil' you mean a power opposite to God and, like God, self-existent from all eternity, the answer is certainly No. There is no uncreated being except God. God has no opposite. . . . Satan, the leader or dictator of devils, is the opposite, not of God, but of Michael" (C. S. Lewis, *The Screwtape Letters* [New York: Macmillan Publishing, 1961], p. vii).

[19]Jeremiah 32:17 literally reads, ". . . not [too] wonderful for you is any thing [or word]." In English it is simpler to rearrange the syntax by attaching the negative to the noun: "nothing is too wonderful for you." The meaning is the same.

[20]The NASB reverses the word order here to "good and evil," though a marginal note concedes that the original order is "evil and good." Though we are more accustomed to speaking of "good and evil" rather than *vice versa*, Bo Johnson sees the original word order as significant and suggestive of Jeremiah's encouragement to the people to hope in God: yes, evil (i.e., disciplinary judgment) has come from God, but good will follow from God as well ("Form and Message in Lamentations," *Zeitschrift Für Die Alttestimentliche Wissenschaft* 97, [1985], p. 67).

[21]The word here is *rhema*. Like its Old Testament counterpart, *dabar*, it can be used in the indefinite sense of "thing" or "matter." Also like *dabar*, however, it is one of the key biblical words for communication generally ("word") and for God's revelation in particular. *Rhema* specifically denotes words, utterances, specific sayings, statements. In defense of this assertion that *rhema* here should be understood not merely in the generic sense of "thing" but the more specific sense of "saying," it is worth noting that F. W. Danker's most recent revision of William F. Arndt's and F. W. Gingrich's standard Greek-English lexicon seems to make room for this interpretation. He lists two definitions for *rhema*: (1) **that which is said, *word, saying, expression or statement of any kind***, and (2) after the Hebrew **an event that can be spoken about, *thing, object, matter, event***. The first example listed under 2 is Luke 1:37. This revised definition appears to reflect a tacit recognition that the concept of speech is native to the word *rhema* even in apparently generic contexts (*A Greek-English Lexicon of the New Testament and Other Early Christian Literature*, revised and edited by F. W. Danker [Chicago: University of Chicago Press, 2000], p. 905). In any case, the context itself seems to be the most decisive argument that the specific "thing" in mind in

each of these passages is the explicit word that the Lord has spoken; however implausible or impossible that promise or prediction might appear, its fulfill-ment is guaranteed, for nothing God says will be impossible for Him to per-form.

[22]For more on finite theism, see Millard Erickson, *Christian Theology* (Grand Rapids: Baker, 1985), pp. 414-17. He also discusses and rebuts another alternative—an excessive Calvinistic determinism (represented by, for example, Gordon Clark) that essentially redefines our notion of "good" to include *whatever* happens, making God the ultimate cause of all things, including sin (pp. 417-19).

[23]Harold S. Kushner, *When Bad Things Happen to Good People* (New York: Avon Books, 1983), p. 43. Kushner cites the example of "an earthquake that kills thousands of innocent victims without reason" (p. 59). Such statements dis-play an unwitting arrogance, an assumed omniscience that (1) the victims are "innocent," and that (2) no good reason for such an event exists, simply because we cannot think of one.

[24]John Boykin, *Circumstances and the Role of God* (Grand Rapids: Zonder-van, 1986), p. 42. Steven Estes bluntly rebuts Boykin's conclusion: "No, the real tragedy is that any Christian would settle for such darkness with the light of the Bible shining so clearly. If God didn't control evil, evil would be uncontrolled. God permits what he hates to achieve what he loves" (*When God Weeps*, p. 84).

[25]*Trusting God* (Colorado Springs: NAVPRESS, 1988), p. 24.

[26]Bridges spends the first three chapters in *Trusting God* establishing the vital connection between God's sovereignty (providence) and His trustworthiness.

[27]Bridges, pp. 110, 114, original emphasis.

Chapter 2

[1]Edward M. Panosian, "The Providence of God in History" in Edward M. Panosian, David A. Fisher, and Mark Sidwell, *The Providence of God in History* (Greenville, S.C.: Bob Jones University Press, 1996), p. 13.

[2]Wilbur Tillett, "Providence," *The International Standard Bible Encyclopedia*, vol. 4 (Grand Rapids: Eerdmans, 1956), p. 2476.

[3]W. B. Pope, *Compendium of Christian Theology* (vol. 1, 456), cited by Tillett.

[4]J. I. Packer, "Providence," *New Bible Dictionary*, ed. J. D. Douglas (Grand Rapids: Eerdmans, 1962), p. 1051.

[5]Stewart Custer, *Witness to Christ: A Commentary on Acts* (Greenville, S.C.: BJU Press, 2000), p. 338.

NOTES FOR CHAPTER 2

[6]H. C. Leupold, *Exposition of Genesis* (Grand Rapids: Baker Book House, 1942), p. 631.

[7]The purposeful repetition in these verses indicates that God intends to make a point, which raises a practical and pertinent question. In light of the explicit assertions of these verses, is it *biblical* to say that God put a William Jefferson Clinton, or a George III, or a Bloody Mary, or a Hitler in charge of his (or her) respective government? It is the only biblical conclusion one can draw. Does that suggest God's approval of such people? Certainly not. But the dynamics of such events within the workings of providence must be discussed elsewhere.

[8]Notice the explicit terminology in this progression of verses in Jonah: "the LORD sent . . . spake . . . prepared." If the reader will allow a slight liberty in terminology for the sake of alliteration, God exercises His providence directly over weather (1:4), "whales" (1:17; 2:10), weeds (4:6), worms (4:7), and wind (4:8)!

[9]*Systematic Theology*, vol. 1 (Hendrickson Publishers, reprint 1999), pp. 575, 581. Charles Hodge devotes an entire chapter (forty pages) to the subject of providence.

[10]*Outlines in Theology* (1860; reprint, Carlisle, Pa.: Banner of Truth, 1983), p. 258. A. A. Hodge gives twenty pages to the topic of providence.

[11]Tillett, p. 2476.

[12]*Concise Dictionary of Christian Theology* (Grand Rapids: Baker, 1986), p. 136.

[13]N. M. deS. Cameron, "Providence," *New Dictionary of Theology*, ed. Sinclair B. Ferguson, David F. Wright, and J. I. Packer (Downers Grove, Ill.: Inter-Varsity, 1988), p. 541.

[14]Packer, pp. 1050-51.

[15]The doctrine of providence can also be dissected by crosscutting it in a slightly different direction. Some differentiate between *general* providence and *special* providence. Puritan John Flavel voices this understanding of providence: "There is a twofold consideration of Providence, according to its twofold object and manner of dispensation; the one in general, exercised about all creatures, rational and irrational, animate and inanimate; the other special and peculiar" (*The Mystery of Providence* [1678; reprint, Carlisle, Pa.: Banner of Truth, 1995], p. 27). *General* providence encompasses all creation, whereas *special* providence focuses especially on man. Theologian G. C. Berkouwer notes a third category of "*very special* providence," which "is limited to believers" (*The Providence of God* [Grand Rapids: Eerdmans, 1952], p. 194). I have chosen to focus instead on the simpler division between preserving and governing providence, both of which extend over all creation generally as well as men (and believers) particularly, as more in keeping with its manifestation and expression in the Bible.

[16]Murray, p. 11.

[17]This definition concisely answers every inductive question about "miracle." *What* is it? (a supernatural act) *Who* does it? (God) *Where* does it happen? (in the natural world) *When* does it happen? (in the natural course of human experience) *How* does it happen? (by exercising His authority over His creation) *Why* does it happen? (to reveal truth about Himself)

[18]In fact, throughout the Bible, God (generally through His spokesmen) utilizes three primary teaching methods: (1) explanation (through discourses), (2) illustration (through parables and metaphors), and (3) demonstration (through miracles). These observations have direct significance for a proper evaluation of the ministry of Christ in particular.

[19]R. C. Sproul, *The Invisible Hand* (Dallas: Word Publishing, 1996), pp.156-57.

[20]Packer, p. 1051.

[21]William Shakespeare, *King Henry V*, Act III, Scene 5.

Chapter 3

[1]John Flavel, *The Mystery of Providence* (1678; reprint, Carlisle, Pa.: Banner of Truth, 1995), p. 28.

[2]In other words, Henry Alford explains, "*out of* God we should have no *Life*, nor even *movement*, nay, not any *existence* at all" (*Alford's Greek Testament*, vol. 2 [Grand Rapids: Guardian Press, 1976], p. 206.

[3]*The Analytical Greek Lexicon* (Grand Rapids: Zondervan, 1977), p. 231, citing this verse specifically.

[4]Acts 17:28*a* comprises a quotation from Epimenides the Cretan. See Stewart Custer, *Witness to Christ: A Commentary on Acts* (Greenville, S.C.: BJU Press, 2000), pp. 253-54; cf. Richard N. Longenecker's commentary on Acts in *The Expositor's Bible Commentary*, vol. 9 (Grand Rapids: Zondervan, 1981), pp. 476-77.

[5]Heathen poets "as creatures of God confronted with divine revelation were capable of responses which were valid so long as and to the extent that they stood in isolation from their pagan systems. Thus, thoughts which in their pagan system were quite un-Christian and anti-Christian, could be acknowledged as up to a point involving an actual apprehension of revealed truth" (Ned Stonehouse, *The Areopagus Address* [London, 1949], p. 37; cited by F. F. Bruce, *The Book of Acts* [Grand Rapids: Eerdmans, 1981], p. 360).

[6]"Paul appeals to God, who 'gives life to' (*zoogonountos*, 'preserves alive') everything" (Ralph Earle, *1, 2 Timothy* in *The Expositor's Bible Commentary*, vol. 11 [Grand Rapids: Zondervan, 1978], p. 386).

[7]The context is instructive. Confronted with the rebellious threat of Korah to usurp his authority, Moses responds to God's wrathful declaration that He will destroy the rebels on the spot (Num. 16:20-21) by appealing to Him as "the God of the spirits of all flesh"—acknowledging that He alone retains the sovereign right to give life and to remove it. The title reflects a truth to which Moses apparently grew fond of appealing, for he uses it again in Numbers 27:16.

[8]Steve Estes, *When God Weeps: Why Our Sufferings Matter to the Almighty* (Grand Rapids: Zondervan, 1997), p. 53.

[9]Cited by Marvin Olasky, "Winning the South," *World* (May 16, 1998), p. 30.

[10]This is a classic line of reasoning employed by atheists and agnostics. For a detailed analysis of this argument and a penetrating response, see John Blanchard, *Does God Believe in Atheists?* (Auburn, Mass.: Evangelical Press, 2000), pp. 499-554.

[11]Despite the similar absence of any written revelation in his day, Job reflected an exquisite understanding of God's sovereign rule over all the events of his life, good and bad: "The Lord gave and the Lord hath taken away. . . . What? Shall we receive good at the hand of God and shall we not receive evil [at the hand of the Lord]?" (Job 1:21; 2:10).

[12]Blanchard, p. 487.

[13]Blanchard recounts a humorously illustrative anecdote. Rising to face a sneering, raucous audience of unbelieving college students whom he was to address, he relates that he decided to employ "shock tactics." He asked them, " 'Have you ever seen a pig giving thanks to God before eating its food?' This produced a puzzled murmur, so I repeated the question and asked them to shout the answer. There was a loud and unanimous 'No!' 'Then let me ask you another question,' I went on. 'Do *you* give thanks to God before eating your food?' This produced another bewildered buzz, but as soon as I interrupted by asking, 'What is your answer?', a massive 'No!' echoed around the hall. 'Thank you very much,' I responded. 'That is a great help to me. You see, I have never been to this school before, and I knew nothing about you. Now I know at least one thing: as far as giving thanks for your food is concerned, you are on the same level as pigs!' " It worked, "and from then on they were as quiet as mice. I admit this was a pretty crude approach, but why would an atheist want to object?" p. 487.

[14]*Mere Christianity* (Nashville: Broadman & Holman, 1980), p. 182.

Chapter 4

[1]The heavenly "host" in Nehemiah 9:6 is traditionally understood to refer to celestial bodies (planets and stars) rather than celestial beings (angels)—consequently, this reference is also included under the next point regarding God's providential preservation of the cosmos. However, the parallelism of the terminology seems to suggest three spheres and their respective inhabitants, all of whom God sustains with life. "Preservest," a Piel form of *chayah,* nearly always refers to giving life to someone or preserving the life of a living being, though it can be used metaphorically with reference to inanimate objects (I Chron. 11:8; Neh. 4:2).

[2]There is some debate over the precise translation of Psalm 104:4 ("He maketh his angels spirits, his ministers a flame of fire"). The translational choice of the NASB and other modern versions is probably unfortunate ("He makes the winds His messengers, flaming fire His ministers"). The flexibility of the Hebrew allows either translation, but the fact that the unambiguous LXX translation is cited to support the point being made in Hebrews 1:7 argues strongly in favor of the traditional translation (see Derek Kidner, *Psalms 73-150* [Downers Grove: Inter-Varsity Press, 1975], p. 369). Underscoring the relevance of Psalm 104:4 to the present argument, Westcott notes that "the Greek Fathers lay stress on the word ["who maketh"] as marking the angels as created beings" (*The Epistle to the Hebrews* [1889; reprint, Grand Rapids: Eerdmans, 1974], p. 25).

[3]*Commentary on the Whole Bible,* vol. 3 (McLean, Va.: MacDonald Publishing, n.d.), p. 628.

[4]See note 1.

[5]E. J. Young, *The Book of Isaiah,* vol. 3 (Grand Rapids: Eerdmans, 1972), p. 57. "One would not be impressed with the knowledge that God is the Creator," Young adds, "unless God continually upheld His creation."

[6]Commenting on Matthew 6:26, D. A. Carson remarks, "The point is not that the disciple need not work—birds do not simply wait for God to drop food into their beaks—but that they need not fret. Disciples may further strengthen their faith when they remember that God is in a special sense *their* Father (not the birds' Father), and that they are worth far more than birds" (*Expositor's Bible Commentary*, vol. 8 [Grand Rapids: Zondervan, 1984], p. 180).

[7]"If the created order testifies to God's 'eternal power and divine nature' (Rom. 1:20), it testifies equally to his providence. . . . This argument presupposes a biblical cosmology without which faith makes no sense. God is so sovereign over the universe that even the feeding of a wren falls within his concern. Because he normally does things in regular ways, there are 'scientific laws' to be

discovered; but the believer with eyes to see simultaneously discovers something about God and his activity" (Carson, p. 180).

[8]J. C. Ryle, *Expository Thoughts on Matthew* (1856; reprint, Carlisle, Pa.: Banner of Truth, 1995), p. 59.

[9]William R. Newell, *Hebrews Verse by Verse* (Chicago: Moody Press, 1947), p. 15.

[10]J. Gresham Machen, *The Christian View of Man* (1937; reprint, Carlisle, Pa.: Banner of Truth, 1984), pp. 91-92.

[11]Machen, pp. 97-98.

[12]John Eadie, *A Commentary on the Greek Text of the Epistle of Paul to the Colossians* (1884; reprint, Grand Rapids: Baker Book House, 1979), p. 57.

[13]A. H. Strong, *Systematic Theology* (Old Tappan, N.J.: Fleming H. Revell, 1907, 1979), p. 311.

[14]Eduard Lohse, *Hermeneia. A Critical and Historical Commentary on the Bible: Colossians and Philemon* (Philadelphia: Fortress Press, 1976); cited by Fritz Rienecker and Cleon Rogers, *Linguistic Key to the Greek New Testament* (Grand Rapids: Zondervan, 1980), p. 568.

[15]Eadie, pp. 57-58, emphasis added.

[16]G. C. Berkouwer correctly objects to a simplistic view of God's preserving providence as though it involved the mere upkeep of a static system. "But God sustains a world that is continually changing and progressively developing. Sustenance is directed toward an end. . . . Sustenance has to do with the entire process in which all things move toward God's arranged end" (*The Providence of God* [Grand Rapids: Eerdmans, 1952], pp. 74-75). This is precisely the point of the inspired terminology in Hebrews 1:3.

[17]Christ "upholds the universe not like Atlas supporting a dead weight on his shoulders, but as one who carries all things forward on their appointed course" (F. F. Bruce, *Hebrews* [Grand Rapids: Eerdmans, 1964], p. 6).

[18]Bruce, p. 6.

[19]J. B. Lightfoot, *Saint Paul's Epistles to the Colossians and to Philemon* (1879; reprint, Grand Rapids: Zondervan, 1976), p. 156.

[20]Newell, p. 13.

[21]An anonymous fifteenth-century text that appears in the second movement of John Rutter's choral work *The Falcon* (London: Collegium Records, 1991).

[22]Isaiah 45:22. Note the contextual connection between vv. 22 and 23, and its connection to Philippians 2:9-11.

Chapter 5

[1]Providential preservation "is not related to Divine government merely as that which preserves the stuff to be governed. It is also purposeful. Sustaining means that God's hand is in all that is and grows and develops according to His purpose. . . . For this reason, again, God's sustenance [preserving providence] and ruling [governing providence] cannot be viewed as two separate deeds. It is, in fact, impossible to think of God's sustaining without at once bringing the rule of God into the picture. . . . God in ruling the world leads it to its designed end, and that *in* this He continues to sustain the world; hence, sustaining and governing together form the one work of Providence" (G. C. Berkouwer, *The Providence of God* [Grand Rapids: Eerdmans, 1952], p. 75).

[2]An example of insisting on more than the Bible affirms is Gordon Clark's unabashed assertion that any and every sinful act is, of logical necessity, caused by God. If a man becomes drunk and murders his family, "it was the will of God that he should do it." He defends this by distinguishing between the preceptive will of God (what God commands) and decretive will of God (what God decrees to happen, which is, as it turns out, whatever happens). This may reduce the complicated experiences of reality to a logically tidy theological package, but such an approach bristles with ethical, moral, theological and exegetical problems. Millard Erickson briefly presents several cogent objections to this view (*Christian Theology* [Grand Rapids: Baker, 1985], pp. 417-19).

[3]*Basic Theology* (Colorado Springs: Chariot Victor Publishing, n.d.), p. 40.

[4]The assertion that God cannot tempt man is distinct from the reality that God may lead us into a place where we will be tempted. Implicit in the prayer "lead us not into temptation" is the recognition that God *may*, in fact, lead us into a temptation. After all, how many places on the earth are utterly devoid of temptation? God can, in answer to our prayer, protect us from the power and appeal of temptation in certain situations. Nevertheless, He often leads us to places and positions where He knows we will be tempted (which is why we are also instructed to pray "but deliver us from evil"). Even then, however, God never instigates or initiates the temptation. After his declaration that God can neither sin nor tempt, James goes on to explain how the temptation process works (James 1:13-16). In short, God cannot tempt us because of what He is; He does not need to tempt us because of what we are. The nature of our world and of our own flesh supply ample opportunity and inclination for us to sin. James caps this vital theological explanation with the admonition "Do not err on this point, my beloved brethren."

John Bunyan puts a very practical face on the importance of this prayer for deliverance from temptation. He attributed much of his struggle with assurance of salvation specifically to not praying that God would protect him from temp-tation: "when delivered from an earlier temptation [to doubt God's saving inter-est in him], I did not pray to God to keep me from later temptations. . . . I should also have prayed that the great God would keep me from the evil that was *before* me. . . . This I had not done, and so I was permitted to sin and fall, because I had not done Matthew 26:41. This truth means so much to me, right up to the present day, that I dare not, when I come before the Lord, get off my knees until I have entreated Him for help and mercy against the temptations that are to come. I plead with you, dear reader, that you also learn through my negligence and my afflictions that went on for days and months and years, so that you will beware" (*Grace Abounding to the Chief of Sinners* [Chicago: Moody Press, rewritten in modern English 1959], pp. 82-83).

[5]Literary genres incorporated into the Bible include narrative history, ge-nealogy, chronicle, prose, poetry, proverb, parable, suspense, law, testimony, drama, debate, philosophical treatise, symbolism, love song, allegory, prophetic oracle, riddle, epic, exposition, biography, autobiography, discourse, letter, ser-mon, theological treatise, hymn, creed, and apocalypse. In other words, God utilized an immense variety of literary media when He inspired the content of His revelation and directed the literary form it would take.

[6]We tend to emphasize the dissimilarity between the Old Testament and New Testament. Nevertheless, God communicated the *bulk* of His Old Testa-ment revelation in two major forms: (1) historical narrative (Genesis-Esther) and (2) prophetic preaching (Isaiah-Malachi). Similarly, God communicated the *bulk* of His New Testament revelation in two major forms: (1) historical narra-tive (Matthew-Acts) and (2) prophetic teaching (Romans-Revelation). This is admittedly a simplification, since both forms incorporate many of the genres listed above as well. For instance, the New Testament form of prophetic teach-ing usually takes the distinctive form of letters/epistles; nevertheless, the writ-ers were divinely designated spokesmen of God addressing His people in very practical, down-to-earth, historically occasioned situations—just as the prophets were divinely designated spokesmen of God addressing His people in very practical, down-to-earth, historically occasioned situations.

[7]The following outline of Joseph's theology, based on his own words about God, is as practical and penetrating as it is comprehensive.

- God is HOLY in His character and expectations (39:9).
- God is OMNISCIENT in His wisdom of our affairs and needs (40:8; 41:16).
- God is TRANSCENDANT in His self-revelation and communication (41:25, 28).

- God is INTERVENTIONAL in His activity in the affairs of men (41:25, 28, 32).
- God is GRACIOUS in His healing of our wounds (41:51).
- God is ABUNDANT in His blessing (41:52).
- God is TO BE FEARED for His knowledge of our actions (42:18, context).
- God is THE SOURCE OF ALL GRACE AND BLESSING in life (43:29).
- God is SUPREMELY SOVEREIGN in all the events of life (45:5, 7, 8, 9; 50:20).
- God OVERRULES in the evil experiences of life and turns them to His own purposes (45:5, 7, 8; 50:20).
- God VINDICATES and blesses those who fear and serve Him (45:8, 9).
- God is THE GIVER OF CHILDREN (48:9).
- God is THE ONLY RIGHTFUL EXERCISER OF MORAL VINDICATION AND VENGEANCE for personal injuries (50:19).
- God is FAITHFUL to keep His promises and DEPENDABLE to fulfill His word (50:24, 25).

Joseph's practice of the presence of God is a model for us as well. His speech about God is so ingrained in his behavior, such a normal and natural part of his conversation, that it affects those around him. Others who come into contact with Joseph begin talking about God, too, including his brothers (42:28; 44:16), his Egyptian servant (43:23), and even Pharaoh (41:38-39).

[8]One of the most egregious examples of this popular but misguided notion of Joseph's cockiness is Douglas Stuart's assessment in *How to Read the Bible for All Its Worth* (Grand Rapids: Zondervan, 1993), pp. 84-85. Stuart is distressingly oblivious to the plain implications of the text. He describes Joseph as an "over-confident, self-centered young man who seems to get into trouble so easily," and refers to "his arrogant dreams of superiority." All this is a speculative mis-reading between the lines, for the Holy Spirit breathes not a syllable of criticism against Joseph. He was, of course, a sinner. But God never lays the blame for what he suffered at the door of Joseph's indiscretion, still less at the door of Joseph's supposed arrogance or overconfidence. As the inspired narrative un-folds, it becomes incontrovertible that the dreams were not "Joseph's" dreams at all, but God-given assurances of His ultimate purpose for Joseph—revelations to which Joseph clung tenaciously with extraordinary faith in the face of all ap-pearances to the contrary.

[9]We need to remind ourselves again that Joseph possessed no written reve-lation from God. In the absence of any written record, dreams were a means of revelation commonly employed by God. It is worth noting that Joseph may well have learned from his father to take such dream revelations seriously. At the age

of six, he had the opportunity to observe both Jacob and Laban acting on the basis of revelatory direction they had received from God through dreams (Gen. 31:10, 11, 24, 29).

[10]My children are not preternaturally healthy eaters. The secret is to sauté the Brussels sprouts in butter.

[11]The "evil report" has been the subject of much discussion and, unfortunately, occasional misrepresentation. The phrase "their evil report" is curious and perhaps often misunderstood. The text does *not* read, "an evil report about them"—as though Joseph were inappropriately snitching on his brothers. *Nor* does it read, "a report of their evil"—as though Joseph were reporting their evil deeds. It is not *Joseph's* report at all; it is *"their* evil report." The word "report" itself is not a generic, neutral term. There are not good "reports" and bad "reports"; this word "report" is bad by definition. The Hebrew word, *dibbah,* carries the negative connotation of defamation, rumor, slander, misrepresentation. This is the same word for the evil report of the land brought by the spies—that is, a misrepresentation, a slander, against the good land God intended to give them (Numbers 13:32; 14:36, 37). Proverbs 10:18 uses the same word ("He that utters a slander is a fool"), as does Proverbs 25:10, which uses it with reference to one's bad reputation ("infamy"). Does this mean Joseph was maliciously slandering his brothers? No. Genesis 37:2 specifies that it was *their* slander/defamation that he "brought" (i.e., relayed) to their father. This seems to refer not to Joseph bringing a bad report of their actions, nor a report of their bad actions, but either (1) relaying to Jacob their own slanderous words (about their father?), or perhaps more likely, (2) relaying the defamatory rumors that were circulating about them, the evil reputation they had acquired, presumably because of their behavior. Either of these would have reflected poorly on the patriarch, Jacob. Following the latter sense, one commentator observed, "It does not mean that Joseph brought accusations against them, but that he . . . repeated what he had heard about them" (Tayler Lewis, in *Lange's Commentary on the Holy Scriptures,* vol. 1 [Grand Rapids: Zondervan, 1960], p. 580). Similarly, H. C. Leupold argues that the pronominal suffix attached to "report" acts as an objective genitive ("their report"), so that it refers "not to his own observations so much as what others said. No doubt Joseph recognized on the strength of what he saw that this report was the truth" (*Exposition of Genesis,* vol. 2 [Grand Rapids: Baker, 1942], p. 954). This understanding colors W. H. Griffith Thomas's comments as well: "What precisely this meant we do not know, but from the wording in the original it was evidently something that was well-known and notorious in the neighborhood" (*Genesis: A Devotional Commentary* [Grand Rapids: Eerdmans, 1946], p. 355). If so, it would not be the first time. Jacob has had previous occasion to bemoan the damage done to his own reputation in the community because of the evil deeds of his sons. After the

vengeful deceit of Simeon and Levi in Shechem Jacob complained, "Ye have troubled me to make me [odious] among the inhabitants of the land" (Gen. 34:30). This same issue seems to be at stake here again. Thus, Joseph's motivation and concern appears to be not merely that his brothers are doing bad things but that their actions are reflecting poorly on their father, Jacob.

[12]In the story of Joseph, "the activity of God is revealed, not as a *deus ex machina*, but *in the* action of the brothers. Their evil plan achieves historical realization, but the historical events are products of the Divine activity. God's good intentions follow the mischievous path of the brothers or, rather, the brothers unwittingly follow the path that God has blazed. . . . The purpose of God lights up the horizon on evil, jealous, malicious activity. The dispute in Jacob's house turns into an important link in the way of God with His people" (Berkouwer, p. 101).

[13]"It was God's intention, already revealed to Abraham (Gen. 15:13-16), to bring the chosen family under foreign domination until 'the iniquity of the Amorites' should be full, and Canaan ripe for possession. So the train of events to lead Israel into Egypt is set in motion through the rivalries and predicaments of the twelve brothers, under the hand of God. The story is a *locus classicus* of providence" (Derek Kidner, *Genesis* [Downers Grove: Inter-Varsity Press, 1967], p. 179).

[14]"The exodus is the most significant historical and theological event of the Old Testament because it marks God's mightiest act in behalf of his people, an act which brought them from slavery to freedom, . . . and from it flows all subsequent Old Testament revelation. . . . In the final analysis, the exodus served to typify that exodus achieved by Jesus Christ for people of faith so that it is a meaningful event for the church as well as for Israel" (Eugene Merrill, *Kingdom of Priests* [Grand Rapids: Baker, 1996], pp. 57-58).

[15]Merrill, p. 47. According to Merrill, the intermarriage of Judah and his sons to Canaanite wives described in Genesis 38 suggests the immediate catalyst and explanation for God's relocation of Joseph (and, subsequently, the family) in Egypt. "There was doubtless a tendency at work for Jacob's sons to be assimilated to Canaanite culture and religion, an assimilation which would certainly be accelerated by intermarriage. . . . The selling of Joseph, then, should be viewed as a divine reaction to the marriage of Judah." That would help explain the abrupt shift in the narrative from the commencement of the Joseph story (Gen. 37) to the marital/moral behavior of Judah (Gen. 38), before resuming with the Joseph story (Gen. 39).

[16]For this reason, therefore, the assertion is correct that "God, not Joseph, [is] the 'hero' of the story" (Kidner, p. 180).

NOTES FOR CHAPTER 5

[17]C. H. Spurgeon, *An All-Round Ministry* (1900; reprint, Carlisle, Pa.: Banner of Truth Trust, 1972), p. 84.

[18]"Coincidence" simply denotes events that happen simultaneously. It refers to co-incidents—that is, two or more incidents that occur at the same time. The word has come to connote chance, but chance is not inherent in the word. Providential coincidence is seen on a number of occasions when God orchestrates the intersection of multiple events at the same time.

[19]The word "himself" is italicized in the AV, indicating that it has been supplied by the translators in the absence of any express object in the original text. The verb "committed" (παραδιδωμι) means to "entrust" or "hand over" (it is the word used in the Gospels for delivering Jesus into the custody of the Sanhedrin and, later, of Pontius Pilate). What did Jesus "commit" to the righteous God? The context emphasizes the importance of obedience and well-doing even at the cost of suffering, and patience even in the face of suffering (I Pet. 2:18-20). In that context, "himself" is a reasonable insertion. Yet why would such a natural and easy pronominal insertion be omitted? Perhaps to accommodate a wider object? Others suggest that He committed "his cause" or "his case" to God. The reference to avoiding retaliation leads some to believe that Christ committed His persecutors to God for vindication. The fact is, when we find ourselves in such circumstances—suffering persecution wrongfully—we can find specific scriptural exhortations to commit *all* of these to God: ourselves, our enemies, our cause, our case, our suffering circumstances. "And it is precisely here that suffering believers can truly walk *in* His steps. As failing mortals they cannot fully place their feet in His sinless footprints, but by His grace they can resolutely determine to follow His example of unreservedly committing themselves to God in all circumstances" (D. Edmond Hiebert, *First Peter* [Chicago: Moody Press, 1984], pp. 174-75).

[20]I am not reading Joseph's faith into the story, nor merely assuming Joseph's trust in God for the sake of artificially making my point. Joseph's own references to God throughout the story, and the profound understanding of the divine purpose behind all that had happened to him that he expressed at the end of the story, underscore an abiding faith that sustained him amid the darkest providences. See also note 7.

[21]*Commentary on the Whole Bible,* vol. 1 (McLean, Va.: MacDonald Publishing, n.d.), p. 224.

[22]I am indebted to my friend Dr. Robert Vincent, assistant pastor at Mount Calvary Baptist Church (Greenville, S.C.), for the three points regarding our delays as God's opportunities.

[23]Walter C. Kaiser Jr., *A History of Israel* (Nashville: Broadman & Holman Publishers, 1998), p. 71.

[24]Joni Eareckson Tada and Steve Estes, *When God Weeps: Why Our Sufferings Matter to the Almighty* (Grand Rapids: Zondervan, 1997), p. 158.

[25]Tada, pp. 173-74.

[26]From *The Letters of C. S. Lewis* (29 April 1959), cited in Wayne Martindale and Jerry Root, eds., *The Quotable Lewis* (Wheaton: Tyndale House, 1989), p. 469.

Chapter 6

[1]When Moses reported to his father-in-law, Jethro, all that God had done in bringing them out of Egypt, Jethro rejoiced and concluded, "Now I know that the LORD is greater than all gods; for in the thing wherein they [the Egyptian gods, cf. 12:12] dealt proudly he was above them."

[2]Pharaoh's "heart 'became hard' (v. 13; there is no reflexive or passive idea to the verb . . . , as so many translations render it)" (Walter C. Kaiser Jr., *Expositor's Bible Commentary,* vol. 2 [Grand Rapids: Zondervan, 1990], p. 347). Actually, very few translations render it that way. The 1611/1769 AV is virtually alone in its translation ("he hardened Pharaoh's heart"). Out of fifteen English translations (and, for the record, six German translations), the only other one that duplicates the AV sense was the Webster Bible (1883, 1995). Why the identical Hebrew phrase translated correctly in 7:22, 8:19, and 9:35 was translated differently in 7:13 is puzzling; in this case, however, the correct translation of 7:13 has significant theological ramifications for a correct perception of the process of God's providential hardening of Pharaoh. Cf. C. F. Keil and F. Delitzsch, *Commentary on the Old Testament,* vol. 1 (reprint, Grand Rapids: Eerdman's, 1983), p. 477; *Lange's Commentary on the Scriptures,* vol. 2 (Grand Rapids: Zondervan, 1960), p. 19; William L. Holladay, *A Concise Hebrew and Aramaic Lexicon of the Old Testament* (Grand Rapids: Eerdmans, 1971), p. 99; *The New Brown-Driver-Briggs-Gesenius Hebrew and English Lexicon* (Christian Copyrights, 1983), p. 304.

[3]"One important observation remains to be made concerning Pharaoh: the king's heart was not actually hardened by God until after he had hardened his own heart by his first refusal of Moses' petition . . . (Exodus 5:2). Once he had of his own free will rejected the request of Moses and Aaron, then God began the process of hardening his heart (7:3, 13, 22; 8:19, etc.), to such an extreme that Pharaoh became almost irrational" (Gleason Archer, *Encyclopedia of Bible Difficulties* [Grand Rapids: Zondervan, 1982], p. 391). Archer's only fault here is that he is a bit sloppy with the texts he cites. If he were to observe the progression of the explicit wording of the texts, it would only strengthen his case all the more.

[4]Matthew Henry, *Commentary on the Whole Bible,* vol. 1 (McLean, Va.: MacDonald Publishing, n.d.), p. 307.

[5]Henry, p. 329.

[6]This represents the essence of Paul's language from a literal rendering.

[7]John 6:44-45, 65.

[8]I am not arguing that God's election was based on His foreknowledge of their personality or responses. I believe Paul's point in Romans 9 (verse 11, for example), God's point in Malachi 1 (verses 2-3), and the testimony of the rest of Scripture emphasizes an unconditional election. I am merely pointing out the correspondence between God's purposes and men's desires as reflected in these biblical accounts. God never hardens someone who wants to believe, nor does He force someone to believe who does not want to. In that respect, I find the term "irresistible grace" unfortunate and misleading; the biblical concept (in John 6, for example) is more accurately reflected in the phrase "persuasive grace"—that is, God effectually works to persuade one to become a voluntary partaker of His grace.

[9]"Esther: The Hand of Providence," in *Men and Women of the Old Testament* (Chattanooga, Tenn.: AMG, 1995), pp. 409-10.

[10]Henry, p. 735.

[11]Jim Berg, *Changed into His Image* (Greenville, S.C.: BJU Press, 2000), p. 42. "Rather than demanding our own way," Berg counsels, "we ought to be begging God never to let us have what our flesh demands. We ought to pray, 'Dear God, limit me, bind me, restrict me. Do whatever you have to, but please don't let me have my own way.' "

[12]The NASB translates, "Now the destruction of Ahaziah was from God, in that he went to Joram." Clearer still is the NKJV: "His going to Joram was God's occasion for Ahaziah's downfall."

[13]Ahaziah was related to the house of Ahab by his marriage to Ahab's daughter, Athaliah, who was in every respect the daughter of her mother, Jezebel.

[14]Berg, p. 42.

[15]Proverbs 21:1 "is a saying about providence, not regeneration. Tiglath-Pileaser (Isaiah 10:6, 7), Cyrus (Isaiah 41:2-4) and Artaxerxes (Ezra 7:21) are all examples of autocrats who, in pursuing their chosen courses, flooded or fertilized God's field as He chose. The principle is still in force" (Derek Kidner, *Proverbs* [Downers Grove, Ill.: Inter-Varsity Press, 1964], p. 141).

Chapter 7

[1]Few verses are more commonly wrenched from their context than the popular promise of Philippians 4:19 (though 4:13 is probably violated even more frequently). This verse is not a blanket promise that can be severed from its context and applied indiscriminately to assure virtually anyone that God will always provide for them. The topic throughout this passage is the Philippians' material provision for the apostle Paul. It explicitly dominates the discussion in verses 10, 14, 15, 16, 17, and 18. It implicitly underlies what Paul says in verses 11-13 as well. In other words, the ground for Paul's assurance, and the Philippians' confidence, that God will (literally) "gloriously fill full all your need" ("in glory" is an adverb) is rooted in their faithful and sacrificial meeting of Paul's material needs. To those who, like the Philippians (or the widow of Zarephath), obey God's instruction to minister materially to God's servants, Paul (or Elijah) could promise under inspiration, "As you have ministered faithfully to me and my needs, I can assure you that my God will minister faithfully and fully to your needs." In fact, Elijah says as much in I Kings 17:13-14. On the other hand, a believer who is selfish and stingy with the resources God gives him and never extends himself to minister materially to God's people has no ground for claiming this promise. To sever such verses from their context and apply them without qualification as if they were isolated excerpts from a book of sacred sayings is to mishandle the Scripture by ignoring the literary context in which God gave it.

[2]Matthew Henry, *Commentary on the Whole Bible,* vol. 2 (McLean Va.: Mac-Donald Publishing, n.d.), p. 666.

[3]I should point out here that many (if not most) commentators make all the neuters in I Corinthians 1:27-28 (foolish things, weak things, base things, despised things, nonexistent things) refer to people (viz., Christians) as viewed derogatorily by the world. I.e., God chooses these very people who are despised and dismissed by the world as "things," accounted as nothing, to confound those who regard themselves as wise and strong and great. Verse 26 would seem to lend its weight to this interpretation. However, the larger context is dominated not by people but by a *thing.* Through what *means* were these mostly ignorant, insignificant, and ignoble converts called? Through *the preaching of the cross.* It is by means of that *message*—dismissed by Greeks as foolishness and by Jews as scandalous (v. 23)—that God effects His calling. It is this message of the gospel, this preaching of the cross, that dominates Paul's discussion from verse 17 through verse 25 and, I believe, virtually through the end of the chapter. Paul's recurrent emphasis rests on this divine message of the cross, and the divinely appointed method of preaching (vv. 17, 18, 21, 23). The neuters in verses 27-28 may refer to believers as the *result* of this "foolish" method of preaching and "scandalous" message of the cross (though it is difficult to see

how believers themselves "confound" or "nullify" unbelievers). But the context seems to argue that these neuters refer not primarily to believers themselves but to the message and method God has chosen to confound unbelievers, by saving and transforming those who, in simple faith, believe the preaching of the cross and receive the message of the gospel. In fact, this is precisely Paul's point throughout verses 19-25; verses 27-28 simply elaborate the same argument with slightly different terminology. If this is the case, then I Corinthians 1:27-28 may legitimately serve as a paradigm for the more general principles I extract from it in this chapter.

[4]A. R. Faussett identifies this phrase "foolish things" as "a general phrase for *all persons and things foolish*. Even *things* (and those, too, [who] are accounted by 'the world' [as] *foolish things*) are chosen by God to confound *persons*. This is the force of the change from neuter to masculine" (Robert Jamieson, A. R. Faussett, and David Brown, *A Commentary on the Old and New Testaments,* vol. 3, part 3 (reprint, Grand Rapids: Eerdmans, 1976), p. 286.

[5]Henry, p. 749.

[6]A few otherwise reliably conservative commentators strangely balk at this account. Walter C. Kaiser Jr., apparently unsure what to make of the rather straightforward terms of the text, says that the Arameans fled suddenly "for some unexplained reason" (*A History of Israel* [Nashville: Broadman & Holman, 1998], p. 333). F. F. Bruce understands the auditory phenomenon in II Kings 7:6-7 to mean that the Syrians "heard a rumour" that a large mercenary army was on its way, causing them to abandon the siege hastily (*Israel and the Nations* [revised by David F. Payne; Downers Grove: Inter-Varsity Press, 1997], p. 39). Though the Hebrew word (*qol*) can be used in the sense of "rumor" or "report," this interpretation requires understanding the text to be saying that they heard a rumor about horses, a rumor about chariots, and a rumor about a large army (v. 6). The obvious intended sense is that they heard what they thought was the sound of horses, the sound of chariots, and the sound of a vast approaching military host—presumably from both directions, north (Hittites) and south (Egyptians). God knows how to incite panic in His enemies.

[7]Some form of the Hebrew term מרר ("to be bitter") occurs three times in 1:13 and 20: (1) the phrase "grieveth me much" is literally "it is more bitter for me than for you" (used here in an intensive sense of being deeply distressed); (2) the name "Mara," and, (3) the "bitter" dealing of the LORD. The same root is used of Hannah's "bitterness of soul" over her barrenness (I Samuel 1:10). More pertinent to this discussion is Job's use of the word to describe how "the Almighty . . . hath vexed my soul [lit., "made my soul bitter"]" (Job 27:2).

[8]"Full" obviously does not mean financially well-off; they left Bethlehem in the first place because of a famine. Goslinga explains: "She had left Bethlehem 'full' (i.e., rich), not in material wealth, but in the company of her husband and sons; but the Lord brought her back destitute" and (almost) alone (C. T. Goslinga, trans. Ray Togtman, *Bible Student's Commentary: Joshua, Judges, Ruth* [Grand Rapids: Zondervan, 1986], p. 528).

[9]Born in 1731, the English poet William Cowper experienced his share of frowning providences. His mother died when he was six. After the death of his father, stepmother, and best friend, he suffered a total mental collapse, attempting suicide on several occasions. Even after his conversion, he continued to suffer periodic bouts of deep depression. Out of these dark circumstances Cowper, along with his close friend John Newton, penned hundreds of hymns to the enormous comfort and encouragement of God's saints ever since. The stanzas cited at the end of this chapter come from a hymn titled "Light Shining out of Darkness" (*The Poetical Works of William Cowper,* vol. 2 [Edinburgh: James Nichol, 1854], pp. 66-67).

[10]Addressing the problem of believers who labor under an ongoing sense of guilt and failure, Michael Barrett appeals: "If only we would realize that regardless of our personal failures, imperfections, and sins, the merit of Jesus Christ encompasses and subsumes all of our service to Him. What we do personally cannot increase or decrease God's acceptance of us. . . . He always sees us together with His Son, His dearly Beloved. . . . [B]ecause I am a Christian, God accepts me on the merits of my Savior" (*Complete in Him: A Guide to Understanding and Enjoying the Gospel* [Greenville, S.C.: Ambassador-Emerald, 2001], p. 94).

[11]"Do not take this truth in the wrong direction," Barrett warns, "and beware of those who do," interpreting God's acceptance of us in Christ as a "license to sin or reason to abandon the pursuit of personal purity. . . . Right thinking about the gospel produces right living in the gospel" (Barrett, p. 95).

Chapter 8

[1]William S. Plumer, *Jehovah-Jireh: A Treatise on Providence* (1865; reprint, Harrisonburg, Va.: Sprinkle Publications, 1993), p. 111.

[2]An example of this unwarranted (in my view) assumption is John C. Whitcomb, *Esther* (Chicago: Moody Press, 1979). This view has been widely popularized as well by, among others, H. A. Ironside's *Notes on the Book of Esther* (New York: Loizeaux Brothers, 1921) and J. Vernon McGee's *Exposition on the Book of Esther* (Wheaton: Van Kampen Press, 1951), which incidentally shows a clear dependence on and duplication of Ironside's comments. Interestingly, however,

few people argue that Ezra and Nehemiah were disobedient for being and remaining in Persia as long as they did.

³One might be tempted to argue that were it not for Mordecai's offending Haman back in Susa, the Jews in Jerusalem—and everywhere else—would have been in no danger in the first place. But that is a far less certain "what if." The Jews were already facing constant threats from their neighbors. If Mordecai had not been there, someone else would have been and some offense likely "would have arisen from another place" (to adapt Mordecai's own words). The Jews have historically stood in danger, not because they have a penchant for annoying other people but because they are integrally tied to God's redemptive purposes for the world through Messiah. That has made them a key target for satanic attack, through a variety of human means, throughout history (cf. Rev. 12).

⁴*Purim* is the Persian word in Esther for the lot that Haman cast to determine the timing of the execution of the Jews; it was that symbol—which to the unbeliever represented "chance" or "fate" but to the believer came to signify God's providential overruling of chance—for which the memorial feast commemorating these events was named.

⁵Abraham D. Cohen, "'Hu-Hagoral':The Religious Significance of Esther," *Studies in the Book of Esther*, ed. Carey A. Moore (New York: Ktav Publishing House, 1982), p. 129.

⁶*The Silence of God* (1907; reprint, Grand Rapids: Kregel, 1978), pp. 16, 10.

⁷One introduction to Esther is certainly correct, therefore, when it asserts that "the author has deliberately refrained from mentioning God or any religious activity as a literary device to heighten the fact that it is God who controls and directs all the seemingly insignificant coincidences that make up the plot and issue in deliverance for the Jews. God's sovereign rule is assumed at every point, an assumption made all the more effective by the total absence of reference to him" (*The NIV Study Bible* [Grand Rapids: Zondervan, 1985], p. 719).

⁸"The Book of Esther, then, does not ignore the presence of divine activity; rather it points to the hiddenness of Yahweh's presence in the world. Because Yahweh's control of history is neither overt nor easily discerned in everyday events, the determination of the shape and direction of history shifts to human beings. This understanding of the hiddenness of Yahweh . . . explains the narrator's emphasis upon individual responsibility for the successful outcome of events. . . . The narrator understandably refrains from any reference to the deity in order to accentuate the role of human responsibility in shaping history, and to indicate the hiddenness of Yahweh's control of history" (Sandra Beth Berg, *The Book of Esther* [Missoula, Mont.: Scholars Press, 1979], pp. 178-79).

⁹Why does so much time elapse between Vashti's dethronement and her replacement? A well-known historical event intervened between chapters 1 and

2—Ahasuerus's (Xerxes') famous, and disastrous, military campaign against the Greeks, culminating in the Battle of Thermopylae in 480 B.C. In fact, it seems likely that Ahasuerus's extended "open house" feast described in Esther 1 doubled as an opportunity for strategy sessions with his commanders in preparation for this massive assault. In any case, the phrase "after these things" in Esther 2:1 marks a gap of about two to three years, when Ahasuerus's attention was distracted by military pursuits. Once those ended, he was free to turn his thoughts back to the matter of locating a new queen.

[10]J. Sidlow Baxter, among others, argues that although the name of God is not directly mentioned in the story of Esther, His name (Yahweh, spelled with just the radicals YHWH) does appear in hidden acrostic form four times in the Hebrew text. Baxter alludes to certain manuscripts that enlarge the key letters in the text to draw attention to the presumably hidden acrostic. Here are the alleged acrostics with the key letters highlighted, along with how they would appear in English:

1:20—King's counselors speaking (Gentiles)

וְנִשְׁמַע פִּתְגָם הַמֶּלֶךְ אֲשֶׁר־יַעֲשֶׂה בְּכָל־מַלְכוּתוֹ כִּי רַבָּה הִיא
וְכָל־הַנָּשִׁים יִתְּנוּ יְקָר לְבַעְלֵיהֶן לְמִגָּדוֹל וְעַד־קָטָן:

"When the king's decree that he will make is proclaimed throughout all his empire, for great is It, Then-all The-wives Shall-give honor to their husbands great and small." In this case, God's name YHWH is allegedly encrypted in the recorded words of *Gentiles* and spelled *backwards* (backwards in Hebrew, that is) with the *first* letter of four consecutive words.

5:4—Esther speaking (a Jew)

וַתֹּאמֶר אֶסְתֵּר אִם־עַל־הַמֶּלֶךְ טוֹב יָבוֹא הַמֶּלֶךְ וְהָמָן הַיּוֹם
אֶל־הַמִּשְׁתֶּה אֲשֶׁר־עָשִׂיתִי לוֹ:

"And Esther said, 'If it please the king, Let-come The-king And-Haman Today to the banquet that I have prepared for him.'" Here YHWH is spelled *forwards* (in Hebrew) by a *Jew* with the *first* letter of four consecutive words.

5:13—Haman speaking (a Gentile)

וְכָל־זֶה אֵינֶנּוּ שֹׁוֶה לִי בְּכָל־עֵת אֲשֶׁר אֲנִי רֹאֶה אֶת־מָרְדֳּכַי
הַיְהוּדִי יוֹשֵׁב בְּשַׁעַר הַמֶּלֶךְ:

"Yet all thiS nothinG availS to-mE every time I see Mordecai the Jew sitting in the king's gate." Here YHWH is spelled *backwards* by a *Gentile* with the *last* letter of four consecutive words.

7:7—Narrator speaking (a Jew or a believing Gentile)

וְהַמֶּ֫לֶךְ קָם בַּחֲמָתוֹ מִמִּשְׁתֵּה הַיַּ֫יִן אֶל־גִּנַּת הַבִּיתָן וְהָמָן עָמַד
לְבַקֵּשׁ עַל־נַפְשׁוֹ מֵאֶסְתֵּר הַמַּלְכָּה כִּי רָאָה כִּי־כָלְתָה אֵלָיו
הָרָעָה מֵאֵת הַמֶּ֫לֶךְ:

"Then the king arose in his wrath from the banquet of wine and went into the palace garden; but Haman stood before Queen Esther, pleading for his life, for he saw thaT was-determineD against-hiM the-evil by the king." Here YHWH is spelled *forwards* by a *Jew* with the *last* letter of four consecutive words.

As intriguing as the data appear, the intentionality of these alleged acrostics has been widely questioned. F. B. Huey notes that even though "the four letters YHWH are written larger than others in some manuscripts to reveal the 'hidden' name . . . no one today takes these rabbinic devices seriously" (*Expositor's Bible Commentary,* vol. 4 [Grand Rapids: Zondervan, 1988], p. 785). After all, the radicals that spell the divine name in Hebrew (YHWH) are among the most common in Hebrew vocabulary. For example, *Y* is a frequent prefix on many verb forms and a possessive suffix on nouns; *W* is customarily prefixed to words as a conjunction and serves as a pronominal suffix as well; *H* also is regularly prefixed to many nouns as a definite article and functions as a common pronominal suffix. Moreover, the alleged hidden appearances of God's name do not occur in thematically significant passages, but in seemingly haphazard places, not only breaking into the middle of statements (1:20; 7:7) but even bridging across a logical, punctuated gap (1:20). These factors suggest a statistical probability that this pattern could be found in virtually any given manuscript and is, therefore, purely coincidental. In an attempt to validate my suspicions of this theory, I scrutinized every line of Hebrew text in both Ezra and Nehemiah, looking for other examples of this pattern. Expecting to find several, I found one, buried in Ezra 8:19 (the backward pattern). I don't know about statistics, but the empirical evidence I have investigated, to my surprise, suggests to me that (1) despite the commonness of the letters, similar examples of this pattern appear to be much rarer than I supposed, (2) the presence of only *one* example of this pattern in all of Ezra-Nehemiah (two longer narratives from nearly the same era) makes the *four* in Esther that much more remarkable, (3) the consistent distribution of those four patterns in Esther between Gentile speakers (the backward pattern) and Jewish speakers (the forward pattern) is additionally extraordinary in light of my own findings (or rather, the lack of them), and (4) though the results of my own admittedly limited investigation neither prove nor disprove Baxter's view of divine intent, it appears to me to be more feasible than I once supposed. Even if these unusual patterns are purely coincidental, a significant theme throughout this book is worth remembering and applying here: God's providence encompasses coincidences.

[11]Commentators are divided between those who assume that the absence of any explicit reference to prayer indicates the absence of prayer (e.g., John A. Martin, *Bible Knowledge Commentary,* vol. 1 [n.p.: Victor Books, 1985], p. 707) and those who argue that the reference to fasting is an implicit reference to praying (e.g., F. B. Huey, *Expositor's Bible Commentary,* vol. 4 [Grand Rapids: Zondervan, 1988], p. 817). The latter makes the most sense. The fasting mentioned in Esther 4:3 could be explained as an expression of grief, but what is the point of the fast mentioned in 4:16 unless it carries an implicitly petitionary purpose? "The omission of any reference to prayer or to God is consistent with the author's intention; absence of any distinctively religious concepts or vocabulary is a rhetorical device used to heighten the fact that it is indeed God who has been active in the whole narrative" (*NIV Study Bible*, p. 725).

[12]Arndt Meinhold, "Theologische Erwagungen zum Buch Esther" in *Theologische Zeitschrift*, cited by Berg, *The Book of Esther,* p. 180). Such veiled allusions "represent indirect references to Yahweh's intervention in history on behalf of His elect people" so that "the unstated recognition of Yahweh's power still remains the vital force behind these expressions" (Berg).

[13]Bernhard W. Anderson, "The Place of the Book of Esther in the Christian Bible," *Journal of Religion* 30, no. 1 (January 1950): 40.

[14]Scottish pastor Robert Bruce (ca. 1554-1631); source unknown.

[15]Ken Connolly, *The Indestructible Book* (Grand Rapids: Baker Book House, 1996), p. 184.

[16]First, the reference in Esther 8:11 to "the power of the people and province that would assault them" literally refers to the armies of any people or province that might rise up against them ("all the forces of any people or province," NKJV; "the entire army of any people or province," NASB). Second, the narrative specifies that the Jews slew only men (Esther 9:6, 12, 15). Third, the Jews refused to take any of their enemies' goods as a spoil (Esther 9:10, 15, 16).

[17]Cohen.

[18]The examples of literary reversals are drawn from Berg, pp. 106-7.

[19]This chiastic analysis of Esther, slightly adapted, comes from Yehudah T. Radday, "Chiasm in Joshua, Judges and Others" in *Linguistica Biblica,* vol. 3 (1973), pp. 6-13, cited by Berg, *The Book of Esther,* p. 108.

[20]Matthew Henry, *Commentary on the Whole Bible,* vol. 2 (McLean, Va.: MacDonald, n.d.), p. 1137.

[21]Henry, p. 1134.

[22]Henry, p. 1135.

[23]For a thorough and helpful discussion of biblical imprecations see J. Barton Payne, *The Theology of the Older Testament* (Grand Rapids: Academie Books, 1962), pp. 201-3.

[24]Elizabeth Barrett Browning, *Aurora Leigh*, Book VII, lines 820-23, in *The Complete Poetic Works of Elizabeth Barrett Browning* (Brighton, Mich.: Native American Book Publishers, n.d.), p. 372.

Chapter 9

[1]The juxtaposition of II Samuel 24:1 (which states that God moved David against Israel to number them) and II Chronicles 21:1 (which states that Satan moved David to number Israel) is a fascinating and instructive one. It sheds some light on God's use of Satan's temptation (which might be described as the amount of leash God allows Satan) as well as natural human tendencies and proclivities (which apart from the intervening grace of God tend naturally to sin and evil), in order to accomplish His larger purposes. God never prompts anyone to sin (James 1:13). Such an action is utterly contrary to His holy nature and, besides, is wholly unnecessary. All God needs to do is lift His operative grace (undeserved in the first place) and allow human nature to take its natural course (James 1:14-15). Left to himself, any man is fully capable of initiating all manner of sin on his own. "You and I have enough evil residing in us that if God were to let us have our own way, we would destroy ourselves" (Jim Berg, *Changed into His Image* [Greenville, S.C.: BJU Press, 1999], p. 42). God merely "manages" it for His own ends and glory. In the case of David, given what we have seen so far of the operation of providence from the case of Pharaoh and of Job, it may be explained that God authorized (permitted) Satan to tempt David along the line of his own voluntary inclination at this time in order to occasion a divine chastening on the nation. Cf. J. Barton Payne, *Expositor's Bible Commentary,* vol. 4 (Grand Rapids: Zondervan, 1988), pp. 406-7.

[2]The same term appears in Job 1:9, "Does Job fear God *for nothing?*" In other words, "Does Job fear God without compensation? Doesn't Job get compensated for fearing You? You bless the work of his hands and build a hedge of protection around him. You pay him off so that he will worship You!" This unmasks Satan's attack as an assault not merely on Job and the integrity of his faith but on God and His integrity. Job did not suffer because of the insinuations and false accusations of a liar. God wanted to demonstrate larger things (to both men and angels) about Himself and His character.

[3]"The God who handed over Job to his torturer was no olympian figure, content to win his victories through others [and at their expense]. He would say, in Christ, to his own more hideous tormentor, 'This is your hour, and the

power of darkness' (Lk. 22:53). Any thinking about the sufferance of evil, and exposure of the innocent to grief, must take its bearings now from that crucial and seminal event" (Derek Kidner, *The Wisdom of Proverbs, Job, & Ecclesiastes* [Downers Grove, Ill.: InterVarsity Press, 1985], pp. 59-60).

[4]"It would be a mistake to see the concession to the accuser as a merely isolated tactic. It reflects the consistent practice of God. Where we might wish to argue that omnipotence ought to have stamped out evil at its first appearance, God's chosen way was not to crush it out of hand but to wrestle with it; and to do so in weakness rather than in strength, through men more often than through miracles, and through costly permissions rather than through flat refusals. Putting the matter in our own terms we might say that he is resolved to overcome it in fair combat, not by veto but by hard-won victory." But why? Someone besides man is watching (the angelic "sons of God" in Job 1:6; 2:1) and, in the process, learning things about the character of their God. "What the prologue makes clear, however, is that this is indeed permission, not abdication; for in both these chapters it is God who sets the limits of the test. The conditions are all that the challenger could desire, but they are of God's choosing, not his" (Kidner, p. 59).

[5]John Flavel, *The Mystery of Providence* (1678; reprint, Carlisle, Pa.: Banner of Truth, 1995), p. 30.

[6]Millard Erickson employs a vivid analogy here, likening God to "a judo expert who redirects the evil efforts of sinful men and Satan that they become the very means of doing good. . . . [O]ur omnipotent God is able to allow men to do their very worst, and still he accomplishes his purposes" (*Christian Theology* [Grand Rapids: Baker Book House, 1985], p. 400).

[7]Erickson, p. 399, acknowledges that his outline is drawn from Augustus Strong's *Systematic Theology* (Old Tappan, N.J.: Fleming H. Revell Co., 1907), pp. 423-25.

[8]The Greek word, *endeiknumi*, means "to prove, demonstrate, display." God "planned a continuing exhibition of his favor to man to cover all the centuries between the ascension and the return of Christ, and after that through all eternity (cf. Jude 25). This eschatological dimension implies that it will be for the benefit of angels as well as men" (E. Skevington Wood, *Expositor's Bible Commentary*, vol. 11 [Grand Rapids: Zondervan, 1978], p. 35).

[9]Readers of C. S. Lewis will recognize this image as an allusion to his Chronicles of Narnia, in which a passageway to perceiving an entire world of spiritual reality is "accidentally" discovered through the back of an otherwise very ordinary-appearing wardrobe.

[10]Charles Bridges, *The Christian Ministry* (1830; reprint, Carlisle, Pa.: Banner of Truth Trust, 1980), p. 1, emphasis added.

¹¹The Greek word, *apodeiknumi*, reflects the same root as *endeiknumi* in Ephesians 2:7 (see note 8 above).

¹²The same truth is just as subtly suggested in the temptation of Christ as well when the celestial audience, stepping forward after Satan's departure, "came and ministered unto him" (Matt. 4:11.)

¹³The Jews interpret Jesus' weeping at the tomb as a manifestation of this same emotionally rooted attachment to Lazarus and the family (John 11:36).

¹⁴Cited by William S. Plumer, *Jehovah-Jireh: A Treatise on Providence* (1865; reprint, Harrisonburg, Va.: Sprinkle Publications, 1993), p. 8.

¹⁵"Light Shining out of Darkness," *The Poetical Works of William Cowper* (Edinburgh" James Nichol, 1854), pp. 66-67.

¹⁶"This arch-fiend plots the ruin of Job," wrote William Henry Green. "We see Satan's design in Job's distresses, and how conspicuously it was foiled. But what did the Lord intend by them? . . . There must have been some end, which, so far as Job himself was concerned, would be an ample justification of the providence of God in permitting him to be treated as he was, and to suffer as he did." God's purposes, according to Green, included "the increase of Job's faith . . . the enlargement of his spiritual perceptions, and his keener insight into religious truth" (*The Book of Job* [New York: Hurst & Company, 1891], pp. 249-53).

Chapter 10

¹Edward Panosian, *The Providence of God in History* (Greenville, S.C.: Bob Jones University Press, 1996), p. 13.

²This passage refers to "our Lord Jesus Christ's appearing, which He will manifest in His own time" (NKJV). The title "King of kings and Lord of lords" reappears more famously in Revelation 19:16 (cf. 17:14). The Greek phrase evokes the image of Christ as the King over the aggregate of human kings, and Lord over the whole group of human lords. In I Timothy 6, however, the phrase appears in a peculiarly forceful form. The words "kings" and "lords" are not nouns, per se, but participles (verbal nouns). The phrase might be literally read that Christ is "the King of the ones kinging and Lord of the ones lording." He is the supreme King over all the ones currently reigning as kings (who think they are the ones in control when, in fact, they are not) and the sovereign Lord over all the ones currently lording their power over men. It often looks to us as if men (and usually, wicked men) hold absolute sway over all our affairs; but as King Solomon himself once hinted, there is one "higher than they" (Eccles. 5:8). A similarly forceful phrase occurs in Revelation 1:5, where Christ is called "the prince [ruler] of the kings of the earth." The word "ruler" is a present participial form that is commonly used as a substantive. A fuller rendering would be that

Christ is "the One ruling over the kings of the earth"—an ongoing reign that is dramatically demonstrated in His activity over the kings of all nations throughout the pages of Revelation (6:15; 10:11; 16:14; 17:2, 10, 12, 14, 18; 18:3, 9; 19:16, 18, 19).

[3]"God worked out the framework of the Roman Empire so that it was a prepared world for a prepared revelation. . . . The apex of human achievement since the Flood was the century of Rome's transition from republic to empire. Under Rome there was one world, one language, one road system, one rule, one citizenship. It was an empire of cities. Do you know that after the fall of Rome there was not to be a Europe of cities for some eleven centuries? What is the significance of cities? Rapid communication of new ideas among great numbers of people. Great numbers heard a new message—the gospel of Jesus Christ—at one time. The preparation of the Roman world for the coming of Christ involved natural circumstances through which God was working out His omnipotent will" (Panosian, pp. 14-15).

[4]New Testament scholar F. F. Bruce in *The Books and the Parchments* (Old Tappan, N.J.: Fleming H. Revell, 1963), p. 162.

[5]Textual expert Adolf Deissmann in *New Light on the New Testament* (Edinburgh: T & T Clark, 1908), p. 95.

[6]Bruce, citing several examples, asserts, "Indications are not lacking in the pagan Greek literature of the last three centuries B.C. that [the Septuagint] was known and appreciated in some Greek circles" (p. 161).

[7]Alfred Rahlfs, "History of the Septuagint Text" in *Septuaginta* (Stuttgart: Deutsche Bibelgesellschaft Stuttgart, 1979), p. LVII. The Septuagint, he adds, "being already everywhere widespread and well-known, was simply adopted by the Christians as the Church's Bible"—while the New Testament was being progressively revealed and penned.

[8]A sample of sources for this section include T. G. Donner, "Logos," *New Dictionary of Theology* (Downers Grove, Ill.: Inter-Varsity Press, 1988), pp. 395-96; Donald Guthrie, *New Testament Theology* (Downers Grove, Ill.: Inter-Varsity Press, 1981), pp. 321-29; Leon Morris, *The Gospel According to John* (Grand Rapids: Eerdmans, 1971), pp. 115-26; J. N. Birdsall, "Logos," *The New Bible Dictionary* (Grand Rapids: Eerdmans, 1962), pp. 744-45; Archibald Alexander, "Logos," *International Standard Bible Encyclopedia,* vol. 3 (Grand Rapids: Eerdmans, 1956), pp. 1911-17.

[9]J. W. Shephard, *The Christ of the Gospels* (Grand Rapids: Eerdmans, 1946), p. i. Cited in J. Dwight Pentecost, *The Words and Works of Jesus Christ* (Grand Rapids: Academie Books, 1981), p. 41.

[10]Alfred Edersheim, *The Life and Times of Jesus the Messiah* (Grand Rapids: Eerdmans, 1971), p. 137. For a detailed and colorful description of Zacharias's experience at the temple see pp. 137-41.

[11]The view that the "prayer" mentioned by the angel had reference to Zacharias's prayer at that moment, in his priestly capacity, for messianic deliverance will be addressed in chapter 13. All the textual details and implications seem, however, to point to his earlier prayers for a child, though perhaps it is even broader and included his lifelong prayer for messianic deliverance as well.

[12]Walter L. Liefeld, *The Expositor's Bible Commentary,* vol. 8 (Grand Rapids: Zondervan, 1984), p. 843.

[13]Cross references such as these are not cited merely for documentation. Rich treasure awaits those who will take the trouble to look them up, the time to consider them thoughtfully, and the meditation to apply them personally.

[14]Edersheim, p. 187.

[15]Pentecost observes that the "glory of the Lord" that illuminated the angelic announcement to the shepherds was the same luminous manifestation of the divine presence that filled both the tabernacle (Exod. 40:34-45) and the temple (I Kings 8:11), and "that Ezekiel saw depart from the temple" in judgment (Ezek. 10:4, 18-19; 11:22-23). "For more than 500 years the nation Israel had been without that visible sign of God's presence among His people, and now the glory for which Israel had waited was revealed to the shepherds in the field, not to the priests in the temple" (p. 61).

[16]For an intriguing treatment of the fulfillment of the Hosea 11:1 prophecy, see Michael P. V. Barrett, *Beginning at Moses: A Guide to Finding Christ in the Old Testament* (Greenville, S.C.: Ambassador-Emerald International, 1999), pp. 256-61.

[17]Herod, described by Josephus as "a man of great barbarity toward all men equally, and a slave to his passions," died a gruesomely diseased death in 4 B.C. Cf. Josephus, *Wars of the Jews*, Book I, 33:5.

Chapter 11

[1]Acts 4:25-26 (NKJV).

[2]Psalm 2:4, 6 (NKJV).

[3]Only two escapes even hint at the possibility of some kind of miraculous intervention. In Luke 4:30, Christ "passed through the midst" of His enemies who were ready to seize Him. In John 8:59, Christ "hid himself" and went "through the midst of them." Though many assume these verses indicate a miracle of some kind, the terminology here is vague and inconclusive. Leon

Morris argues that "hid himself" (John 8:59) should be rendered as a pure passive ("was hidden"), adding that "John is perhaps hinting that God protected His Son," that "He was concealed by Another" (*The Gospel According to John* [Grand Rapids: Eerdmans, 1971], p. 474). Similarly, the description of Christ's "passing through the midst" of His enemies communicates nothing inherently miraculous. The simple fact is that the narrative avoids offering any unambiguous explanation of exactly what happened—the point being that God was (providentially) preserving the life and safety of His Son, in the face of repeated and growing hostility, until His "hour" had come.

[4]Interestingly, this would have been a valid application of the passage previously twisted out of context by Satan in the temptation of Christ—only a few months earlier (Luke 4:10-11).

[5]Walter L. Liefeld, *Expositor's Bible Commentary,* vol. 8 (Grand Rapids: Zondervan, 1984), p. 869.

[6]My references to the days of the Passion Week in this chapter reflect calculations based on my belief in a Thursday crucifixion.

[7]D. Edmond Hiebert, *Mark: A Portrait of the Servant* (Chicago: Moody, 1974), p. 291.

[8]*The Gospel of Matthew* (Grand Rapids: Baker Book House, 1973), pp. 897-98.

[9]Morris, p. 797.

[10]We may be tempted to think that the Father's special protection and preservation of Christ was to be expected since that was, after all, His unique, beloved Son. Naturally we cannot expect the same kind or degree of protection, right? But this is to miss two vital biblical truths that God has revealed to counter this kind of thinking. (1) As believers we are *in* Christ (a theme so pervasive throughout Paul's epistles that references are unnecessary; make a search for yourself and it will be one of the most profitable studies you have ever pursued) so that God regards us with the same protective care and concern with which He views His own Son. This is not abstract positional psychology to make us feel good; this is practical reality. (2) The risen Christ Himself, the head of the church, clearly acts and intervenes on this very principle. See Acts 9:1-5, and compare what Saul was doing with how Jesus characterized it. The Father's special care for His Son is *entirely* relevant to His posture toward us.

[11]I am indebted to the careful and substantive preaching of my pastor, Dr. Mark Minnick, for first calling to my attention several of the details in this section.

[12]E. J. Young suggests that the verb "appoint" may have "a modalistic shade," indicating that they "wanted to appoint" his grave with the wicked ones (*The Book of Isaiah,* vol. 3 [Grand Rapids: Eerdmans, 1972], p. 352).

[13]See J. Dwight Pentecost, *The Words and Works of Jesus Christ* (Grand Rapids: Academie Books, 1981), p. 491; cf. Robert Mounce, *The New International Biblical Commentary,* vol. 1 (Peabody, Mass.: Hendrickson, 1991), p. 261.

[14]The quotations of Luther and More are cited by C. S. Lewis in *The Screwtape Letters* (New York: Macmillan, 1961), p. 5.

[15]A. T. Robertson, *Epochs in the Life of Simon Peter* (Nashville: Broadman Press, 1974), p. 79.

[16]See note 6 above.

[17]For a provocative discussion of Judas's motives, see A. B. Bruce, *The Training of the Twelve* (Grand Rapids: Kregel, 1971), ch. 23.

[18]Merrill C. Tenney, *Expositor's Bible Commentary,* vol. 9 (Grand Rapids: Zondervan, 1981), p. 140.

[19]Alfred Plummer, *A Critical and Exegetical Commentary on the Gospel According to S. Luke* (1896; reprint, Edinburgh: T. & T. Clark, 1981), p. 490.

[20]To put it more colloquially, if you are a northerner "you" in the AV always means "you guys"; if you are a southerner, "you" in the AV always means "y'all."

[21]Cf., for example, Plummer, p. 503.

[22]Plummer, p. 513.

[23]Details in the medallions painted on the Sistine Chapel ceiling, depicting various scenes from the Books of Kings, were delicately outlined with gold leaf by Michelangelo—an unnecessary but visually attractive and aesthetically pleasing touch by the master.

[24]Robin Richmond, *Michelangelo and the Creation of the Sistine Chapel* (New York: Crescent Books, 1992), p. 96.

[25]"The relation between Divine and human activity is illuminated also in the role played by Caiaphas. . . . Caiaphas' suggestion is the turning point in Christ's path of suffering; but God acts in this human act too. John makes this explicit by way of a two-verse parenthesis (John 11:51-52). Caiaphas does not speak merely out of his free thoughts as a man, but officially as high priest and prophet" (G. C. Berkouwer, *The Providence of God* [Grand Rapids: Eerdmans, 1952], p. 106).

[26]Morris, p. 567.

[27]"In Caiaphas's extremist opposition to Jesus, God's revelation of the meaning of Christ's suffering and death becomes more clear. He unintentionally gives a definition of substitutionary suffering. This is not a matter of Caiaphas's cunning or guileful ingenuity, but a revelation of the profound congruity between God's and man's actions. Schilder remarks pointedly, 'When Caiaphas formulated his answer thus, *one must die for all,* he ended the last sacrifice-hungry priestly discourse with the same conclusion, the same aphorism that was

written before all time in the Book of God as the principle and ultimate rationale of the covenant of peace: *one for all, one for all*'" (Berkouwer, pp. 106-7).

[28]See John A. Broadus, *Commentary on the Gospel of Matthew* (Valley Forge, Pa.: Judson Press, 1886), p. 563.

[29]Broadus also sees a functional side: "This curious interruption from Pilate's wife gave time for the rulers to move about among the crowds and persuade them to ask for Barabbas" (Broadus).

[30]"Abba," a term of endearment for one's father, becomes a New Testament epithet for God (Rom. 8:15; Gal. 4:6). There may be an additional element of providence about Barabbas's name that even further highlights the imagery of substitution. Barabbas is not a first name but a patronym that indicates one's family (somewhat like a last name; cf. Simon *Barjonah*). According to some ancient texts, as well as the early church father Origen, his full name in Matthew 27:16-26 was *Jesus* Barabbas. If this is correct, "it adds pungency to Pilate's offer— 'Jesus Barabbas or Jesus Christ?'" (A. F. Walls, "Barabbas" in *The New Bible Dictionary*, ed. J. D. Douglas [Grand Rapids: Eerdmans, 1962], pp. 132-33).

[31]For these reasons, Morris notes, "The question of whether the Jews could or could not inflict the death penalty is a perplexing one" (p. 765). Nevertheless, the bottom line is that in pressing for the sentence of crucifixion from Pilate, they were unwittingly fulfilling the prophetically expressed divine will.

[32]Morris, p. 766. "John sees it as necessarily (and the Jews as demanding) a death by crucifixion. I do not see how this is to be explained other than by reference to the curse: 'he that is hanged is accursed of God' (Deut. 21:23). Caiaphas would see this as a way of discrediting Jesus, John as the way Jesus took away the sin of the world."

[33]Alfred Edersheim, *The Life and Times of Jesus the Messiah,* vol. 2 (Grand Rapids: Eerdmans, 1971), p. 590; D. H. Wheaton, "Crucifixion," *New Bible Dictionary* (Grand Rapids: Eerdmans, 1962), p. 282.

[34]G. Campbell Morgan, *The Crises of the Christ* (Old Tappan, N.J.: Fleming H. Revell, 1936), p. 325.

[35]Hiebert, p. 395.

[36]Hiebert adds that "darkness and judgment are often associated in Scripture (Isa. 5:30; Joel 2:31; 3:14-15; Amos 8:9-10)," p. 395.

[37]Edersheim, p. 611.

[38]It should be pointed out that those who were raised did not appear in the form of ghosts or spirits. Spirits are not resurrected because spirits do not "die"—upon death they pass immediately either into God's presence or out of it. Bodies are resurrected. Those who "appeared unto many in Jerusalem" were bodily resurrected Old Testament saints. Without entering into a detailed dis-

cussion of the doctrine of resurrection, the New Testament indicates that there are two kinds of resurrection—the "first" a resurrection to life, the other a resurrection to damnation. Moreover, while the latter is a one-time bodily resurrection of all the damned (Rev. 20:11-15), the "first" is divided into several stages: (1) resurrection of Christ as the firstfruits of the first resurrection; (2) resurrection of Old Testament saints after Christ's resurrection (Matt. 27:52-53); (3) resurrection of dead church age saints at rapture (I Thess. 4); (4) resurrection of the two witnesses (Rev. 11); (5) resurrection of tribulation saints (Rev. 20:4).

[39]Plummer, p. 256.

[40]Plummer, p. 429.

[41]Plummer.

[42]Berkouwer, pp. 105-6. "The New Testament sees human actions as being nonetheless fully responsible," he insists. "Christ was nailed to the cross by unrighteous, responsible men." This is clear, for instance, in Peter's accusations (Acts 3:15, 17).

[43]*Desiring God* (Portland, Ore.: Multnomah, 1986), pp. 26-27.

[44]Stewart Custer, *Witness to Christ: A Commentary on Acts* (Greenville, S.C.: BJU Press, 2000), p. 26. Commenting on Acts 4:27-28, he adds: "This is the mystery of God's predestination and man's free will. Herod and Pilate were free moral agents who chose to murder an innocent Man; God is the sovereign Lord who chose to accomplish the atoning sacrifice for the sins of the world by this action. The mystery of the intersection of these purposes in the cross vastly transcends the ability of man to explain" (p. 53).

[45]Joni Eareckson Tada, *When God Weeps: Why Our Sufferings Matter to the Almighty* (Grand Rapids: Zondervan, 1997), pp. 131-32.

[46]Alister McGrath, as quoted by John Blanchard, *Does God believe in Atheists?* (Auburn, Mass.: Evangelical Press, 2000), p. 577.

[47]Maltbie D. Babcock, "This Is My Father's World."

Chapter 12

[1]John R. W. Stott's observations regarding the value of the record of Ananias and Sapphira are noteworthy and instructive: "It illustrates the honesty of Luke as a historian; he did not suppress this sordid episode. It throws light on the interior life of the first Spirit-filled community; it was not all romance and righteousness. It is also a further example of the strategy of Satan. Several commentators have suggested a parallel between Ananias and Achan. . . . F. F. Bruce sees a further analogy: 'The story of Ananias is to the book of Acts what the

story of Achan is to the book of Joshua. In both narratives an act of deceit interrupts the victorious progress of the people of God'" (*The Spirit, the Church and the World: The Message of Acts* [Downers Grove, Ill.: InterVarsity Press, 1990], pp. 108-9).

[2]Stott elaborates on "at least three valuable lessons" from this narrative: (1) the "gravity" of the sin of hypocrisy; (2) the "sacredness of human conscience" and the inherent danger of brazenly violating it; (3) the "necessity of church discipline" (pp. 111-12).

[3]*John G. Paton: Missionary to the New Hebrides* (1889; reprint, Edinburgh: Banner of Truth Trust, 1984), pp. 196-97.

[4]Rosalind Goforth, *How I Know God Answers Prayer* (Chicago: Moody Press, n.d.), pp. 49-51.

[5]The verb, *diapriomai*, occurs only in Acts 5:33 and 7:54. The words "to the heart" (KJV) or "to the quick" (NASB) are not in the Greek text but are supplied by the translators to fill out the sense of the verb.

[6]Stewart Custer, *Witness to Christ: A Commentary on Acts* [Greenville, S.C.: BJU Press, 2000], p. 70.

[7]This account, related by Kimbrough himself, comes from B. F. Riley, *History of the Baptists in Texas* (Dallas: B. F. Riley, 1907), pp. 302-3, cited in E. Wayne Thompson and David Cummins, *This Day in Baptist History* (Greenville, S.C.: Bob Jones University Press, 1993), p. 262.

[8]David Daniell, *William Tyndale: A Biography* (New Haven, Conn.: Yale University Press, 1994), pp. 186-89.

[9]Daniell, pp. 189-95.

[10]The following anecdote, including quotations, is taken from "Hall's *Chronicle* of 1548" cited by Daniell, pp. 196-97.

[11]The conversation here represents a slightly paraphrased version of Hall's account (see note 10).

[12]Ken Connolly, *The Indestructible Book* (Grand Rapids: Baker Book House, 1996), pp. 141-42.

[13]I am not suggesting that the break with Rome was immoral, but the king's primary personal motivation for doing so was his desire to divorce his wife and legitimize his adulterous affair with Ann Boleyn by marrying her instead. God *can* use personally sinful choices to further His purposes, without either approving those actions or absolving people of their responsibility for making them.

[14]A photograph of this page can be seen in Figure 11 between pages 214 and 215 in Daniell.

[15]Timothy A. McKeown, "Peace, if not safety," *World* (April 11, 1998), p. 29. He adds that he often asks those who pray for him "that they focus not so

much on our 'safety' as on our 'faithfulness' in whatever circumstances our Sovereign God might call us to minister." That is not to say that safety is unimportant for God's servants. "I do not advocate foolish and irresponsible 'risk-taking,'" McKeown explains. "However, biblical reality dictates that there are, indeed, times in which God will lead us into the valley of the shadow of death, where our prayer needs to be for faithfulness as reflections of his light and saltiness in this needy world."

[16]Stott, p. 146.

[17]The "Candace" mentioned in the text was not a personal name but a dynastic title, like "Pharaoh" or "Caesar." The queen is specified because in ancient Ethiopia, the kings served as the religious leaders, while the queens governed the civil and political affairs of the nation (Custer, p. 111).

[18]Olive Fleming Liefeld, *Unfolding Destinies* (Grand Rapids: Zondervan, 1990), pp. 230-42. Mrs. Liefeld's account of this milestone in the history of missionary martyrdom was recently republished by Discovery House Publishers (1998).

[19]"On the one side was the authority of Herod, the power of the sword and the security of the prison. On the other side, the church turned to prayer, which is the only power which the powerless possess" (Stott, pp. 208-9).

[20]I do not mean to imply that no request was made to God for Peter's deliverance, but I am deliberately downplaying that request because it is so commonly assumed to be *the* obvious content of their prayers. Certainly they remembered the miraculous deliverance in Acts 5:19, and it is perfectly natural to assume that at least part of their prayer was that the Lord would do likewise this time, should He see fit. But that last qualification is an important one. I have heard this passage taught as a paradigm for how we can be positively certain we will get what we ask God for—the assumption being that the church was obviously asking for Peter's deliverance and, sure enough, he was delivered. But at least three considerations must be weighed in our handling of this text: (1) What about the focus of their previous prayer (Acts 4), the only inspired and explicit precedent we have of the nature of the church's prayer? (2) What about James (Acts 12:1-3)? Surely one cannot assume that they failed to pray for this apostle, yet he was not delivered. (3) What about the Spirit-inspired ambiguity regarding the content of the prayer (Acts 12:5)? A sound hermeneutic is not governed by assumptions; the ambiguities of the sacred text are as important to observe in interpretation as its certainties.

[21]*Travels of William Bartram* (New York: Dover, 1955), pp. 44-45.

[22]William Owen Carver in *The Acts of the Apostles*; cited by D. Edmond Hiebert, *In Paul's Shadow* (Greenville, S.C.: Bob Jones University Press, 1992), p. 50.

[23]Hiebert, p. 50. As he points out, "We have no positive scriptural evidence that Paul and Barnabas ever worked together again" (p. 51).

[24]Custer, p. 225.

[25]J. B. Williams, *The Lives of Philip and Matthew Henry* (1828; reprint, Carlisle, Pa.: Banner of Truth, 1974), p. 54. In this statement Williams was expressing a lesson learned by Philip Henry, Nonconformist pastor and father of the more famous Matthew Henry.

[26]Both Paul and Barnabas were right, as evidenced in the positive outcome of Silas, who proved himself a valuable and faithful companion in ministry, and Mark, who became the author of the second Gospel (Custer, p. 226).

[27]Hiebert, p. 51.

[28]The fact that both Silas and Mark are later found together with Peter (I Pet. 5:12-13) "becomes very suggestive" of the healing of any breach or suspicion between these two men (R. J. Knowling, *Expositor's Greek Testament,* vol. 2 [reprint, Grand Rapids: Eerdmans, 1976], p. 331).

[29]H. B. Swete, *The Holy Spirit in the New Testament* (London: MacMillan & Co., 1919), p. 106.

[30]*Journal of John Wesley* (Chicago: Moody Press, n.d.), pp. 126-27.

[31]Paton, pp. 214-15.

[32]Paton, pp. 206-7.

Chapter 13

[1]Charles Hodge, *Systematic Theology,* vol. 3 (reprint, Grand Rapids: Eerdmans, 1999), p. 692.

[2]Hodge, p. 709.

[3]For a further discussion of how something can be logical yet erroneous, see the appendix "Salvation: Divine Determination or Human Responsibility?"

[4]Terrance Tiessen, professor of theology and ethics at (appropriately) Providence Theological Seminary in Manitoba, explains his motivation for writing *Providence & Prayer: How Does God Work in the World?* (Downers Grove: InterVarsity Press, 2000): "my desire to research and write this book grew out my discovery that the way my students prayed was often not consistent with the doctrine of providence they confessed" (p. 13).

[5]For example, Matthew 6; Mark 11:24; Luke 18:1; Acts 2:42; Romans 12:12; Ephesians 6:18; Philippians 4:6; Colossians 4:2; I Thessalonians 5:17; II Thessalonians 3:1; I Timothy 2:1, 8.

[6]Tiessen, p. 20.

[7]Charles Spurgeon, *Twelve Sermons on Prayer* (Grand Rapids: Baker, 1977), p. 105.

[8]Spurgeon, pp. 115-16.

[9]John Piper, *Desiring God* (Portland, Ore.: Multnomah, 1986), p. 135.

[10]Piper, pp. 133, 140.

[11]"Indeed, prayer is one of the most effective means we have to discern the invisible hand of Providence. . . . When we are praying in general we tend to see the work of Providence likewise 'in general.' When we pray specifically, we begin to be overwhelmed by the specific answers to our prayer that vividly display His hand to us. By this our faith is strengthened, and our confidence in His Providence is intensified" (R. C. Sproul, *The Invisible Hand* [Dallas: Word Publishing, 1996], p. 207).

[12]Alfred Edersheim, *The Life and Times of Jesus the Messiah* (Grand Rapids: Eerdmans, 1971), p. 137.

[13]That their childlessness did occasion some quiet tongue clucking among the neighbors seems apparent from this woman's words when their situation changed (Luke 1:25).

[14]Their agedness is, in fact, the major stumbling block to Zacharias's faith (Luke 1:18).

[15]For an instructive and beautifully descriptive account of Zacharias's experience in the temple, see Edersheim, pp. 137-41.

[16]Some have suggested that the "prayer" mentioned in Luke 1:13 was not Zacharias's past prayer for a child but his priestly prayer just offered in conjunction with the incense offering—presumably a prayer for the redemption of Israel—which was about to be answered immediately in the birth of John as the forerunner of Messiah (e.g., J. Dwight Pentecost, *The Words and Works of Jesus Christ* [Grand Rapids: Academie Books, 1981], p. 41). Walter Liefeld mentions this latter view, though he opts for the former (*Expositor's Bible Commentary*, vol. 8 [Grand Rapids: Zondervan, 1984], p. 826). The latter view seems to me more speculative and less likely for several reasons, including (1) the text's emphasis on their past childlessness and present old age, (2) the aorist tense in Luke 1:13 (see next endnote), and (3) the announcement's immediate focus on John himself, rather than on the nation. Nevertheless, it would not substantively change the larger point being illustrated—the conjunction between prayer and promise.

[17]The present tense translation "thy prayer is heard" might be misconstrued to suggest that God had only just now finally heard Zacharias's prayer. The verb is actually an aorist passive, "thy prayer was heard." God had, in fact, heard all of Zacharias's prayers when they were offered day after day for many years. It is also worth observing that the angel does *not* say, "thy prayer will now be answered." Zacharias's prayers *were heard* when offered, and *were answered* with di-

vine silence—which early on would be interpreted as "wait" and was eventually assumed to mean "no." Prayers are not "answered" only by a divine "yes" (i.e., when we receive what we ask) any more than a child's request is "answered" only when the parent gives him what he asks. "No" and "wait" are answers as legitimate and necessary for God as they are for any parent.

[18]Another similar example would be the birth of Samuel. Though his coming was never foretold as John's was, he is so pivotal to Israel's history and the crucial transition from judgeship to monarchy, one cannot imagine Hebrew history without him. Yet, humanly speaking, his providential birth was the result of the earnest prayer of another godly yet barren woman, Hannah.

[19]The Qal form of *zakar* means "remember"; the Hifil form found here indicates a causative sense, "cause to remember, remind," hence in this passage to "call upon" (*The New Brown-Driver-Briggs-Gesenius Hebrew Lexicon* [Christian Copyrights, 1979], p. 270).

[20]Interestingly, the same participial form used here is also translated "recorder" to denote the official writers of the royal chronicles (Isa. 36:3, 22)—records intended to serve as accurate reminders of past events (see also II Sam. 8:16; 20:24; I Kings 4:3; II Kings 18:18, 37; I Chron. 18:15; II Chron. 34:8). That, incidentally, is why the KJV translates it "make mention" (since you remind someone of something by mentioning it to them). The question is, does it here mean "make mention *of* the Lord" (as in preaching or verbal testimony) or "make mention *to* the Lord" (as in praying)?

[21]"The participle expresses the thought of calling something to God's attention, i.e. engaging in importunate prayer" (Edward J. Young, *The Book of Isaiah,* vol. 3 [Grand Rapids: Eerdmans, 1972], p. 471.)

[22]Young, p. 467. Young believes that the reference to setting watchmen (62:6) confirms that the speaker is God.

[23]R. C. H. Lenski, *The Interpretation of the Epistles of St. Peter, St. John and St. Jude* (Minneapolis: Augsburg Publishing, 1966), p. 348.

[24]Of the handful of New Testament occurrences and the nearly seventy uses of *speudo* in the Septuagint version of the Old Testament, the consistent sense of *speudo* is that of hurrying either an action (e.g., the Israelite ambush hurried to set the city of Ai on fire, Josh. 8:19) or an object (e.g., the priests were commanded to hurry the collection of funds for the temple repair, II Chron. 24:5). Passages are listed in W. F. Moulton, A. S. Geden and H. K. Moulton, eds., *A Concordance to the Greek Testament* (Edinburgh: T. & T. Clark, 1978) and Edwin Hatch and Henry A. Redpath, eds. *A Concordance to the Septuagint* (1897-1906; reprint, Grand Rapids: Baker, 1998).

[25]Translations adopting the sense of "hastening the coming" of that day include NASV, NKJV, NIV, RSV, NRSV, NEB, New Berkley, Rotherham, Darby,

Williams, Weymouth, 20th Century N.T., Montgomery, Moffatt, and Good-speed. Most of these are listed in D. Edmond Hiebert, *Second Peter and Jude: An Expositional Commentary* (Greenville, S.C.: Unusual Publications, 1989), p. 163.

[26] *The Holy Bible, 1611 Edition, King James Version* (1611; reprint, Nashville: Thomas Nelson, 1993), original spelling. The ASV (1901) likewise opted for the sense of "earnestly desiring" but includes the alternate sense of "hastening" in the margin (see also *The Amplified Bible*).

[27] Hiebert, pp. 163-64.

[28] This is admittedly a loaded question. Hiebert cites Michael Green who "insists that 'the timing of the advent is to some extent dependent upon the state of the Church or of society'" (Hiebert, p. 164). The issue of whether the timing of this eschatological event is tentative or open-ended raises the question of the openness of the future, which tumbles into the arena of openness theology. For a critique of a recent, popular defense of openness theology, see my review of Gregory Boyd's *The God of the Possible* in *Biblical Viewpoint* (Greenville, S.C.: BJU. November 2000), pp. 139-44.

[29] In citing this prayer in Matthew 6:10 as an example of how we hasten the coming of the day of God, Hiebert includes Isaiah 62:6-7 as a parallel cross reference (p. 164).

[30] J. C. Ryle, *Expository Thoughts on Matthew* (1856; reprint, Edinburgh: Banner of Truth, 1986), p. 51. John Broadus elaborates: "It is therefore perfectly legitimate for us to use the petition with our minds specially directed towards the consummation of Christ's reign, the complete establishment of his kingdom, his final glorious triumph, when the kingship (sovereignty) of the world, shall become our Lord's and his Christ's" (*Matthew* [1886; reprint, Valley Forge, Pa.: Judson Press, n.d.], p. 134). D. A. Carson ties the personal and immediate sense to the theological and ultimate sense: "To pray 'your kingdom come' is therefore simultaneously to ask that God's saving, royal rule be extended now as people bow in submission to him . . . and to cry for the consummation of the kingdom (cf. I Cor. 16:22; Rev. 11:17; 22:20)" (*The Expositor's Bible Commentary*, vol. 8 [Grand Rapids: Zondervan, 1984], p. 170).

[31] Charles Bigg in *A Critical and Exegetical Commentary on the Epistles of Peter and Jude*, cited by R. H. Strachan, *The Expositor's Greek Testament*, vol. 5 (reprint, Grand Rapids: Eerdmans, 1976), p. 146.

[32] Carson, p. 182.

[33] Geoffrey W. Grogan, *Expositor's Bible Commentary*, vol. 6 (Grand Rapids: Zondervan, 1986), p. 337. Grogan adds, "This passage may well furnish part at least of the OT background to the parables of importunate prayer told by our Lord (Luke 11:5-10; 18:1-8)."

[34]John A. Martin, *The Bible Knowledge Commentary,* vol. 1 (n.p.: Victor Books, 1985), p. 1117.

[35]Matthew Henry, *Commentary on the Whole Bible*, vol. 4 (McLean, Va.: Mac-Donald Publishing, n.d.), p. 964. Henry adds that even so certain a prophetic promise as the Father's giving the nations to Christ for His inheritance is secured only upon the Son's *asking* the Father for them (Psalm 2:8).

[36]Sproul, p. 205.

[37]Tiessen, p. 342.

[38]Tiessen, p. 337.

[39]D. Edmond Hiebert, *Working with God Through Intercessory Prayer* (Greenville, S.C.: Bob Jones University Press, 1991), p. 108.

[40]"In prayer God learns nothing new about us, but we are ever learning about Him. . . . In prayer we have the opportunity to learn of the character of the Father" (Sproul, pp. 206-7).

[41]Tiessen, p. 337. "We do not seek to change God's mind, we seek to change the situation in the world through an understanding of how God wishes things to be [*an understanding acquired through His Word*] and through fervent petitions that he will do what is necessary for that state of perfect shalom to be realized. . . . It is God, however, and not prayer that changes things, even though his doing so is in answer to prayer" (p. 342).

[42]The 70-year prophecies present some challenging difficulties. The central question is, of course, what is the period's precise *terminus a quo* and *ad quem* (beginning and ending date)? Several passages must be taken into consideration: (1) According to Jeremiah 25:1, 9-13, Judah and the surrounding nations would serve the king of Babylon 70 years; then *after* the 70 years were *completed*, God would bring upon the land of Babylon all His words against it through Jeremiah. In this passage the focus of the 70 years is on the nations' servitude to Babylon. The difficulty is that this prophecy comes in the first year of Nebuchadnezzar (605 B.C.). Cyrus the Mede took over Babylon in 539 B.C.—a maximum of only 67 years (counting 605 and 539). We do know, however, that Babylon and Media, among other enemies of the Assyrian empire, allied after the death of Ashurbanipul, king of Assyria, in 526 B.C., and that they captured and destroyed Assyria's capital, Ninevah, in 612. What exactly was the nature of the Babylonian kingdom prior to Nebuchadnezzar (between 612 and 605)? Was there an overlapping co-regency? Or, given the power vacuum and the ensuing vying for international dominance among the surviving kingdoms, could the prophecy have already been in effect among some of the surrounding nations in terms of their servitude to Babylon prior to Nebuchadnezzar? (2) According to Jeremiah 29:1-2 and 10, after God accomplished His 70 years determined for Babylon

(not Jerusalem), He would intervene to bring His people back into their land. In this passage the focus of the 70 years is what has been determined "for Babylon." (3) According to II Chronicles 36:20-21, the emphasis again is on the completion of 70 years, this time with specific reference to the land of Judah. This passage marks the beginning of the 70 years *for* Jerusalem at 605 B.C., since it makes reference to the beginning of Judah's captivity. The difficulty remains as to what year the return occurred. Though Cyrus took Babylon in 539 B.C., many historians regard the "first year of Cyrus" to be 538 B.C. (or more specifically, March 538-March 537). We are told when Cyrus's decree was issued (his first year, though that could have been as late as the beginning of 537), but we are not told how long the Jews' preparations or the return journey took, or exactly when they actually returned to the land. A year's preparation and return time is not unreasonable to assume, which would place them back in the land in 536 B.C. This would handily accommodate the 70 years prophesied on Jerusalem beginning in 605. (4) Finally, according to Daniel 9:1-2, in the first year of Darius (evidently appointed governor/king over the former Babylonian realm just conquered by Cyrus, king of Persia), Daniel noticed in his study of the Scriptures Jeremiah's prophecy that 70 years were determined "for the completion of the desolations of Jerusalem." This was after the fall of Babylon to Persia, but prior to the Jews' restoration to the land. Consequently, he prays for God's fulfillment of this promise. In this passage the focus is on the fulfillment of the 70 years, which would culminate in the return and restoration of God's people to the land, a time period which began in 605 B.C. and, as discussed under the previous reference, likely ended in 536 B.C.

Attempting to account for the data in all of these passages, the 70-year prophecy seems potentially fulfilled on two or three levels simultaneously. (1) Seventy years of **domination by Babylon** (609-539), after which Babylon would be punished (Jer. 25:11-12). (2) Seventy years of **desolation on Jerusalem**, after which the Jews would be restored (Jer. 29:10; II Chron. 36:20-21; Dan. 9:1-2). This second aspect allows for two feasible time frames: (a) 605-535, from the initial exile to the return, and (b) 586-516, from the temple's destruction to its completed rebuilding. The difficulty has to do not with the 70 years prophesied on Jerusalem until the restoration; that is easily resolved by either (a) or (b) above. Given the emphasis of II Chronicles 36 (on the land enjoying its sabbaths), the former seems the more likely intent, though both are clearly workable. The difficulty has to do with the Jeremiah 25 prophecy, which specifies that "when seventy years are completed I will punish the king of Babylon and that nation." From the time that prophecy was given (605, unless there was an as-yet undiscovered overlapping co-regency which could date Nebuchadnezzar's "first year" earlier than 605) until "the king of Babylon" was punished (539) appears to have been not 70 but, at most, 67 years, unless one or more of the considerations suggested above helps to explain it.

[43]It is difficult to know how much Daniel perceived chronologically. In retrospect, we reckon the 70 years from the first phase of the Babylonian takeover—the 605 deportation. It is not clear whether Daniel automatically calculated from that date, or whether he might more naturally have assumed the final takeover of Judah and decimation of Jerusalem in 586 as the starting point. Gleason L. Archer Jr. reads into Daniel's response a considerable degree of acuity on this point. "Moved to claim the promise implied by the number seventy," Archer remarks, "he implored the Lord God to reckon those years from the year of his own exile and to ensure the reestablishment of the Commonwealth of Israel in the Land of Promise by seventy years from the first Palestinian invasion of King Nebuchadnezzar" (*Expositor's Bible Commentary*, vol. 7 [Grand Rapids: Zondervan, 1985], p. 107).

[44]Daniel 2:20-21; 4:25-26; 5:18-23.

[45]Ezekiel's prophecy appears to include a similar assurance regarding Israel's cleansing and restoration. Like Isaiah 60-63, Ezekiel 36:23-38 describes Israel's future millennial blessing. A string of unequivocal divine declarations of what God will do in and for Israel (the oracle contains over a dozen unconditional sovereign assertions of "I will" in as many verses) is followed by an equally certain expression of human participation: "Thus saith the Lord GOD; I will yet for this be inquired of by the house of Israel, to do it for them" (Ezek. 36:37). Many of the commentators are unhelpfully silent on verse 37*a*, though most seem to interpret 37*b*-38 as the specific object of this prayer (viz., that God would greatly multiply their population in answer to their prayers to that effect), rather than to the preceding prophetic promises in verses 23-36.

[46]John Walvoord adds, "Daniel realized that the Word of God would be fulfilled only on the basis of prayer, and this occasioned his fervent plea as recorded in this chapter. On the one hand, Daniel recognized the certainty of divine purposes and the sovereignty of God which will surely fulfill the prophetic word. On the other hand, he recognized human agency, the necessity of faith and prayer, and the urgency to respond to human responsibility as it relates to the divine program" (*Daniel: The Key to Prophetic Revelation* [Chicago: Moody Press, 1971], p. 205).

[47]Walvoord, p. 205.

[48]Archer elaborates on the intriguing (though unverifiable) possibility that Daniel might well have also been aware of Isaiah's Cyrus prophecy, which described centuries in advance the appearance of a man named Cyrus whom God would use to overthrow Babylon and rebuild Jerusalem (Isa. 44:24–45:13).

Archer imagines Daniel's thrill at seeing the rise and dominance of this one named Cyrus as the fulfillment of these prophecies and as a powerful incentive to Daniel to pray that God would continue to fulfill all His word through this man (pp. 107-8).

[49]Hiebert, *Working with God Through Intercessory Prayer.* p. 107.

[50]Garry Friesen, *Decision Making and the Will of God* (Portland, Ore.: Multnomah Publishing, 1980), pp. 91-92.

[51]Friesen, p. 13.

[52]Other passages curiously absent from a book about seeking God's will and biblical decision making include Joshua 9:14 (when the Israelites believed the Gibeonites' ruse and "asked not counsel at the mouth of the Lord") and Genesis 13-14 or II Peter 2:6-8 (Lot's disastrous and prayerless choice).

[53]John Flavel, *The Mystery of Providence* (1678; reprint, Carlisle, Pa.: Banner of Truth, 1995), pp. 188-89.

[54]Ephesians 1:15-23; 3:14-19; Philippians 1:9-11; Colossians 1:9ff.

[55]Romans 15:30-33; Ephesians 6:18-20; Colossians 4:2-4; II Thessalonians 3:1-2.

[56]Oswald Chambers, *My Utmost for His Highest* (Westwood, N.J.: Barbour and Company, 1935, 1963), p. 160.

Appendix E

[1]*Mere Christianity* (Nashville: Broadman & Holman, 1996), p. 142. Lewis applies this illustration brilliantly to the paradox of the nature of God, to which I have already alluded. "On the human level one person is one being, and any two persons are two separate beings—just as, in two dimensions (say on a flat sheet of paper) one square is one figure and any two squares are two separate figures. On the Divine level you still find personalities; but up there you find them combined in new ways which we, who do not live on that level, cannot imagine. In God's dimension, you find a being who is three Persons while remaining one being, just as a cube is six squares while remaining one cube. Of course we cannot fully conceive a Being like that: just as, if we were so made that we perceived only two dimensions in space we could never properly imagine a cube. But we can get a sort of faint notion of it. . . . It is something we could never have guessed, and yet, once we have been told, one almost feels one ought to have been able to guess it because it fits so well with all the things we know already" (pp. 142-43).

[2]The allusion is to J. R. R. Tolkien, *The Fellowship of the Ring,* Part One of *The Lord of the Rings* (Boston: Houghton Mifflin, 1965), p. 372.

[3]"But," some will protest, "I Peter 1:2 explicitly says 'elect according to the foreknowledge of God.' See? He chose on the basis of whom He foreknew would accept." Check the text again. (1) It does not say "elect according to God's foreknowledge of response." Any such explanatory insertion is the encroachment of logical assumption into the text. "But what else could it possibly refer to?" It need refer to nothing more than God's election based on His foreknowledge of His own sovereign purposes and intentions. The point is, the text itself does not explain foreknowledge here; only theologians do. (2) The literal reading of the text makes the above assumption even more remote: "To the elect strangers scattered throughout Pontus, Galatia, Cappadocia, Asia and Bithynia, according to the foreknowledge of God." The syntax may even suggest that their scattering was not accidental but providential, "according to the foreknowledge of God." (3) If God is omniscient, He must foreknow all responses—not only who will accept but who will reject. Yet Romans 8:29 indicates that all those "whom he did foreknow, he also did predestinate to be conformed to the image of his Son." It is difficult to assert that "foreknowledge" means foreknowledge of response, since He foreknows both positive and negative responses, yet Paul asserts here that those whom He foreknew He also predestined to conformity to Christ. That cannot be true of those whose rejection He foreknew. This alone suggests that "foreknowledge" must mean something beyond mere prescience.

[4]While they are not soteriologically oriented, the implications of two passages in Acts previously discussed in chapter 10 of this book are worth pointing out here. (1) Acts 2:23—Christ, "being delivered **by the determinate counsel and foreknowledge of God,** *ye have taken, and by wicked hands have crucified and slain.*" (2) Acts 4:27-28—"For truly *against Your holy Servant Jesus, whom You anointed, both Herod and Pontius Pilate, with the Gentiles and the people of Israel, were gathered together to do* **whatever Your hand and Your purpose determined before to be done.**"

[5]D. Edmond Hiebert, *The Thessalonian Epistles* (Chicago: Moody, 1971), p. 52.

[6]Leon Morris, *The First and Second Epistles to the Thessalonians* (Grand Rapids: Eerdmans, 1959), p. 237.

[7]John Eadie, *Commentary on the Epistles to the Thessalonians* (1877; reprint, Grand Rapids: Baker, 1979), p. 294.

[8]Jamieson, Robert, A. R. Faussett, and David Brown, *A Commentary Critical, Experimental and Practical,* vol. 3 (reprint, Grand Rapids: Eerdmans, 1976), p. 393.

[9]"Esther: The Hand of Providence" in *Men and Women of the Old Testament* (Chattanooga, Tenn.: AMG, 1995), pp. 409-10.

[10]Excerpt from Handley C. G. Moule, *Charles Simeon* (1892; reprint, London: Inter-Varsity Fellowship, 1956), p. 79. Simeon was the godly pastor of the Church of the Holy Trinity in Cambridge for over half a century spanning the late 1700s and early 1800s.

[11]The NT consistently presents the gospel as a message that demands a response; that response is described not only as belief but obedience. See Romans 10:16; II Thessalonians 1:8; I Peter 2:7; 4:17; and John 3:36 (where "believe not" is not $\alpha\pi\iota\sigma\tau\epsilon\upsilon\omega$ but $\alpha\pi\epsilon\iota\theta\epsilon\omega$).

[12]Read carefully through the phraseology of Ephesians 1—predestined "according to the good pleasure of His will," redemption and forgiveness "according to the riches of his grace," the revelation of his will "according to his good pleasure," predestined "according to the purpose of him who worketh all things after the counsel of his own will." The piling up of these qualifying phrases, one on top of another, gives the inescapable impression of God's absolute initiative in salvation. This is a needed corrective to a prevalent anthropocentric view of the gospel. "Unless we begin with God in this way, when the gospel comes to us, we will inevitably put ourselves at the center of it. We will feel that our value rather than God's value is the driving force in the gospel. We will trace the gospel back to God's need for us instead of tracing it back to the sovereign grace that rescues sinners who need God. . . . He was not coerced or constrained by our value. He is the center of the gospel. The exaltation of his glory is the driving force of the gospel" (John Piper, *The Pleasures of God* [Portland, Ore.: Multnomah, 1991], p. 19).

SELECT ANNOTATED BIBLIOGRAPHY

A number of books directly or indirectly related to the subject of God's providence are available. The following list is intended as a guide to further reading and study in this area.

Berkouwer, G. C. *The Providence of God*. (Grand Rapids: Eerdmans, 1952). 294 pp. For the more advanced reader, Berkouwer (former professor of systematic theology at the Free University of Amsterdam) presents a sometimes weighty but biblically moored theological discussion of God's providence.

Bridges, Jerry. *Trusting God*. (Colorado Springs: NavPress, 1988). 215 pp. A superb and soundly biblical treatment of issues relating to the sovereignty and providence of God, and how to translate faith in those truths into everyday living. Covers the Bible's teaching on God's providence over people, nations, nature, adversity—and how it all relates to human responsibility and our need to rest in God's trustworthiness. Very readable for the layperson, biblically accurate and insightful without being technical. I discovered this book only days after I finished teaching through my series on providence for the second time and found in it a remarkably kindred spirit. Reading it was gratifying and reaffirming as I came across numerous points of similarity with my own conclusions; two men went separately to the same well (the Bible) and brought up the same water—which is as it should be.

Flavel, John. *The Mystery of Providence*. (1678; reprint, Edinburgh: Banner of Truth, 1995). 221 pp. A rich and thought-provoking study from the pen of a godly Puritan. Flavel lays solid theological foundations, but spends most of his time on the simple and practical but far-reaching ramifications of God's providence in our lives. Rewarding reading.

Murray, John J. *Behind a Frowning Providence*. (Carlisle, Pa.: Banner of Truth Trust, 1990). 30 pp. A brief, reverent and insightful study focusing specifically on God's "dark providences"—their purposes and our comfort in them.

Panosian, Edward M., David A. Fisher, and Mark Sidwell. *The Providence of God in History* (Greenville, S.C.: BJU Press, 1996). 44 pp. Six essays on various topics related to the importance of God's providence in history and in the teaching of history. A valuable resource especially for teachers.

Plumer, William S. *Jehovah-Jireh: A Treatise on Divine Providence* (1865; reprint, Sprinkle Publications, 1993). 233 pp. An old but helpful meditation on the implications of providence, including an impressive array of quotations by a chronologically wide assortment of sources.

Sproul, R. C. *The Invisible Hand*. (Dallas: Word Publishing, 1996). 210 pp. Some good, helpful material—some less helpful. The author has a penchant for unnecessary Latin phrases, complicated theological analysis, and retelling biblical stories; but he also offers some significant insight. (A more extended review of this book is available in *Biblical Viewpoint* [Greenville, S.C.: BJU, November 1997], pp. 93-94.)

Tada, Joni Eareckson and Steve Estes. *When God Weeps: Why Our Sufferings Matter to the Almighty*. (Grand Rapids: Zondervan, 1997). 255 pp. An excellent treatment of providence as it relates to suffering. The authors display a compassionate "bedside manner" but avoid the popular focus on the sufferer as "victim." Despite Estes's penchant for a "relevant" literary style (Eareckson's portions are much better in this regard), the message of the book is thoroughly Bible-oriented, unfailingly God-centered, and eminently practical. The authors' first-hand experience of and exposure to deep human suffering lends compelling weight to the authority of their theology of God's providence over suffering and His purposes in it. (A more extended review of this book is available in *Biblical Viewpoint* [Greenville, S.C.: BJU, April 1999], pp. 97-101.)

SCRIPTURE INDEX

SCRIPTURE INDEX

SUBJECT INDEX

SUBJECT INDEX